the NELSON
FIRST CERTIFICATE
course

the NELSON
FIRST CERTIFICATE
course

Susan Morris, Alan Stanton

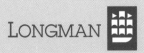
LONGMAN

Addison Wesley Longman Limited
Edinburgh Gate
Harlow
Essex
CM20 2JE
England

and Associated Companies throughout the world.

© Susan Morris, Alan Stanton, 1993, 1996

First published by Thomas Nelson and Sons Ltd 1993

This edition Longman Group Ltd 1996

Set in Helvetica

Printed in Spain
by Gráficas Estella

ISBN 0-17-557129-5

Reprinted 1996

Publishers' Acknowledgements

The publishers would like to thank the following for permission to reproduce copyright material. They have tried to contact all copyright holders, but in cases where they may have failed will be pleased to make the necessary arrangements at the first opportunity.

Texts
You Magazine/Solo for the article 'My Body and I' Helen Pickles (page 11);
Saska Greville for the article 'All About Cindy' (page 12);
The European for the articles 'My Favourite Village' by Michael Cacoyannis (page 22), 'Living with my own Legend' by Boris Becker (page 140), 'Clinging to Life by the Finger-tips' by Kalpana Vora (page 203);
The Independent/Independent on Sunday for the articles 'Looking forward to the time of our lives by Celia Dodd (page 31), 'The Worst of Times' by Danny Danziger (page 32), 'Coatbridge and Chelsea: a Tale of Two Diets' by Susan Strickland (page 51), 'Little Girls Dressed to Kill' by Michael Durham (page 85), 'How we met – Caroline and William Waldegrave' by Shirley Lowe (page 96), 'The lifelong penalty facing football-crazy youngsters' by Sharon Kingman (page 119), 'Lessons on a life of crime' by Isabelle Anscombe (page 149), 'The major league' by Liz Jobey (page 102);
New Internationalist for the text 'Friday Night Burnout' by George Fisher (page 38);
David Rose for the article 'The rails that narrow the mind' published in *The Guardian* (page 41);
The Guardian for the articles 'Tying the knot: portraits of modern marriage' by Joanna Moorhead (page 75), 'Dressing to kill leads to murder in Chicago' by Simon Tisdall (page 146), 'Teenage conman gets four years' (page 159), 'High-flyer ready for take-off' by Jon Ronson (page 180);
Carcanet Press Ltd for the poem 'Subway Piranhas' from 'Collected Poems 1990' by Edwin Morgan (page 43);
The Devon Association of Tourist Attractions for material from the leaflet 'Devon's Best Attractions' (page 44);
BBC Enterprises Ltd for the introduction to 'the BBC Diet' by Barry Lynch (page 52);
Carcanet Press Ltd for the poem "This is just to say" by William Carlos Williams (page 53);
The Telegraph Magazine for the article 'First Person: Designer Catherine Walker' by Margaret Rooke and Ruby Millington (page 56);
Good Housekeeping for the extract from the interview by Geraldine Bedell with Anita Roddick entitled 'Love and work are the only important things in life' (page 72);
Woman Magazine for the article 'I'm serving a sentence too' by Alison Leigh-Jones (page 76);
Sunday Mirror for the article 'Dolphin's mystery powers cure slim-mad Jemima' by Alan Burns (page 82);
Company Magazine for the extracts from the article 'You've Got a Problem' by Donna Dawson (page 92);

She for the extract from the article 'Beating the Bullies' by Angela Phillips (page 95);
The cartoon 'Look don't judge me by ...' by Haefeli is reproduced by permission of *Punch* (page 97);
TV Quick for the article 'My God, what have I done?' by Dave Thomas (page 105);
Faber and Faber Ltd and Wendy Cope for the poem 'Some More Light Verse' from 'Serious Concerns' by Wendy Cope (page 107);
The Radio Times for the article 'My kind of day' by David Gillard (page 110);
19 Magazine/Solo for the article 'Survivors'. First appeared in Britain in *19 Magazine* (page 120);
Young Telegraph for the cartoon strip 'Custer's last stand', words by Claire Watts, illustration by Patrick Williams (page 139);
Gareth Parry for the article 'Two armed raiders killed in shoot-out with police' published in *The Guardian* (page 150);
Family Circle Magazine for the letter 'Moment of Truth' (page 156);
Daily Express for the article 'Four Years' Jail and a Ruined Life for Conman, 18' by Jane Langston and Michael O'Flaherty (page 159);
Barclays Bank Plc for the extracts from an advertisement (page 161);
The Evening Standard Magazine for the article 'The man who fell to earth' by Simon Walsh (page 164);
Empire for the article 'A Star is Made' (page 183);
Abner Stein and *Transworld* for the extracts from the book 'Extraordinary People: An Exploration of the Savant Syndrome' by Darold A Treffert (pages 184 and 194);
The Observer for the article 'Grow up – get a set of vegetable dishes' (page 210);
The Observer Life Magazine for the article 'Children's Seaside' by Louise Nicholson (page 219).

Cover Illustration
Hanife Hassan O'Keeffe

Illustrations
Rachel Ross
Tim Oliver

Photographs
A.G.E. Fotostock (page 168); Action Plus (page 87); Allsport Photographic (pages 7, 178, 203); Barnaby's Picture Library (pages 23, 26, 124, 205); Stuart Boreham Photography (pages 114, 144 and 151); Bridgeman Art Library (pages 134 (2), 168); Bubbles Photo Library (pages 100, 114); J. Allan Cash (pages 6, 13, 16 (2), 23, 80, 188); Colour Sport (pages 141, 185); Colour Sport/Ross Wearing (page 141); Sally & Richard Greenhill (pages 6, 26, 67 (2), 80, 100, 188, 215); Hampton Court Palace (page 195); Hutchison Photo Library (page 6); Image Bank (pages 36, 46, 87, 195); Lifelife (page 114); Marshalls (page 178); Musée Légèr/The Bridgeman Art Library (page 168); Observer/Richard Mildenhall (page 208); Panos Pictures (page 124); The Photo Shop Limited (page 70); Picturebank (pages 36, 77); Rex features (page 33); Rex features/Peter Brooker (page 175); Rex features/Nils Jorgensen (page 154); Chris Ridgers Photography (pages 46, 87); Science Photo Library (pages 36, 67); Frank Spooner (page 90); Sporting Pictures (page 6); Sygma (page 175); John Timbers (page 107 (2)); Topham Picture Source (page 198).

Recordings
Rebecca Brown, Alasdair MacPherson, Helen Mosby, Katherine Nock, Claire Skinner, Betty Stankowski.

contents

unit 1
PEOPLE AND CLOTHES

Lead-in	6
Reading: Who are these People?	8
Grammar: present simple, present continuous	9
Listening: In a Shop	10
English in Use: comparatives and superlative	10
Reading: My Body and I	11
Reading: Looking Good	12
Talking Points: What to Wear	13
Listening: The Clothes I Wear	14
Writing: Describing People	14
English in Use: finding errors; word-formation	15

unit 2
A PLACE OF YOUR OWN

Lead-in	16
Reading: Doing up a Derelict House	18
Grammar: past simple, present perfect	19
Listening: A Good Crop	20
English in Use: prepositions, household vocabulary	20
Reading: A Room of My Own	21
Reading: My Favourite Village	22
Talking Points: Houses and Flats	23
Listening: My Own Place	24
Writing: A Letter to a Friend	24
English in Use: phrasal verbs; countable, uncountable nouns; word-formation	24

unit 3
MAKING A NEW START

Lead-in	26
Reading: A Change for the Better	28
Grammar: past continuous, past simple	29
Listening: Going to University	30
English in Use: *hope, expect, wait for, look forward to; gain, win, earn; get used to, be used to*	30
Reading: The Times of our Lives	31
Reading: The Worst of Times	32
Talking Points: Major Changes	33
Listening: Immigrants	34
Writing: Telling a Story	34
English in Use: gap-fill; phrasal verbs; word-formation	35

unit 4
GETTING ABOUT

Lead-in	36
Reading: Friday Night Burnout	38
Grammar: ways of talking about the future	39
Listening: An Incident on the Motorway	40
English in Use: *other, others, another; journey, travel,* etc.	40
Reading: The Rails that Narrow the Mind	41
Reading: Taking the Wrong Path	42
Talking Points: Public Transport, Holidays	43
Listening: Planning a Journey	44
Writing: A Letter of Advice	44
English in Use: phrasal verbs; *so, neither;* word-formation	45

unit 5

CAKES
AND ALE

Lead-in	46
Reading: A Dinner Party	48
Grammar: sentences with *if*	49
Listening: Being a Vegetarian	50
English in Use: finding errors	50
Reading: A Tale of Two Diets	51
Reading: Eating the Healthy Way	52
Talking Points: Favourite Foods	53
Listening: In a Restaurant	54
Writing: A Letter to a Friend	54
English in Use: prepositions; phrasal verbs; word-formation	55

Exam Practice 1	56

unit 6

HOW
THINGS WORK

Lead-in	60
Reading: The Magic of the Silver Screen	62
Grammar: passives; *anything, something, nothing*	63
Listening: Surviving Air Crashes	64
English in Use: *must be, could be*; *invent, discover, find*	64
Reading: Holiday in Space	65
Reading: Enter a New World	66
Talking Points: Computers	67
Listening: Supermarket Checkouts	68
Writing: Describing a Process	68
English in Use: *too, enough*; *rise, raise, arise*; phrasal verbs; word-formation	69

unit 7

THE
FAMILY

Lead-in	70
Reading: Anita Roddick	72
Grammar: present perfect	73
Listening: A Family Photo	74
English in Use: prepositions, finding errors	74
Reading: Weddings	75
Reading: I'm Serving a Sentence Too	76
Talking Points: The Elderly	77
Listening: Childhood Memories	78
Writing: A Letter of Advice	78
English in Use: *look like* and *be like*; phrasal verbs; word-formation	79

unit 8

GOOD
COMPANIONS

Lead-in	80
Reading: Dolphin's Mystery Powers	82
Grammar: present perfect continuous	83
Listening: Pets as Therapy	84
English in Use: definite article	84
Reading: Little Girls Dressed To Kill	85
Reading: An Extraordinary Flatmate	86
Talking Points: Recreation	87
Listening: Losing a Friend	88
Writing: A Letter Requesting Information	88
English in Use: phrasal verbs; word-formation	89

unit 9

EMOTIONS
AND FEELINGS

Lead-in	90
Reading: Problems	92
Grammar: *who, which, that*	93
Listening: Embarrassing Moments	94
English in Use: finding errors	94
Reading: Beating the Bullies	95
Reading: How We Met	96
Talking Points: Feeling Confident	97
Listening: Difficult Situations	98
Writing: A Letter of Apology	98
English in Use: gap fill; phrasal verbs; word-formation	99

unit 10

MAKING THE
MOST OF YOURSELF

Lead-in	100
Reading: Being a Fashion Model	102
Grammar: mixed modals; any-, some-, no-, every-; *whose; used to*	103
Listening: Talking About Interviews	104
English in Use: *like, as, as if, alike*	104
Reading: What Have I Done?	105
Reading: People Who Made The Break	106
Talking Points: Self-improvement	107
Writing: A Leaflet	108
Listening: How To Study	108
English in Use: *about to; bound to; a little, a few*; phrasal verb; word-formation	108

Exam Practice 2 — 110

unit 11

THINGS THAT
GO WRONG

Lead-in	114
Reading: Unfortunate Incidents	116
Grammar: past perfect	117
Listening: An Accident on a Motorbike	118
English in Use: *wound, injury, damage; heal, cure, treat;* prepositions	118
Reading: The Lifelong Penalty	119
Reading: Survivors	120
Talking Points: Everyday Disasters	121
Listening: Narrow Escapes	122
Writing: A Letter to a Company	122
English in Use: phrasal verbs; word-formation	123

unit 12

WEATHER
AND CLIMATE

Lead-in	124
Reading: Storms Sweep Britain	126
Grammar: conditionals	127
Listening: Weather Forecasts	128
English in Use: *bath, bathe, sunbathe;* short forms	128
Reading: Is Winter a Disease?	129
Reading: Water, Water Everywhere	130
Talking Points: Weather and Climate	131
Listening: Freak Weather	132
Writing: An Article	132
English In Use: *what, which;* phrasal verbs; word-formation	133

unit 13

HEROES AND HEROINES?

Lead-in	134
Reading: Grace Darling	136
Grammar: revision of past tenses	137
Listening: Women to Admire	138
English in Use: memory words; adjectives in *-ing* and *-ed*	138
Reading: Custer's Last Stand	139
Reading: Boris Becker	140
Talking Points: Popular Figures	141
Listening: Oliver Cromwell	142
Writing: Biography	142
English in Use: gap fill; phrasal verbs; word-formation	143

unit 14

VICTIMS AND VILLAINS

Lead-in	144
Reading: Dressing to Kill	146
Grammar: revision of conditionals	147
Listening: Being Arrested	148
English in Use: *rob, steal; fault, blame*	148
Reading: Lessons on a Life of Crime	149
Reading: Two Armed Raiders	150
Talking Points: Punishment	151
Listening: Witnessing a Crime	152
Writing: Story Writing	152
English in Use: phrasal verbs; *in prison, in the prison*; word-formation	153

unit 15

LIES, TRICKS AND DECEIT

Lead-in	154
Reading: Moment of Truth	156
Grammar: indirect speech (1)	157
Listening: The Great Tortoise Mystery	158
English in Use: prepositions; finding errors	158
Reading: A Young Conman	159
Reading: The Tichborne Case	160
Talking Points: Tricks and Cheating	161
Listening: Deceiving People	162
Writing: A Letter Giving Advice to a Friend	162
English in Use: gap fill; phrasal verb; word-formation	163

Exam Practice 3	164

unit 16

A THING OF BEAUTY IS A JOY FOREVER

Lead-in	168
Reading: Works of Art	170
Grammar: indirect speech (2)	171
Listening: Visiting Museums	172
English in Use: *so, such* (a)	172
Reading: Untitled	173
Reading: Just as Good as the Original?	174
Talking Points: Spending a Fortune	175
Listening: Restoring Works of Art	176
Writing: A Report	176
English in Use: *I wish, if only*; phrasal verbs; word-formation	177

unit 17

A SENSE OF ACHIEVEMENT

Lead-in	178
Reading: From Scholar to Entrepreneur	180
Grammar: gerund and infinitive	181
Listening: A Sense of Satisfaction	182
English in Use: *could* and *was able to*; *manage* and *succeed*	182
Reading: A Star is Made	183
Reading: Alonzo Clemons, Sculptor	184
Talking Points: Winners and Losers	185
Writing: Applying for a Job	186
Listening: Writing a Song	186
English in Use: money words; gap fill; phrasal verbs; word-formation	186

unit 18

TIME AFTER TIME

Lead-in	188
Reading: Give Us Back Our Eleven Days!	190
Grammar: gerund and infinitive with or without *to*	191
Listening: Telling the Time	192
English in Use: measurements; *last, latest, least*	192
Reading: Time Travel	193
Reading: The Calendar Calculators	194
Talking Points: Past and Future	195
Listening: Samuel Pepys	196
Writing: Telling a Story	196
English in Use: *for, during, while*; phrasal verbs; word-formation	197

unit 19

EXPLORATION, ADVENTURE, INVENTION

Lead-in	198
Reading: Inventions	200
Grammar: connectors	201
Listening: My Favourite Invention	202
English in Use: finding errors	202
Reading: Clinging to Life by the Finger-tips	203
Reading: The Adventures of Isabella Bird	204
Talking Points: Desert Island and Inventions	205
Listening: Sewing Machines	206
Writing: Telling a Story	206
English in Use: gap fill; word-formation; phrasal verbs	207

unit 20

CONTRASTS

Lead-in	208
Reading: Get a Set of Vegetable Dishes	210
Grammar: Adverbs	211
English in Use: common errors; *else*	212
Reading and Listening: The Store Detective's Story	213
Reading: Mission Accomplished	214
Talking Points: Boys and Girls	215
Listening: Town and Country	216
Writing: Arguing a Point of View	216
English in Use: phrasal verbs; word-formation	217

Exam Practice 4	218
GRAMMAR NOTES	222
EXAM HINTS	242

unit 1 PEOPLE AND CLOTHES

Lead-in **1** How good are you at describing people? Work with a partner. Describe one of the people in the photos. Can your partner identify who you are describing? You may find the following words useful:

> uniform   fringe   helmet
> watch   suit
> overalls

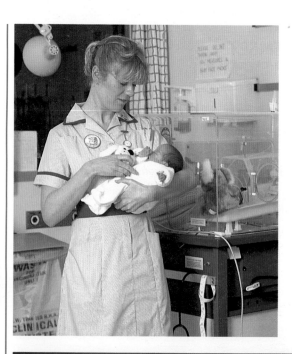

2 Match the words to the correct parts of the body.

a	thumb	h	wrist
b	throat	i	ankle
c	calf	j	elbow
d	heel	k	knee
e	forehead	l	thigh
f	knuckles	m	cheek
g	jaw	n	forearm

3 Complete the passage on the right using the following words:

patched	greasy	frayed	wig
cream	face-lift	bags	pimples

ohn Brown looked at his reflection in the mirror. He didn't like what he saw. His skin was dry, he had several .... (1) on his chin and there were .... (2) under his eyes.

He was unshaven and his hair, what little there was of it, was .... (3). His teeth were uneven and he was developing a double chin. The rest of him wasn't any better. His shoulders drooped, his stomach was flabby and his knee-joints ached if he sat down for too long.

He opened his wardrobe to look at his clothes – old shirts with .... (4) collars and buttons missing, shabby suits with wide lapels, ties covered with stains, socks with holes in and old-fashioned pullovers.

What could he do to improve matters? A more nutritious diet, perhaps, or try something really drastic like plastic surgery. A .... (5) might make him look younger and perhaps his dentist could straighten his teeth. Maybe he should take up weight-training to improve the shape of his body. He certainly needed some .... (6) on his face. There wasn't much he could do about his hair except wash it more often, unless he wanted to wear a .... (7).

All these things would take a lot of time and effort and money. Perhaps it wasn't worth bothering, he thought, pulling on a pair of .... (8) trousers. After all, he still looked better than a lot of other twenty-five year olds.

Reading

Who are these people?

 Read these short descriptions of people and think of one or two words to describe who they are. Compare your answer with a partner.

EXAMPLE:

She's wearing a long, high-necked dress which has long sleeves and lots of frills. There is a veil over her face and she is carrying a large bouquet of yellow roses.

She must be a ......*bride*......

1 She's got short blond hair and bright blue eyes. She isn't wearing any make-up or jewellery. She looks fit and energetic. She's wearing tracksuit trousers over a black leotard and brand-new trainers on her feet.

   She must be a ....

2 He's wearing strong leather boots and thick woollen knee-length socks. He's carrying a small rucksack on his back and holding a map in one hand. Underneath his waterproof jacket, there is a thick pullover.

   He must be a ....

3 He is shuffling along the street, occasionally bending down to pick something up. He is clutching two plastic shopping bags in one hand and a can in the other. His face is unshaven, his teeth are yellow and crooked and his fingers are grubby. He is wearing a shabby overcoat tied with string.

   He must be a ....

4 He is wearing well-polished black shoes with laces, a blazer with a badge on the breast-pocket, a white shirt with a striped tie and long grey trousers. He is carrying a satchel over his shoulder. His face is covered in freckles.

   He must be a ....

5 She's wearing a dark blue uniform and black shoes. She looks very serious. She is holding something in her hand and turning the pages slowly, occasionally looking up at the person at the other side of her desk.

   She must be a ....

2 Use the following words to describe the people in the pictures.

Height: tall short of average height

Weight/build: slim overweight

Colouring/complexion: dark fair tanned

Hair: long short shoulder-length curly straight bald parting fringe

Facial characteristics: moustache beard freckles

Nose: long straight

Grammar: *present simple, present continuous*

1 Choose a verb from the box to complete the following sentences. Use the verb in either the *present continuous* or the *present simple* tense. You can use the same verb more than once. (Grammar Notes **1.1** and **1.2**)

EXAMPLES: think
I _think_ I'll send John a postcard.
I _'m thinking_ of going to see them in person.

> meet   make   melt
> wear   see   pay

1 They .... every afternoon at 4 p.m.

2 'I ....,' said John. 'So that's why you kept it a secret until now?'

3 Sam always .... rubber gloves to do the washing up.

4 Mrs Thomas .... a dress for her daughter's wedding.

5 I .... both of them for the first time at 10 a.m. tomorrow.

6 For this recipe, you first .... the chocolate in a pan and then …

7 Stories of such dreadful cruelty .... me sick.

8 Look! He .... in cash. I wonder why.

9 The snow on this mountain .... (not) ...., even in summer.

10 John .... a hat! I've never seen that before.

11 I can't see you now – I .... all the heads of section in five minutes.

12 I .... (not) .... this story up! It's completely true.

13 He .... all his restaurant bills with his credit card.

14 Increasing temperatures .... the Earth's ice-caps.

15 Jennifer .... wedding dresses for well-known designers.

16 Tom .... a model of the ship the *Santa Maria* to enter in the competition.

17 You just put two ice-cubes in a glass and then what happens? The ice ....

2 Use the same verb in each sentence. One sentence needs the *present simple* tense and the other the *present continuous*. Note that they are all questions.

1 stay
a Jackie, ... for the party after the concert?
b .... in hotels when you visit Paris, Bernard, or with friends?

2 eat
a .... a lot of fish in your country?
b .... this steak for lunch today, Mary, or shall I put it in the freezer?

3 cook
a .... this before eating it?
b What a lovely smell! What ...., Tony?

4 think
a What .... of the new Kurosawa film, Bob?
b You're very quiet. What .... about?

5 walk
a .... home tonight, Charlotte?
b .... to work every day, Tim?

6 look
a Andrew could at least pretend to be interested. .... as bored as that at every meeting?
b Can I help you? .... for someone?

7 put
a Why .... stamps on it, Sally? It's a FREEPOST envelope.
b Where .... my signature?

8 go
a Why .... to work by bike, John? You would save a lot of money.
b 'Where ...., Amanda?' 'It's none of your business, Mum.'

9 sleep
a It's ten o'clock and he's still in bed! .... as late as this every morning?
b .... the baby still ....? I'll try not to make a noise.

Listening

In a shop

A Listen to the short dialogues on the cassette and complete the sentences below with *too + adjective*. The words you need are not on the cassette. The first one has been done for you as an example. (Grammar Notes **1.3**).

1 The shoes are ...... *too small* ......
2 The handbag is ....
3 The trousers are ....
4 The T-shirt is ....
5 The colour is ....
6 The material is ....
7 The coat is ....
8 The jacket is ....
9 The dress is ....
10 Friday is ....

B Listen to the dialogue between a shop assistant and a customer and answer the questions below.

1 What did Jane take to the shop?
2 Why did she take it to the shop?
3 Who gave it to her?
4 What was wrong with it?
5 What did the assistant ask for?
6 Did Jane have it?
7 What kind of shop was it?
8 Did Jane get what she wanted? Give a reason for your answer.
9 What finally happened?

English in Use

1 Comparative, superlative

Write two sentences which mean the same as the original sentence.

EXAMPLE: Charlotte and Anne are both twenty.

Charlotte is as old as Anne.
They are the same age.

1 John and Edward are both 1m 80 tall.
2 The suitcase and the bag both weigh 20 kilograms.
3 The diamond ring and the emerald ring both cost £7000.
4 The kitchen and the bathroom both measure 4m × 4m.
5 The bottom shelf and the top shelf are both 1m long and 20cm wide.
6 The Tropic of Cancer and the Tropic of Capricorn are both 2,000 km from the Equator.
7 In Tokyo and London today it is 30°C.
8 My motor-bike and my car can both reach 200 kph.

2 Rephrase each of the following sentences using the superlative form of the adjective. (Grammar Notes **1.4**).

EXAMPLES:

I have never heard a funnier joke.
It's the funniest joke I have ever heard.

She has never heard a more ridiculous excuse.
It's the most ridiculous excuse she has ever heard.

He had never seen a worse film.
It was the worst film he had ever seen.

1 Richard has never lifted a heavier weight before.
2 I have never eaten a more delicious meal.
3 We have never had a drier summer.
4 Michael had never handled a more poisonous snake.
5 I have never owned a more accurate watch.
6 John had never heard a more outrageous proposal.
7 The doctor had never been called to a worse accident.
8 P.C. Smith had never arrested a more dangerous criminal than Jake Carter.
9 I had never seen a sadder sight.
10 Margaret had never received a nicer birthday present.

Reading

 A Is keeping fit important in your life?
What do you do to keep fit?
What do life-guards do and how do they keep fit?

My Body and I

KEEPING FIT is a vital part of a lifeguard's job, especially if, like Gary Lee, you also coach local and national lifesaving teams. This is a boy every mother would love her daughter to marry. Kind, considerate, clean, selfless, hard-working, strong and healthy. What's more, he has already devoted more than half his life to the care and safety of others. In his spare time, Gary is a volunteer lifeguard.

Gary, a mechanical engineer by profession, has one mildly irritating streak. He refuses to get excited about what he does. 'Drowning accidents are overdramatised,' he points out when I ask how many lives he's saved. 'Most are not a rescue, but more a case of giving a helping hand to someone, offering a bit of advice.' But how many people are now walking around thanks to you, I ask impatiently. 'I don't count them,' he replies stiffly. I discover later, after much effort, that there are at least three people alive today thanks to Gary: a businessman who'd collapsed in the street, a woman being swept out in a stormy sea off Crete, and a man training for his lifesaving award, treading water fully-clothed. 'I got distracted, looked back and he was underwater. That's the funny thing, you know – people drown so quietly, there's none of this thrashing about.'

To keep in a state of peak alertness, Gary follows a training programme of Olympian proportions: Monday – circuits; Tuesday pool lifesaving session; Wednesday – water-polo; Thursday – open water lifesaving; Friday – competitive swimming training followed by water-polo; weekends are left free for lifesaving competitions and preparation. Such a regime has produced a powerfully packed body in Gary's 1m 68 frame. Is that what I have to look like to be a lifeguard? 'Oh no,' he laughs, 'you don't have to be as fit as me to be a lifeguard. You can always help someone. But you have to know your own limitations.' He pauses, as though to assess mine. 'Just shouting for help, for example, is useful.'

Does Gary take such care of his body because he just enjoys being fit rather than because he wants to be constantly ready to save lives? 'Anyone who can swim can potentially save a life. So not to have bothered to learn would have been terrible. But I also derive great joy from competing. Being able to lifesave and keep myself fit enough to compete are equal reasons.'

B Find the word or phrase in the passage which in context means the same as the following:

Paragraph 1
1 very important
2 train
3 thoughtful
4 unpaid

Paragraph 2
5 annoying
6 because of
7 stopped concentrating
8 strange

Paragraph 3
9 maximum
10 a way of living
11 consider carefully

C Work in pairs. Find the answers to the following questions:

1 Describe Gary's physical appearance.

2 Describe Gary's character.

3 How does Gary help other people to develop their skills?

4 What makes Gary desirable as a son-in-law?

5 What is Gary's attitude to life-saving?

6 What does Gary do when he is asked about people he has helped?

7 Describe the three occasions on which Gary saved someone's life.

8 What does Gary do to keep fit?

9 Does Gary think all life-guards are like him?

10 What does Gary think is important if you want to help someone?

Reading

 A What do people do to improve their appearance?
Is it worth spending a lot of money on clothes
and cosmetics?

LOOKING GOOD
Cindy Crawford, a model, reveals her top tips:

LONG HAIR works best for me. Unlike many models, I haven't been tempted to have a shorter haircut. The most I ever have is a quick trim. It's important to make the most of the type of hair you have. I need frequent-use shampoos and conditioners since I often wash my hair more than once a day on photographic shoots. For my work, it's essential to keep my skin, as well as my body, looking its best. Good skin takes special attention, and even if I weren't a model, I'd make an effort. I don't have an extensive beauty routine. Twice daily I cleanse, tone and moisturise. And then, once a week, I give my skin a deep steam clean over a pan of boiling water. That helps to keep my skin looking healthy. When I'm being photographed, I have to wear a lot of make-up. In my spare time, I prefer a natural but polished look that makes the best of my features. For a big occasion like a movie premiere, I have to look my best. I take more time with the extras. I may create a bit of drama with eyeliner or wear a vibrant lipstick. I also always wear my favourite perfume.

I'm lucky enough to have personal fitness trainers in two cities. When I'm in New York or Los Angeles, I work out with them twice a week. Otherwise, walking is a good alternative and I love to go swimming. I also allow myself the great luxury of having a massage about twice a month. I have a busy social life which involves a lot of dining out. I make sure I don't eat or drink too much at these events. I prefer natural foods, avoiding anything fried or fatty.

I have a reputation for being very professional, always prepared and on time for a job. This means being ready to work and not exhausted with bags under my eyes. I need eight hours sleep a night to look my best. Over the years, I've modelled the best clothes from the most talented designers worldwide. That has given me a taste for the best and I adore luxurious fabrics and colours. Having said that, I feel best in Levi's and a white shirt.

To look good, you have to be yourself and wear what makes you feel best. It's a waste of time trying to copy someone else's style. Try lots of different clothes, be adventurous. Only by doing that can you find your own level of comfort. The same holds true of cosmetics. It's all right to experiment but once you find what makes you look great, stick with it. Make the most of your features but do it naturally – and with style.

B Put these words into three groups under the headings **skin**, **eyes** or **hair**.

> trim   cleanse   shampoo
> perfume   massage   bags
> moisturise   conditioner

C Choose the best answer according to the text.

1 What does Cindy recommend people to do with their hair?

  A keep it long
  B be sure to have it cut regularly
  C have a fashionable cut
  D find out what suits their hair type

2 If Cindy weren't a model, she would

  A adopt a different exercise routine.
  B go to bed earlier.
  C treat her skin in the same way.
  D dress in jeans all the time.

3 When not working, Cindy

  A is able to eat whatever she likes.
  B goes without make-up.
  C reduces the amount of make-up she wears.
  D pays no attention to her clothes.

4 To give herself a special treat Cindy

  A goes to exercise classes.
  B has a swim.
  C goes for a walk.
  D has a massage.

5 Which of the following statements sums up Cindy's advice to people who want to look good?

  A Keep up with changes in fashion.
  B Find your own personal style.
  C Vary the colours and styles you wear.
  D Copy the style of someone you admire.

Talking Points

Section 1

Work with a partner.

What is the person in the photo doing?

What kind of clothing is this person wearing?

Why is this clothing being worn?

What other situations can you think of where people have to wear special clothing?

Section 2

Discuss these questions in groups of three.

What kind of clothes would you wear to:

school   a party   a wedding   a disco

What clothes would you take with you if you were going:

– camping
– to the beach
– on a two-week language course in another country

Section 3

With a partner, act out the following situations. In each situation, one of you will take each role.

1   You are in a shop and you need to buy the following items:

> a pair of trousers for your brother
> a glass vase for your mother's birthday
> a present for your best friend
> something special to wear to a party

> Talk to the shop assistant and ask for help in order to get what you want.

2   You recently bought one of the following and when you got it home it was not satisfactory. Take it back to the shop and talk to the shop assistant about it. Make it clear what you want, and do not leave the shop until you are satisfied with the situation.

> a leather bag
> a T-shirt
> a compact disc

3   While you were travelling, you left your suitcase behind. You have gone to the Lost Property desk. Talk to the assistant and provide full details of where and when you lost your suitcase, giving a description of the case and its contents.

Listening

The clothes I wear

 A Listen to Alasdair, talking about clothes and answer the questions.

1 What colour are Alasdair's trousers?

2 What kind of trousers are they?

3 What kind of shirt is he wearing?

4 What is his sweater made of?

5 What kind of clothes does he wear for work?

6 What kind of clothes is he going to wear for his wedding?

7 What are the two occasions on which he would wear a suit?

B Now listen to Helen.
Match the clothes she mentions with the appropriate occasions.

1 trousers   a interview
2 skirt   b relaxing
3 dress   c dinner party
4 comfortable shoes   d working away from home
5 tights   e working at home
6 something bought especially for the occasion

Writing

Describing people

A Read the description below, and look back at the short paragraphs written about each person on page 8. Look carefully at the details the writer has chosen to provide. The important information about each person is given, and details that are true, but not important, are left out.

EXAMPLE:

Jenny is in her seventies. She has a happy face and there is always a smile on her lips. She wears large glasses to help her see. She has short brown curly hair that frames her face. She is not a tall woman and is rather plump. Her clothes are carefully chosen and are always neat. Although her poor eyesight causes her difficulty, she is always cheerful.

B Work in pairs. You are each going to describe a well-known person. Write down the important points first in note form and include a description of:

hair
eyes
height
clothes
and any special characteristics.

Then describe the person to your partner. Can your partner guess who you are describing?

C Write three paragraphs of approximately seventy words each describing the appearance of:

– a member of your family
– a friend
– someone you saw whose appearance was unusual

English in Use

 Finding errors

In Paper 3 of the First Certificate exam, Part 4 is a text which contains errors in the form of extra words that should not be there. Most lines will contain an error but 3–5 lines will be correct. You have to identify the wrong words and also the correct lines. You do not have to correct the text.

How to find the errors:

1 Read the entire passage, including the title, in order to understand what it is about.

2 Study the first two lines, which are examples. One line is correct, the other contains an error.

3 Read each sentence carefully. Remember that although the errors are in the lines, the sentences may be longer than one line so you will have to read the whole sentence to find the error. Although there is only one error in a line, there may be more than one error in a sentence.

Pay special attention to the following points:

Decide if the following example sentences are correct or incorrect. Identify the wrong word in the incorrect sentences.

1 Articles: Look for the wrong use of *the*, *a* and *an*.
John, an experienced climber, liked to be close to the nature.

2 Auxiliary and modal verbs: Look for words such as *has*, *were*, *been*, *can* and *should*, especially in passive constructions.
The train should have been arrived one hour ago.

3 Prepositions/particles: Check for wrong prepositions. Pay special attention to the word *to* which may be a preposition or part of the infinitive. Look out for wrong use of phrasal verbs.
Mr Brown didn't object to helping us. In fact, he didn't mind to helping us at all.
John set out his alarm clock for 5.30 a.m.

4 Comparatives: Look for wrong uses of *more*, *than* and *as*.
The journey was longer more than I had expected.

5 Relatives: Look for wrong pronouns in combination with *which* or *who*. Also, remember that the extra word must be wrong, not just unnecessary.
John bought the painting which he had first seen it the day before.
He told me that the price was very low for such a good painting.

6 Such: Check that you know what this word refers to.
The coach was impressed by the team. He had never been seen such good players before.

7 Familiar phrases: You may think a word is missing from a familiar phrase. This is not so. There are no missing words.
He prepared a lot salad to eat with the steak.

8 Unusual phrases: You may see an unfamiliar phrase and think there is a mistake when there isn't. Remember that the wrong word cannot appear twice in the same line.
They allowed us in in groups of eight.

9 Nouns and adjectives: Although most of the wrong words will be short structural words, you may find some nouns or adjectives that do not make sense.
Wreckage was floating on the upper surface of the sea.

2 Word-formation

Complete the sentences with the correct form of the word in capitals.

EXAMPLES: Tim is always losing his temper. He is the most <u>impatient</u> man I know.   PATIENT
We apologise for the delay but it was <u>unavoidable</u> .   AVOIDABLE

1 I won't go back to the shop again. The assistants are always so ....   POLITE

2 John likes giving people presents, but the things he chooses are usually quite ....   SUITABLE

3 We'll have to have a new car soon. Our present one is totally ....   RELIABLE

4 It's a lovely jacket, but quite .... for work.   PRACTICAL

5 The coat was an .... bargain in the sale.   EXPECTED

15

A PLACE OF YOUR OWN

Lead-in **1** Describe what you can see in each photograph. Which place would you prefer to live in?
List the features that make a place good to live in.

You may find these words useful:

traffic   noise   lively atmosphere
park   entertainment   peace and quiet
natural landscape   crops
farming   seasons

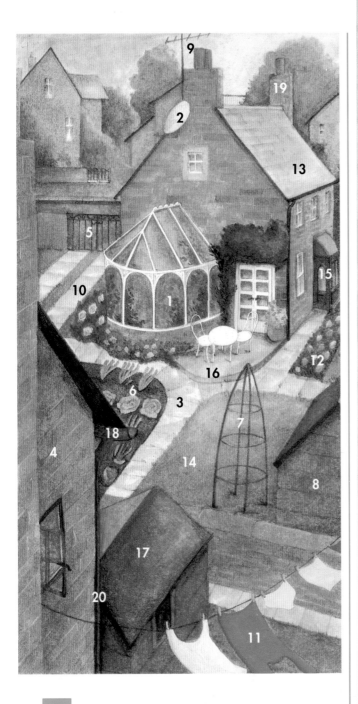

Complete the passage using the following words and phrases:

> gossip   live   amenities   doorstep
> facilities   lack   drawbacks   crime-rate
> home background   beautiful scenery
> major city   leisure activities   on campus
> social life   cost of living

The place where you grow up shapes your view of what the world is like. It is difficult to appreciate the advantages that are on your own ....(1). If you grow up in a small, provincial town, you are likely to find the idea of living in a ....(2) attractive. You think of all the ....(3) that would be around you, the ....(4) you could take part in and the opportunities you would have. You might choose to ignore the ....(5) of life in a city, such as the frightening ....(6), the need to travel long distances from one side of the city to the other, and the much higher ....(7). If you live in a small village in the countryside, you are surrounded by .... (8) but there is little for young people to do. There is a serious problem with ....(9) of transport, particularly in the evenings. This makes it difficult to have a good ....(10). In small communities, you know everyone and everyone knows you. People ....(11) about everything you do!

No wonder students who go away to college appreciate the chance to get away from their ....(12) and experience life in a different place. Life ....(13) in a hall of residence meets many students' needs. With a study/bedroom and shared cooking and washing ....(14) you can be independent and ....(15) your own life.

2 Match these parts of the house with the numbers on the picture.

a	drainpipe	k	vegetable plot
b	aerial	l	lawn
c	roof	m	patio
d	satellite dish	n	climbing-frame
e	chimney pot	o	drive
f	gutter	p	gate
g	bricks	q	conservatory
h	clothes line	r	porch
i	shed	s	tiles
j	flowerbed	t	path

Reading

 A Discuss in pairs:

Which would you prefer to live in – a new modern house or an old traditional house?
Would you be willing to spend a lot of time and money doing up a house?
Would you like to design your own house?

DOING UP A DERELICT HOUSE

JOHN AND MARY KING dreamed of escaping from their poky inner-city flat and setting up home in the country. They longed for fresh air, green fields and the sound of birds. Seven years ago they saw a chance of
5 making their dream come true. 'We were driving along a narrow country lane,' says John, 'when we spotted three houses in a short terrace which must have been farm labourers' cottages in the past. There was a FOR SALE notice outside. No-one lived there, of course, because they
10 were in such terrible condition, virtually derelict, in fact. Even without getting out of the car we could see that tiles had slipped off the roof, so rain was getting into the houses. The gutters were hanging down and almost every window was broken. Inside, things were even worse.
15 Doors were hanging off their hinges, several floorboards were rotten, birds had made their nests everywhere and there was even a tree growing inside one of the houses. Obviously, they had been deserted for years. The houses were quite uninhabitable, but the position was idyllic,
20 with uninterrupted views over the surrounding countryside, so we contacted the estate agent and made the owner an offer which was accepted immediately – I think he was glad to get rid of them.'

It has taken the Kings seven years of hard work to
25 create the beautiful home that they live in now. They knocked the three cottages into one in order to create spacious rooms. 'The inside has been transformed', says Mary. 'We started from scratch and changed things to suit our own taste but the outside hasn't changed much
30 and still retains the character of the original buildings. The worst problem was with one of the end walls. The surveyor advised us to knock it down and build it up again on new foundations. Fortunately, we were able to re-use the old stones so you can't tell the difference. We
35 did most of the work ourselves because we prefer to do it that way, and it's cheaper, but occasionally we had to call in professional help.' At first, the house had no water and no power and because of its isolated position it was necessary to dig long trenches for the pipes and
40 cables that link the house to the mains. 'It was like living on a building site,' says John,' and it cost a fortune. In fact, we spent much more on repairing and restoring the house than we did on buying it. It's definitely been worth it, though, in every way. I'd much
45 rather live here than in a city.'

However, the Kings cannot enjoy the fruits of their labours yet. They have devoted all their energy to transforming a ruin into a dream home, but the garden, still a tangled wilderness, needs their attention.

B Explain the meaning of the following expressions:

Paragraph 1
1 poky inner-city flat
2 virtually derelict
3 quite uninhabitable
4 glad to get rid of them

Paragraph 2
5 from scratch
6 link the house to the mains

Paragraph 3
7 the fruits of their labours
8 a tangled wilderness

C With a partner ask and answer these questions:

1 Why did the Kings want to leave the city?
2 Name four things that were wrong with the houses that they saw.
3 Why was it obvious that no-one had lived in the houses for a long time?
4 Why did the Kings want to buy the houses?
5 Why was it easy to buy them?
6 What were the three biggest changes that the Kings made?
7 How many houses do the Kings own now?
8 Which part of the house has changed the least?
9 What advice did the surveyor give them?
10 What must the Kings do next?

Grammar: *past simple, present perfect*

A Complete the following dialogues using the verbs in the box. Use *past simple* and *present perfect* tenses. Sometimes you need a question, negative or short answer. You can use some verbs more than once. (Grammar Notes **2.1** and **7.1**)

> hide choose say do see find refuse
> tear leave win lose meet give
> be bring eat

EXAMPLE: a __Have__ you __seen__ the latest production of *Macbeth*?
b Yes, I __have__ . I __saw__ it last Saturday.

1 a .... John's plane .... on time?
   b Yes, it .... But the airline .... to take one of his bags so I .... it back here. What shall we do with it?

2 a The police .... the money yet, ... they?
   b No, the robbers .... it straight after the robbery and so far none of them .... where it is.

3 a .... you .... Elizabeth recently?
   b No, I .... We .... for lunch three weeks ago but I .... her since.

4 a What .... Jack .... with the letter when you .... it to him?
   b He .... nothing and then .... it into tiny pieces.

5 a .... the coach .... Michael for next Saturday's team?
   b I .... the list yet but he .... last time.

6 a How many races .... this horse ....?
   b Four so far this year, plus the ten he .... last year. He .... any yet.

7 a .... you .... in this café before?
   b No, but I .... a lot of Italian food when I .... on holiday there last year. .... you ever .... there?

B Complete the following sentences using the past simple form. Note that you cannot use the past simple form for **three** sentences. Identify these three and complete them correctly with another tense.

EXAMPLE: Louis Bleriot __flew__ across the Channel in 1909.

1 I .... a new fridge yesterday – it was reduced in the sale.

2 Sally and Charlotte .... friends since they were at university.

3 The lake .... a few days ago and people are skating on it now.

4 Peter .... in Barcelona from 1981 to 1989.

5 I .... in this house for twenty years and I do not intend to leave.

6 Roderick .... on June 12 and no-one has seen him since.

7 When one of the pipes burst last winter, I didn't .... it myself. The plumber ....

8 I .... rose-bushes in the garden when the postman called to me over the fence.

9 When I was a boy, we .... all our own vegetables.

10 Bill and Jim .... when they were at school together.

C A burglar broke into Mr Campbell's house yesterday and stole some valuable items. You have to interview Mr Campbell and find out as much as you can about what happened. Write the actual questions that you will ask, using the notes below.

You want to know:

1 what time Mr Campbell left home.
   What time did you leave home, Mr Campbell?
2 if he locked the door.
   Did you lock the door?
3 where he went after leaving home.
   Where ....
4 when he returned home. ....
5 what he saw first of all. ....
6 how he knew something was wrong. ....
7 when he called the police. ....
8 if he spoke to anyone else. ....
9 why the burglars chose his house. ....
10 what the burglars stole. ....

Listening 🔲

A Good Crop

A Listen to this man talking about his garden. Tick the box if he mentions the vegetables in the list:

1	potatoes	8	carrots	
2	tomatoes	9	cabbage	
3	peas	10	onions	
4	beans	11	lettuce	
5	garlic	12	cucumber	
6	courgettes	13	cauliflower	
7	pumpkins	14	spring onions	

B Look at the diagram of the speaker's garden. It is incorrect in six ways. List the mistakes. Make an accurate diagram.

English in Use: *prepositions, household vocabulary*

1 Complete the sentences with a suitable preposition.

1 Tim and Susan live .... the main road

2 Their friends, Sheila and George, have a house just .... the corner from them.

3 Mary's house is .... the other side of the street.

4 Mary has always wanted to have a house .... a large garden.

5 .... the end of the street, there is a block of flats.

6 Mr Forrester has a two-bedroomed flat .... a balcony .... the third floor.

7 Mr Smith, a pensioner, is usually .... home during the day. Everybody else is .... work.

8 Mrs Campbell moved .... this area two years ago.

9 Jane Ranson lives .... the flat .... to mine.

10 Jane shares her flat .... two other girls.

2 Change each of the phrases given below so that you have an adjective in front of each noun.

EXAMPLES:
a house with three bedrooms = *a three-bedroomed house*
a house with good insulation = *a well-insulated house*

1 an avenue lined with trees
2 a house designed by an architect
3 a house with central heating
4 a kitchen with good ventilation
5 a house with a timber frame
6 a house in a good situation.

3 Match the container with the contents.

Container	**Contents**
1 a vase	A money and other valuables
2 a safe	B rubbish
3 a wardrobe	C medicines
4 a linen basket	D sweaters and underclothes
5 a dustbin	E clothes that are hanging up
6 a chest of drawers	F dirty clothes
7 a trunk	G flowers
8 an album	H old things you have put away
9 a bathroom cabinet	I newspapers
10 a magazine rack	J photos

Reading

A Have you ever had to look for a place to live? What difficulties did you encounter? What are some of the problems of sharing accommodation with other people?

A ROOM OF MY OWN

When I first moved to London I stayed with a friend for a few days while I looked for a place to live. It was a depressing, soul-destroying experience, phoning up and finding that places had already gone, visiting flats and finding that they were dark and
5 poky with threadbare carpets and shabby furniture, talking to landlords and finding that many of them were extremely odd. Any flat that was merely reasonable was always described as 'a luxury flat'. After a few days I despaired of ever finding anywhere but then I had a stroke of luck. I was given an
10 address by an agency and the rent that they mentioned seemed unusually low, so low in fact that I thought it might not be worth even going to see the flat. It was bound to be a dump. Obviously, a lot of other people had thought the same because when I got there it was still available. The rent was low
15 because it was in a poor and rather rough area of London but the flat itself was very spacious. It was much bigger than anything else I had seen and within walking distance of the place where I worked. I decided to take it. There were two other people in the flat, which was on the first and second floor above
20 a shop. Since there were two floors, it was, strictly speaking, a maisonette. We each had our own room and there was a kitchen, living-room, bathroom and toilet plus a little paved patio at the back.

My room was very large with a huge carpet covering almost all
25 the floor. Right in the middle of the floor was a big patch of a different colour where the carpet had been repaired. I learned later from one of the other tenants that the landlord, who was very mean, had bought a carpet extremely cheaply, thinking he had got a bargain, only to find when he rolled it out that it had a patch in
30 the middle, but since he was not going to live in the room he didn't care. After a few weeks I bought a rug and covered the patch up. The other problem was that all the walls were covered with dark blue wallpaper, and, despite the large bay window, the room was rather gloomy. I spoke to the landlord about this and he agreed
35 that if I paid for the paint and did all the work myself, I could paint the walls white – so I did. It didn't cost much to buy the paint, although it did take a long time to do since I had to give the walls three coats of paint. It was worth the effort though, because afterwards the room looked even bigger and a lot lighter.

40 In my delight at finding a cheap and spacious room I had given no thought to what the other tenants were like. In fact, they were all right. One was a man from Newcastle who was very fond of curry, which he cooked every night. The flat usually smelt of curry but I didn't mind. The other was a zoologist who worked with
45 chimpanzees. When she came home from work her clothes stank of chimpanzee, as did her room. The two smells, curry and chimpanzee, sort of cancelled each other out. Our front door was opposite a bus stop and people waiting for a bus would sometimes get bored and write rude words on our door. Another problem was
50 that I would often be woken up late at night by the sound of shouting, broken glass, screams and police sirens. Once, on my way to work one morning I saw a group of policemen sprinkling sawdust on a large pool of blood on the pavement. However, I soon got used to all these things. I was glad to have a room of my own.

B Find a word or phrase in the text which, in context, is similar in meaning to:

Paragraph 1
1 thin and worn
2 much-used and in poor condition
3 gave up hope
4 a dirty and unattractive place
5 to be precise

Paragraph 2
6 unwilling to spend money
7 a small carpet
8 unpleasant, almost dark
9 layers

Paragraph 3
10 smelt badly
11 scattering

C Choose the best answer to the following questions.

1 When he tells us about his search for a flat, how many specific problems does the writer mention?

A two   C four
B three   D five

2 Why was he reluctant to go and see the flat that he eventually rented?

A The rent seemed too low.
B It was in a rough area.
C The landlord was odd.
D He didn't believe what the agency told him.

3 Why was he impressed by what he saw?

A It was near where he worked.
B It was big.
C He had his own room.
D The rent was low.

4 How many changes did he make to his room?

A one   C three
B two   D four

Reading

 A Discuss these questions in pairs.

What places do you remember from your childhood?
Why are those places special?
What memories are associated with those places?

MY FAVOURITE VILLAGE

Michael Cacoyannis, the actor and film director, writes about Platres, a village in Cyprus.

TO BEGIN with, I am not a very 'village' person, although I like villages for short visits. I can appreciate their picturesque qualities and idyllic life, but my idea of peace and quiet is not necessarily connected with village life. Having said that, it's childhood memories of the Cypriot
5 village of Platres that still keep me awake at night.

Although I'm not a very nostalgic person, I often try to re-immerse myself in my childhood and relive all the sounds of Platres, the sound of running brooks, the songs of birds and the distant chatter of people in the night. I manage it up to a certain point before it just evaporates and I
10 find myself back in the sad reality of my old age.

My family used to visit Platres every summer until I was seventeen. The setting high up in the pine-covered mountains of Trodos, was particularly stimulating. We used to rent a house in the hills and would move there for two months every summer taking all our furniture with us.
15 Sometimes we would stay in hotels, which suited me even better because of the wonderful dances held in the ballrooms there. When I wasn't allowed to attend them, I'd creep downstairs and spend ages watching the elegant ladies dancing. I was always entering dance competitions when I was there. I used to think I was great at the tango, but I never won
20 anything! It was in Platres that I acquired my first dinner jacket at the age of fourteen when I was allowed to go to the dances.

Nowadays I return to Cyprus about three times a year and I always make a point of visiting Platres. I make sure I stock up with a year's supply of the famous Platres biscuits. Of course, I never recapture the old
25 thrill of arriving which signalled the end of the most horrible torture because I was so car-sick as a child. Nowadays you can do the trip in half an hour. But in those days it was three hours of winding mountain lanes. It was always marvellous when we finally reached the cool of the mountains after the heat of Limassol where we lived.
30 In Platres, I got my first taste of the world beyond Cyprus. Children of all nationalities were there – people from Athens, Egypt, Lebanon, England. You could always find old friends or make new ones. We took the games we played together very seriously. For instance, we'd divide into two camps and declare war. There would be casualties and nurses
35 and we would weep. It was in Platres that I first got married. I was seven years old. I'd sort of fallen in love with a girl of six and we decided to get married. We performed a whole ceremony under the trees by a brook and we made crowns of flowers while somebody played the priest and put them on our heads. The poor girl was punished terribly by her
40 parents who thought it was a shocking thing to do. My mother laughed.

I'll never forget one time my aunt visited us at Platres. She was a prima donna, a famous opera singer in Vienna, and she used to come and stay with us in the summer. She was a crazy person although very exotic and beautiful. One night we were all in bed when we were suddenly
45 woken up by an operatic burst of incredible vibrancy. We all crept out of bed and found her singing in the hall.

Platres has since become fashionable among rich Cypriots and is almost swamped during the summer months by coach-loads of day-trippers. It's changed a lot and hasn't the magic it used to have. I find it
50 much drabber and uglier. All its old stone buildings have either been pulled down or replaced. I never spend the night there now.

B Find the word or phrase in the text which is similar in meaning to:

Paragraph 1
1 like a picture
2 perfect
3 calmness

Paragraph 2
4 having pleasant feelings about the past

Paragraph 3
5 move slowly, quietly and secretively
6 got

Paragraph 4
7 obtain a large amount of
8 twisting

Paragraph 5
9 cry
10 small stream

Paragraph 6
11 amazing energy

Paragraph 7
12 too crowded
13 charm
14 duller and more ordinary

C Are the following statements *true* or *false*, according to the information given in the text? If a statement is false, can you correct it?

1 The writer would like to live in a village.

2 Platres is situated near a mountain.

3 As a boy the writer preferred staying in a hotel rather than a rented house.

4 The writer wasn't allowed to attend dances until he was fourteen.

5 The writer felt sick in Platres because he had eaten too many biscuits.

6 The main difference between Platres and the place the writer's family normally lived was that Platres had a much smaller population.

7 The children in Platres did not get on well and fought a lot.

8 The writer and his friend were punished for their 'wedding'.

9 The writer's aunt visited Platres only once.

10 People still find Platres attractive.

Talking Points

Section 1

With a partner, look at the pictures of these two houses. Describe these houses, and then say what you like and dislike about them. You may find the following words useful.

a detached house
a semi-detached house   brick   burglar
alarm   bay windows   porch   lawn
flowerbed   attic

Useful phrases

What I like/dislike about the house is ....
I don't really like the ....
I'm not too keen on ....

Do you and your partner agree?

Section 2

Look at the layout of the flat below. If you had to live in this flat, what changes would you make?

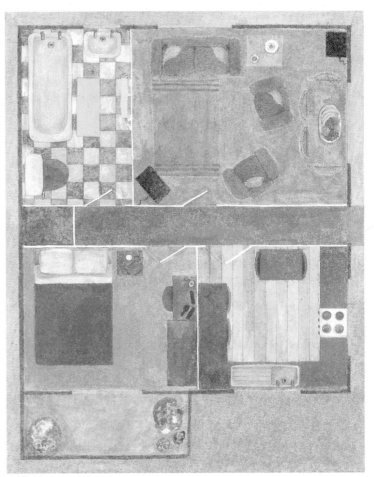

Section 3

What is your ideal room?

Think about these questions:

Where is your room?
How big is it?
What is it for?
What view is there from the window/s?
What kind of furniture do you have?
What is the colour-scheme and decoration like?
What's in the room?

In groups of three, talk about your ideal room and see what differences there are.

Listening

My own place

1 Listen to David describing his house and answer the questions.

1 What do people say when they go into David's house?

2 Why do they say this?

3 Describe his house when he first bought it.

4 What additions has he made to his house?

5 What does he use the third bedroom for?

2 Listen to Alasdair talking about the village where he grew up and answer the questions.

1 What is Fort William famous for?

2 How far did Alasdair live from Fort William? from Inverness?

3 What was his father's job?

4 When did Alasdair go to Glasgow?

5 How many pupils attended his school?

6 What has happened to his school?

Writing

Letter to a friend

You have agreed to take part in an exchange programme organised by your college. You will spend a month living in the home of a foreign student and that student will then stay for a month in your home. Write a letter to that student describing your home, your town and what to expect on the visit. Write about 150 words. Before you write, study this letter carefully. Pay attention to the position of the address, the date, the number of paragraphs, and how the letter begins and ends.

31 Montpelier Avenue
Sheffield
S1 7SG

7th May 1992

Dear Carlos,

Thank you for your letter. I'm pleased to hear that your flight is now confirmed. I'll meet you at the airport. I thought I would explain a few things to you before you come so that you know what to expect. Firstly, it can be quite cold and windy even in the summer, so you should bring some warm clothes. It also rains a lot. The area where I live is very hilly, so nobody rides bicycles much. We usually travel about by bus, so I'll get you a one-month bus pass, which costs £18.

The house I live in is semi-detached and has a large garden. There are six bedrooms, so you will have a room of your own. In the summer we spend a lot of time in the garden. My father grows lots of different vegetables, so you can be sure that you will eat well – if you like fresh vegetables.

There is plenty to do in Sheffield. The sports facilities are excellent. You can go swimming and riding, play tennis and football, do aerobics and martial arts – I remember you saying that you were keen on judo. In fact, whatever sport you want to do, you can do it here. There are plenty of museums, cinemas and other places of entertainment. Outside Sheffield there are some historical buildings which are worth visiting and it is enjoyable to walk in the countryside. It's very hilly so there are wonderful views. Bring a good pair of walking shoes!

I'm looking forward to meeting you.

Best wishes

Tony

English in Use

1 **A Phrasal verbs**

Compare these sentences. Which one sounds more urgent?

'Hurry!' said John.
'Hurry up!' said John.

Many verbs have a more emphatic meaning if we add *up*.

Add a suitable word to these sentences.

1 .... up! We can't hear you!

2 .... up your dinner or you won't get any cake.

3 .... up the house before you leave.

4 .... up, the bar is closing soon.

5 .... up so that everybody can see you.

B In these examples, the meaning of the main verb is exactly what it appears to be but the exact meaning is modified by adding *up*, *out*, *through* or *down*.
Match the sentence to the meaning.

1　The house burned all night.
2　The forest fire burned out.
3　The satellite burned up in the atmosphere.
4　The office block burned down.
5　The acid burned through the metal floor.

a　burned until there was nothing left to burn.
b　burned until it was completely destroyed.
c　burned from one side to the other.
d　was on fire.
e　burned and collapsed.

C What are the differences in meaning between these sentences?

1　I'm tired
　　I'm tired out.

2　Joe was beaten with a stick.
　　Joe was beaten up.

3　Can you spell it?
　　Can you spell it out?

4　He read the orders.
　　He read the orders out.

5　He counted the money.
　　He counted the money out.

D What is the difference in meaning between *pick* and *pick up*, and between *grow* and *grow up*? Look at these sentences.

Mary *picked* the apples from the tree while her daughter *picked up* the ones on the ground.

Martin has *grown* a lot taller and he has a very *grown up* manner now.

Complete the sentences with the correct form of *grow*, *grow up*, *pick*, *pick up*.

1　The trees .... a lot since last year.
2　We .... some wild flowers in the forest.
3　I always .... potatoes in my garden.
4　................................ your toys and put them in the box.
5　In the stressful wartime conditions, children .... quickly.

2 **A** Countable, uncountable nouns

Divide these words into two groups – words which are normally countable and words which are normally uncountable. (Grammar Notes **2.2**).

people	news	information	feet
children	luggage	teeth	money
sheep	luck	mice	spaghetti
traffic	advice		

B Now complete these sentences with *much* or *many*.

1　John wasn't able to give me very .... advice.
2　Not .... people came to the party.
3　How .... spaghetti shall I cook?
4　I didn't think there would be so .... traffic on this road.
5　There isn't .... news in this newspaper – it's just scandal about film stars.
6　How .... legs has a centipede got?
7　We don't have .... information about this product.
8　John didn't have .... luck in the competition.
9　Mrs Brown doesn't have .... of her own teeth left.
10　This passenger doesn't seem to have .... luggage.
11　Not .... sheep survived the extreme weather conditions.
12　We haven't got .... money left, so don't be extravagant.

3 Word-formation
Complete the sentences with the correct form of the word in capitals.

EXAMPLES:　The gunman ___terrorised___ the people in the bank.　TERROR

The film ___frightened___ the very young children in the audience.　FRIGHT

1　They were .... the road which meant that there were long traffic delays.　WIDE
2　Many people buy old cottages and then spoil them when they attempt to .... them.　MODERN
3　Those scissors won't cut anything – they need ....　SHARPEN
4　Mandy has to pay so much rent for her flat that she has had to .... on other things.　ECONOMY
5　I have dreadful neighbours – the noise they make when they have a party is ....　DEAF
6　They've tied the tree to a post in order to .... it.　STRAIGHT
7　The builder .... all the work to be done.　ITEM
8　The surveyor said the wall was not strong enough and should be ....　STRENGTH
9　It would be wrong to .... about the effect of accidents on different people.　GENERAL
10　If we knocked down the wall, it would .... the sitting room by three metres.　LENGTH

25

unit 3

MAKING A NEW START

Lead-in **1** What is happening in each of the pictures?
What is going to happen to the people?
How do you think they feel?
What changes are the events in the pictures going to bring about in these people's lives?
What have been the major changes in your life?

2 Choose the correct word or phrase for the gap in each sentence.

> settle down   feel at home   inherited
> mature   refugees   making   lifestyle
> redundant   widen   lottery

1 Going to college gives you the chance of .... lots of new friends.

2 It took Tom more than a year to .... in his new job.

3 Jenny began to .... after she'd been living in the house for a few weeks.

4 After he was made ...., Tim could no longer afford to go out with his friends.

5 There was such persecution of minorities that the whole family was forced to leave the country as ....

6 When his grandfather died, John .... enough money to buy a house.

7 All the shop assistants had bought a .... ticket together and it won.

8 Caroline accepted the job abroad in order to .... her experience.

9 Since Terry started his first job, he has become much more ....

10 'How did your .... change when you won the prize?' asked the interviewer.

3 Choose the correct word for the gap in each sentence.

> deported   evicted   evacuated
> released   retired   discharged
> dismissed   expel   dropped   leave

1 Sally was .... from her first job because she kept taking days off.

2 The player had performed badly in the last three matches and was .... from the team.

3 The criminal was .... to his own country when he finished his sentence.

4 Mr and Mrs Jones were behind with the rent and so they were .... from their home.

5 After the accident, Peter spent three months in hospital before he was finally ....

6 Frank was .... from prison last year but has found it hard to adapt to life as a free man.

7 At what age do most pupils .... school?

8 The school decided to .... the student who had tried to set fire to the chemistry laboratory.

9 The area had been polluted by an explosion at the chemical factory and all the residents were ....

10 My father .... at the age of 65, but I'd like to do so at 50.

Reading

How To Handle A Gapped Text

 A gapped text is a piece of writing with sentences or paragraphs removed.

There are many things you can do to help you fill in the gaps.

Step 1:
Read all the way through the 'base text', the piece that has had the extracts removed. Concentrate on the meaning of the piece.

Look at the ideas in each paragraph.

Look at the way these ideas are developed from one paragraph to another, and the way they progress through the piece.

Step 2:
Now look at the extracts that have been removed from the text. Think carefully about the ideas that are expressed there and which part of the text they might appear in. For example, are they likely to be at the beginning, near the end or somewhere in the middle?

Step 3:
Go back to the base text, and look at the first gap. Look at the sentence before the gap and the one after it, and try to predict what kind of information is likely to occur in the gap.

There are a lot of things that can help you:

- look for repetition of vocabulary: the same word or a different word with the same meaning may occur in the extract and the base text, e.g. *twenty years ago* and *all that time* in the following article.
- decide if the gapped sentence is an example of what is said in the previous sentence. Is it a development of the argument? Is it a contradiction?
- look at the words that make connections between sentences and paragraphs, e.g. *such, this, that, so, therefore*.
- look for ordering words, such as *first, secondly, then, finally*.
- look for words that show a contrast – *on the other hand, however, in fact*, or a result – *so, consequently*.

Step 4:

When you think you have found the correct extract for the gap, check that the extract you have chosen follows from the sentence before it and leads to the one that comes after it.

Check the pronouns, to make sure that what is referred to in the gap fits correctly, e.g. if the previous sentence refers to *my father* and the gapped sentence is also about him, check that the pronoun is *he* or *him*. Check possessives in the same way.

Check that the verb is in the correct form, singular or plural depending on the subject, and that it is in a suitable tense, in the context.

Step 5:

Fill the rest of the gaps in the same way.

Step 6:

When you have completed all the gaps, check the whole piece:

- first, read it all the way through to make sure that it now makes sense as a whole, and that what you have put in each gap is logical. If anything does not make sense, check that particular gap and see that you haven't made a mistake. If you have, you will need to check all the other gaps too.
- finally, check each gap again by reading the whole paragraph and then checking again the sentence before and the one that comes after it.

 A Before you read the text, discuss these questions:

Have you ever had to move from a place where you have lived for a long time? Or have you had to make a big change in the way you live? How did you react?

 B Now read the text below about how the members of the Long family reacted to the possibility of a major change. Eight sentences have been removed from the article. Choose from the sentences A–I the one which fits each gap (1–7). There is one extra sentence that you don't need to use. The first sentence has been done for you as an example.

A CHANGE FOR THE BETTER

Ever since he left university twenty years ago Geoffrey Long has worked as a civil servant at a government ministry in London. (0) .... *C* .... However, he is now about to make a radical change in his lifestyle. A distant relative died recently and left Geoffrey a small hotel by a loch in Scotland. (1) .... 'It came as a complete surprise,' he says, 'but I see it as a great opportunity to do something different with my life.' His wife, Elizabeth, shares his enthusiasm but is a little apprehensive about their lack of business experience. 'Neither of us has ever worked in a hotel before, so we have no experience of managing staff or looking after guests. I hope we will be able to make a go of it, but if we don't we can always sell up and try something else. I'm looking forward to going there, and I'm sure we will succeed in running the hotel as a profitable business.'

Their daughter, Sarah, aged fourteen, is not so keen to go. (2) .... Moreover, the education system in Scotland is not quite the same as in England. She dreads moving but she has no choice but to accompany her parents. Her elder brother, Christopher, couldn't care less about the move. (3) .... 'I don't really mind where my parents live,' he says, 'except that if they are in Scotland I will have to travel a long way to visit them in the holidays, but I might not bother anyway, wherever they are. I've got my own life to lead now.'

(4) .... He is determined to go. 'The only alternative for me is twenty more years of boring routine office work. If I chose to do that, it would drive me mad. (5) .... I'm looking forward to being my own boss and making my own decisions. It will be a challenge, but I can't wait to get started. I'm committed to doing this and there will be no turning back. (6) .... She'll enjoy having more open space and opportunities for skiing and other sports.'

They are moving at the end of September, by which time they will have sold their London house. (7) ....

A She will miss her friends and have to start a new school at a time when she has to take important exams.

B I'm going to take this opportunity and make the most of it.

C During all that time he has made the same journey to work and spent all day in the same office doing much the same work, returning home in the evening to his semi-detached three-bedroomed house in a South London suburb.

D There is no likelihood of Geoffrey Long changing his mind.

E They hope to be ready to open the hotel, which they are first going to refurbish, in the spring of next year.

F I have to concentrate on my studies now and I don't expect to have lots of free time to be able to use any of the leisure facilities that may be available.

G Geoffrey did not expect to inherit a hotel.

H I know that Sarah isn't enthusiastic about moving but she will quickly get used to living in a new place.

I He is going to start university in a couple of months and will not be living at home anyway.

Grammar: *past continuous, past simple*

A Complete these dialogues using a verb in the *past simple* or *past continuous*. Use the words in the box. You can use some words more than once. (Grammar Notes **2.1**, **3.1**)

> work stop come rehearse wait decide
> go arrest leave do write make think

1 a What .... Sarah .... when you .... to her house?
  b She .... a report, but she .... doing that and we .... out for a meal.

2 a What .... John .... when you phoned him?
  b I don't know but he .... whatever he .... and .... round to my house immediately.

3 a How long .... you .... the play last night?
  b Until 10 p.m. but the director .... we .... (not) much progress so we .... to stop.

4 a .... the police .... Jack at his hotel?
  b No, later when he .... for a train.

5 a .... the others still .... when you .... the office?
  b Yes, they .... I .... back after an hour and we .... until 10 p.m.

B Complete these sentences. Put one verb in the *past simple* and one in the *past continuous*. Look carefully at the meaning of the sentence and the order of tenses.

EXAMPLE: Jim ....*burned*.... his fingers when he was ....*making*.... toast.

1 I .... at books in a second-hand bookshop when I .... a rare first edition. (look, find)

2 Janet .... her essay when she .... a spelling mistake. (check, spot)

3 Peter .... on the lake when the ice .... (skate, give way)

4 Sarah .... her ankle when she .... hockey. (twist, play)

5 John .... at 200 kph when a police car .... him. (drive, overtake)

6 I .... an art exhibition when I .... an old friend. (visit, meet)

7 I .... when a beach ball .... me on the head. (sunbathe, hit)

8 The minister .... a speech when someone in the crowd .... an egg. (make, throw)

9 Nick .... his finger when he .... onions. (cut, peel).

10 A thief .... Mr Brown's wallet when he .... the parade. (steal, watch)

11 The soldier .... towards the enemy position when a sniper .... him in the leg. (run, shoot)

Listening 🔘

Going to university

Listen to Claire talking about going to university. Complete the form according to the information she gives.

```
CANDIDATE  NAME:        Claire Harrison
PROPOSED
COURSE  OF  STUDY:           1
LENGTH  OF  COURSE:          2
SUBJECTS  STUDIED  AT  SCHOOL:
                             3
                             4
                             5
PREVIOUS  EXPERIENCE:
in veterinary practice: YES/NO
with animals (tick as appropriate)
          sheep      dogs
          cows       other
          horses
```

English in Use

1 Complete the sentences with *hope*, *expect*, *wait for* or *look forward to*. (Grammar Notes **3.2**).

EXAMPLE: Sheila _is looking forward to_ her trip to France.

1 We've been .... Tim since 8 o'clock, but he still hasn't got here.

2 Mary's .... a baby at the end of May.

3 Anna's .... to visit China next year, but the trip hasn't yet been confirmed.

4 I .... I'll get there in time, but with this bad weather I don't .... I will.

5 I .... Robert will be late – he usually is.

6 'Do you think Richard will be at the party?' 'I .... not.'

7 Sally .... her mother to tidy up her room.

8 I wasn't .... my visit to the dentist, but it wasn't really that bad.

2 Complete the sentences with *gain*, *win* or *earn*. (Grammar Notes **3.3**).

EXAMPLE: Jim was the favourite, but he _didn't win_ the race.

1 How do you intend to .... your living?

2 He has never .... a prize in his life.

3 Sally knew the job wasn't well-paid but decided to take it in order to .... experience.

4 The actor's performance in the film .... him many fans.

5 What do you stand to .... from undertaking this project?

6 It's always better to .... than to lose.

7 The baby .... weight steadily.

8 She has had to .... every penny she has spent.

3 Complete the sentences with the correct form of *get used to* or *be used to*. (Grammar Notes **3.4**).

1 This is a new machine and I .... not .... it yet.

2 When you are in a foreign country, it's often difficult to .... the food.

3 John had been a soldier for twenty years and he found it hard to .... life outside the army.

4 She became a big star but never .... living in the limelight.

5 My grandmother didn't mind being alone – after being a widow for twenty years she .... it.

6 The children .... not yet .... their new school.

7 It took me hours of practice to .... my new computer.

8 I sometimes think I .... never .... living away from the city.

9 Robin made a big effort to .... his new life in another country.

10 The candidates made lots of mistakes in the exam because they .... not .... the type of questions.

Reading

A When young people leave home, what do they expect to do?

Looking forward to the time of our lives

Students about to go to university talk about what they expect and want from the experience.

IMOGEN CASEBOURNE

I see my degree as something which will make me more perceptive as opposed to improving my chances of getting a job. Nowadays no-one seems to want to broaden their minds. I do.
5 Obviously I'd want to earn enough to keep me above the breadline. But I wouldn't mind doing a boring job to save money to travel. Being unemployed doesn't worry me. It'll be quite strange going away. I've never been
10 taken away and put in a totally new environment. It should be interesting. I'm leaving my boyfriend behind. I intend to write to him a lot and see him in the holidays. But I don't want to be rushing home at weekends. I
15 hope university changes me. I've experimented with different ideas and ways of doing things already. I see university as the next step.

ANDREY KOTLARCZYK

20 I told someone I was going to Oxford and he said, 'Are your parents rich then?' Other friends say, 'I hope you still speak to us when you come back.' They think I'm going to become stuck up or something. I hope I
25 never will be. I don't worry about being a boy from a comprehensive school at Oxford. At the interview all the public school people were in one corner and we were in the other. But I think once everybody knows each
30 other the barriers will break down. My college is mixed, with a nine-to-seven ratio of men to women – pretty good, I thought. It

adds a bit of flavour; it tends to make it more friendly. I don't think university is
35 going to change me as much as it could if I'd had a really strict upbringing. Hopefully after three years at university I will have matured. I'll be more worldly. Most of all I'm looking forward to meeting lots of rich girls!
40 If you don't have a good time at university, when can you have a good time?

TESSA MURRAY

You don't really think about what you're doing unless you have a year off. Now I'm
45 more aware of the work aspect of university and how it does determine how you start off in your career. I am ambitious – I'd like to get into the media. I know it sounds square but I'm looking forward to studying and testing
50 my brain. I'm not going to sit in my room every night but I don't feel under pressure to go out. I'll have fewer distractions because I know what I want from university. All the attractions of university life and the freedom
55 don't seem so appealing any more, now that I've had a year off and had the experience of living in Africa. I hope I don't get too carried away with thinking I'm independent. I won't really have left home until I start earning my
60 own wage. As long as Dad gives me an allowance, I can't feel independent.

CHAN ROBERT GUPTA

The impression I get of university life is that students hardly study and they're out every
65 night. If friends ask me out there's no chance of me studying. That's going to be the main difference, that I'm going to be so free. I'm looking forward to running my own life. But I

am a bit nervous because I don't know how to
70 cook or anything. The thing that really worries me is work. I've worked in an accounts office so I know I don't want a boring nine-to-five job. I want a company car and a good wage and all that stuff. Everyone says that university is the
75 best years of your life – that's what I want it to be. But if it's boring I'll have to stick with it.

ELLIE STOREY

I think university will make a big difference to my life. All through school we had it
80 drummed into us that you need a degree to get a job. I chose law because I thought a vocational degree would be a good idea; at the moment, I think I might try to get into the business side of law. When I think about
85 university, the thought of a lecture or anything academic doesn't even cross my mind. A year ago I was looking forward to going to university. Then it was a big thing – leaving school and having a lot of freedom.
90 Now that I've had a good time without going to university I'm not looking forward to it quite so much. In the year since I left school, everyone's changed. Most people are much more confident, and they've tended to
95 broaden their views. After five months' travelling I'm much more confident. Boarding school gives you a slight advantage – I won't get homesick, I'm used to having a bank account and not over-running my allowance.
100 But life at an all-girls boarding school was quite claustrophobic and everyone at school used to be obsessed with talking about men. I am looking forward to mixing with more men. I think I'll find it easier to treat them as
105 human beings having had a year off.

B Look at the points in the next column, and match each of these to the student whose name appears in the box. Some of the points refer to more than one student.

A IMOGEN
B ANDREY
C TESSA
D CHAN ROBERT
E ELLIE

1 mentions financial matters

2 is leaving a boyfriend at home

3 want to develop intellectually

4 talks about the need to get a good job

5 has been away from home before

6 expects to gain more experience of life

7 talks about the way other people view him/her

8 emphasises having a good time

Reading

A When you were thirteen years old, what were the most important things in your life? What difficulties do people have when they move to another country?

THE WORST OF TIMES

I grew up in Evanston, Illinois, a suburb of Chicago, rather pleasant, I thought, with my older sister and brother. My mother got ill and was operated on, and the operation went wrong, so she was paralysed and almost didn't live, it was a
5 real struggle for her to get back to walking and talking. During this time, my father got a job at Oxford as Professor of English Literature, and we moved to Oxford.

One July we came over, and the first thing was this long, rainy summer when I didn't meet anyone my own age. I lay on
10 my bed a lot, hoping I would die in my sleep. I had great hopes of England, I thought it would be full of people like famous pop stars, handsome long-haired young men. But on the trip from the airport to Oxford I couldn't see any. I was looking for a replacement for my boyfriend, but meanwhile I was busy
15 writing to him daily.

My mother sort of disappeared form my life; she was still barely able to speak. My father was terribly unhappy and distressed about her. He was at the hospital all the time and had no time for us. Oxford High School for Girls was not
20 welcoming to Americans, to strange ones, particularly, and very unhappy, bitter, resentful ones, especially. I'd been ostracised before, in America, for riding a tricycle too long and having academic parents. I wasn't bullied, they weren't interested enough in me for that. But those girls treated me with a degree
25 of revulsion I had never encountered before. I became convinced there was something very wrong with my facial features that people had kindly never told me about before.

I wore a coat and hat all the time, it looked as if I was ready to leave at any moment, but I did it to cover up my body which
30 was ballooning under the effects of English cuisine. I got more and more withdrawn into this coat.

The only trouble with being thirteen is that six months makes a huge difference, and when I went back to America for the Easter vacation, my friends had moved on. And the
35 boyfriend pretended that we hardly knew each other … That was real bad. I went back to Oxford with no further hopes for myself. I became energyless, the effort of getting dressed was too much to bear, so eventually I took to sleeping in my school uniform.
40 My mother got better, but she never became a close figure again; I couldn't talk to her, partly because my father told us not to worry her. I was caught for shoplifting make-up – and I never wore make-up, I just did it to show off. It did cure me of stealing, it was so humiliating. I was sentenced to two years'
45 probation and psychiatric care, and the court made me go to a shrink until I grew myself sane.

B Find the word or phrase in the text that means the same as the explanation given below:

Paragraph 1
1 unable to move
2 very difficult

Paragraph 3
3 extremely upset
4 silently angry
5 made to feel unwanted
6 treated in an unpleasant way by people who are bigger and stronger
7 strong dislike
8 sure

Paragraph 6
9 stealing from a shop
10 demonstrate your abilities in order to impress people
11 making you feel ashamed
12 normal and healthy in your mind

C Now answer these questions about the text:

1 What did Lucy think of the place where she grew up?

2 What happened to her mother?

3 Why did Lucy move to Oxford?

4 How old was she then?

5 Was she looking forward to the move?

6 Who did she leave behind?

7 How was Lucy treated by the girls at her new school?

8 Why was it necessary for her to keep her coat on?

9 What kind of reaction did she get on her first trip back to the States?

10 What did Lucy do to draw attention to herself?

Talking Points

Section 1

What has happened?
What changes will there be for these people?

Section 2

Changes, good or bad, cause people stress.
With a partner, look at the list of changes and
discuss how people are affected by them.
Put them in order with the one that causes
most stress *first*, and the one that causes
least stress *last*.
Then compare your order with that of another
pair of students.

changing schools
moving to another country
leaving home   starting a training course
getting married   having a baby
losing a close relative
changing your job
having a row with your partner or a close friend
breaking up with a partner
moving to a new house
taking up a new hobby   going on holiday

Listening

Immigrants

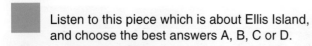 Listen to this piece which is about Ellis Island, and choose the best answers A, B, C or D.

1 The largest number of immigrants arrived in

   A 1892.
   B 1900.
   C 1907.
   D 1931.

2 How many American citizens are estimated to have ancestors who passed through Ellis Island?

   A 14 per cent
   B half a million
   C 40 per cent
   D 12 million

3 Some immigrants did not have to go through Ellis Island. Who were they?

   A Those who were ill.
   B Those with relatives who met them in New York.
   C Those who seemed well off.
   D Those whose papers were in order.

4 What experience did Giuseppe Santi have?

   A He enjoyed travelling on the ferry.
   B He was surprised by the view of New York.
   C He thought the reception building was wonderful.
   D He was frightened by the officials.

5 Which people have been recorded on the tape?

   A immigration officials
   B actors reading from immigrants' letters
   C descendants of immigrants
   D people who arrived as immigrants

Writing

Telling a story

Your college magazine is running a competition to see who can write the best story, using between 120 and 180 words, beginning:

My life has never been the same since that day.

The prize is five videos of your choice.

Before you write your entry, look at the hints below.

First, decide *what* to write about:

What day are you going to write about?
What happened on that day?
Why did your life change?

Write down your ideas like this and any extra points you want to make.

The day we moved to our new house in a new town
Lots of new things to see
Met Maria who became my best friend

Second, decide *how* you are going to write:

One of the main things to consider is what *tense* you are going to use. Here you need to write a story with events that took place in the past so you will need to use the *past simple tense* to talk about them. You may have to use the past perfect and the past continuous as well.

Start off with the important point in the first paragraph. You can develop this in the next paragraphs. You should have three paragraphs for this composition.

Plan all your ideas before you start writing.

Now write your entry.

English in Use

1 Complete the passage using one word for each gap.

Starting at College

It was Jenny's first day at college. She LOOKED (1) up at a quarter to seven, dressed IN (2) the clothes she had chosen the night before, had a quick cup of coffee and was off. As she stood WAITING (3) for the bus she realised how excited she felt. She was getting away from school and all its rules and regulations, was going to meet lots of new people and was about to start a COURSE (4) she really wanted to do, business studies. She was determined to have a successful CAREER (5) in business and doing the course was the first step.

The entrance hall was full of new students just LIKE (6) her. She looked at the notice board and saw where the business studies students WERE (7) supposed to meet. She found her WAY (8) to a large room where there were about fifty other students WHO (9) all seemed to be the SAME (10) age as Jenny. Then a member of staff came in and introduced himself

AS (11) their course tutor. He explained how the course was organised and what work would be EXPECTED (12) from the students. There was also a lot of practical information to do WITH (13) the college and its buildings. Then the whole group was taken to the library, where they learned where to find books and journals RELEVENT (14) to their studies. They were also shown the study centre which contained computers for student use and the 'quiet' room, a place where work COULD (15) be done without ANY (16) noise or distractions.

Jenny went to have lunch in the canteen with some people from her course and found that they came from a HOST (17) of different schools in the area. After lunch they ATTENDED (18) their first class, and Jenny realised that she was going to have to work hard IF (19) she was going to do well. In the evening she went OUT (20) with some of her new friends to celebrate the start of life at college.

---

2 Phrasal verbs

Complete the following sentences with a phrasal verb based on *set*.

EXAMPLE: He rolled up his sleeves and <u>set about</u> clearing the garden of leaves.

1 Jim is determined to .... his own business as soon as he is qualified.

2 The bad weather .... the day we arrived at the resort and completely spoiled our holiday.

3 The trainer .... the conditions which would apply to anyone who was chosen to be a member of the team.

4 The rescue party .... on their search for the missing climber.

5 John couldn't get the information he wanted from his parents and .... getting it himself.

6 'What time do we .... tomorrow?' the travellers asked the guide.

7 The bus .... passengers outside the entrance to the air terminal.

8 The alarm was .... by someone trying to enter the house.

9 Mary is .... acting as a career.

10 Robert's background .... him .... from the other students.

---

3 Word-formation

Complete the sentences with the correct from of the word in capitals.

EXAMPLES: All his staff think Mr Smith is a good <u>employer</u>   EMPLOY

There were seven <u>competitors</u> in the race.   COMPETE

'Why don't you like Frank?' 'He's a <u>liar</u>'   LIE

1 It's a fascinating job being a private ....   INVESTIGATE

2 The .... in the factory wanted an improvement in the canteen facilities.   WORK

3 The shop is waiting for a delivery of goods from the ....   SUPPLY

4 Ask the telephone .... to put you through to the number you require.   OPERATE

5 This aircraft carries two people – the pilot and the ....   NAVIGATE.

6 The man's a convicted ....   MURDER

7 The company has ten .... on the board.   DIRECT

8 We realised economic conditions in the country were bad because of the number of ....   BEG

9 Sally earns her living as a ....   TRANSLATE

10 .... broke into the shop and took away all the electrical goods.   ROB

unit 4 GETTING ABOUT

Lead-in 1 What are the pleasures and
discomforts of these activities?
What are the dangers?
Which would you most like to do?
Is there any other form of travel you
would particularly like to experience?

2 Choose the correct word for the gap in each sentence.

trip	boarded	take	journey
ride	on	drive	by	take off
	catch	land		

1 Richard hates travelling by car and goes everywhere he can .... foot.

2 The best way to get around the city is .... bus.

3 Alison learnt to .... a motorbike as soon as she was old enough to get a licence.

4 You can .... a bus at the stop on the corner.

5 Learning to .... a car takes most people quite a long time.

6 The best way to get here from the airport is to .... a taxi.

7 The plane couldn't .... until all the passengers had ....

8 Because of the fog, the plane was not able to .... and was diverted to another airport forty miles away.

9 How long does the .... to work take you?

10 We're going on a three-day .... to Paris.

3 Label these pictures of the outside and inside of a car.

windscreen	headlights	bonnet
wheel	number plate	roof

a

GO18 NHV

steering-wheel	handbrake	speedometer
accelerator	gear stick	fuel gauge

b

Reading

A Before you read the text discuss these questions:
Do cars play an important part in your life?
Do cars tell us something about the personality of the driver?

B Now read the following article about young people and cars. Five paragraphs have been removed from the article. Choose from paragraphs A–F the one which fits each gap (1–5). There is one extra paragraph that you do not need to use.

In Unit 3, page 28, you saw an example of a text from which sentences had been removed. Now you have an example of a text where paragraphs have been removed.
Use the techniques described on pages 27 and 28 to help you, remembering that now you are looking at whole paragraphs rather than sentences.

FRIDAY NIGHT BURNOUT

Teenagers and cars are a volatile combination. Three young Australians talk about their attachment to the automobile.

Rick started work at sixteen. In the three years since then he has owned five cars. Two were stolen and stripped (Australia has the highest rate of car theft in the world). Another was damaged beyond repair after a drinking session with his mates.

(1) ....

Even though he'd upgraded each machine, Rick also lost financially on each deal. He kept the car – and the repayments – even when unemployed for six months. 'I spend around a third of my pay on my car, and I still owe $6,000.' Rick calls his car a 'mean-looking custom V8', a phrase which his insurance company translates as 'high risk'.

(2) ....

Rick is a skilful driver, probably more skilful than he is with the machinery at work. And there's the additional benefit of not having a factory supervisor to tell him when he's made an error. The feeling of control both excites and frees him. Driving and cornering quickly – especially with passengers – gives him a thrill.

(3) ....

Sharon bought her wheels of independence when she was seventeen and still at school. 'I couldn't afford to move out of home but the car's the next best thing.'

(4) ....

Sharon's two brothers also have their own cars but she doesn't see much point in sharing. 'That'd be like wearing hand-me-down clothes or eating leftovers all the time. There's no way I could do that and still save face with my friends.'

(5) ....

'I'll need it for work,' he says bluntly. 'It's not a luxury. I need an impressive-looking car to impress potential employers.' Riding in Kevin's car is about as quiet as the office he hopes to call his own. There's an air of silent efficiency and of luxury, an image he's happy to display.

A She drives a small yellow two-door which is kept tidier than her room but demands a good deal more pocket money. 'I couldn't survive without a car. I don't want to be depending on guys for lifts. I don't want to give them that advantage. All my friends have cars and mine's probably the cheapest.'

B It also makes him a sure target for the highway patrol. 'All the guys at work drive hot cars. There's a regular burnout on Friday nights.' And Rick's convinced the girls love it too. 'A lot of them wouldn't go out with you if you were driving a pram or a shopping trolley.'

C The highway patrol is busiest on Saturday nights and they say that female drivers are increasingly forming part of their workload. The number of speeding offences committed by females in the 17–25 age-group is fast approaching that of young males.

D Kevin has just enrolled on an accountancy course at college. He bought an imported sports coupé on credit (with a little help from his parents) – a car costing twice his probable starting salary.

E His car has a loud exhaust which is almost as deafening as the factory where he works, but totally within his control. And of course he's got a car stereo that can also deafen. Not surprisingly, his usual way of driving is 'windows down'. Rick isn't easily amused, but he says with a smile 'I turn heads. Yeah. I know that.'

F Rick is one of the statistical 'high-risk under 25's'. Last year, car accidents cost Australians almost $6,000 million. Almost 3,000 people were killed, and more than 29,000 were injured.

Grammar: *ways of talking about the future*

 Which response seems more natural? (Grammar Notes **4.1**)

EXAMPLE:
The window is open.

I'll *close it.*
I'm *going to close it.*

(The first sentence is natural and appropriate, *will* or *'ll* is used for spontaneous offers to do things)

In making your choice, consider the following points:

1 Are you making a spontaneous, immediate decision at the moment of speaking or is it something you think will inevitably happen? Use *'ll.*
2 Is it something that you intend to do and have already decided to do, or is it obvious what is going to happen? Use *going to.*
3 Is it something that you have already made definite arrangements to do? Use the *present continuous.*
4 Is it something that you can find on a timetable, calendar or similar time-schedule? Use the *present simple.*
5 Are you thinking now about something you have arranged to do in the future? Use the *future continuous.*

Now choose the best response. There may be *one* or *two* good answers.

1 When is your meeting with Mr Thomas?
   a I'll see him at 10 a.m. tomorrow.
   b I'm seeing him at 10 a.m. tomorrow.
   c I see him at 10 a.m. tomorrow.

2 What time is your train?
   a It leaves at 7.30 p.m.
   b It's going to leave at 7.30 p.m.
   c It is leaving at 7.30 p.m.

3 I'm going to phone for a pizza. Do you want one?
   a Yes, I'll have one too.
   b Yes, I'm going to have one too.
   c Yes, I have one too.

4 Goodbye.
   a Goodbye. I'm going to see you soon.
   b Goodbye. I'll see you soon.
   c Goodbye. I see you soon.

5 … and what about the third day of our tour of Mogul India?
   a On the third day, you travel by train to Agra.
   b On the third day, you are going to travel by train to Agra.
   c On the third day, you'll be travelling by train to Agra.

6 Look at the skater! I think she's in danger!
   a Yes, the ice breaks!
   b Yes, the ice is going to break!
   c Yes, the ice will break!

7 You must be looking forward to going.
   a Yes, this time next week I'll be spending all day on the beach.
   b Yes, this time next week I'm spending all day on the beach.
   c Yes, this time next week I spend all day on the beach.

8 Bill is standing for election next month, isn't he?
   a Yes, but he doesn't win.
   b Yes, but he won't win.
   c Yes, but he won't be winning.

9 John is getting very nervous. Why is that?
   a He'll perform in the concert on Saturday.
   b He's performing in the concert on Saturday.
   c He'll be performing in the concert on Saturday.

10 You like Charles Dickens, don't you?
   a Yes, next year I'll read all his novels again.
   b Yes, next year I'm going to read all his novels again.
   c Yes, next year I'm reading all his novels again.

11 Does Michael know about the change of date?
   a No, but if I see him I'll tell him.
   b No, but if I see him I'm going to tell him.
   c No, but if I see him I'll be telling him.

12 Have you bought your new house yet?
   a Yes, we are moving in next month.
   b Yes, we'll move in next month.
   c Yes, we move in next month.

13 You look pale. Are you all right?
   a I'll be sick!
   b I'm going to be sick!
   c I'm being sick!

14 Your new radio doesn't work.
   a I know. I'm going to take it back.
   b I know. I'll take it back.
   c I know. I'll be taking it back.

15 …so I'm afraid we can't refund your money, madam.
   a I'm not satisfied. I'll take this matter further.
   b I'm not satisfied. I'm going to take this matter further.
   c I'm not satisfied. I'm taking this matter further.

Listening

An incident on the motorway

Listen to James describing an experience he had while driving and say whether the following statements are *true* or *false*.

1 He was driving in the morning.

2 There wasn't much traffic.

3 It was Friday.

4 His car was old.

5 He still has the same car.

6 He knew that there was something wrong with the car.

7 He was alone in the car.

8 He changed from one lane to another.

9 The car in front of him stopped.

10 He managed to brake just in time.

11 His car didn't suffer any damage.

English in Use

1 Complete the sentences with: *other*, *another*, *the other(s)*, *others*. (Grammar Notes **4.2**)

EXAMPLES: One of his sons became a politician and ...*the other*... a famous writer.
One of his daughters is an actress, ...*another*... a doctor and his youngest is at university.

1 That was a very nice cup of tea. Can I have .... one?

2 There are only two cakes left – you have one and I'll have ....

3 I've found one of my shoes but I can't find .... one.

4 Let's stop and rest. .... will soon catch us up.

5 .... mountaineers had climbed the mountain but only Hans had done it alone.

6 She saw her ex-boyfriend on .... side of the room.

7 I saw Michael just .... day in Hyde Park.

8 Heather goes to her cottage in the country every .... weekend.

9 We looked at each .... in amazement.

10 'I have done all I can,' said Professor Wright. '........................ must finish my work.'

2 Complete the sentences with one of these words. You will need to use some words more than once. (Grammar Notes **4.3**)

trip	journey	travel	travels
voyage	flight	pilgrimage	cruise

1 Mr and Mrs Edwards went on a four-week Mediterranean .... during which they visited several interesting ports.

2 I really enjoyed reading 'The .... of Marco Polo'.

3 When she finished her .... and Tourism course at college, Lucy got a job as a .... agent.

4 Joseph loves going on .... to places of religious significance.

5 During the .... the pilot left his cabin and spoke to the passengers.

6 Next week Mr Hardy will be away on a business .... to Berlin.

7 People say that .... broadens the mind.

8 Columbus's first .... across the Atlantic took just over five weeks.

9 Alan hated his long .... to work every day.

10 Bernard said that the .... would be quicker if we took the motorway.

Reading

A Before you read the text discuss these questions in pairs.
When did you last make a long journey by train? What was it like?
What are the advantages and disadvantages of travelling by train?

THE RAILS THAT NARROW THE MIND

By the time the boat had left Dover, the class division between the passengers was clearly visible. Cross-legged on the deck were the backpackers, the Interrailers, the young and poor, making do with stale baguettes and warm beer. The owners of the expensive cars below, the yuppy tourers and families on their way to their villas, were crammed into the restaurant, or consuming picnics at round plastic tables outside. They were elevated both physically and in status from the hardier folk on the deck. The only thing the two groups had in common was their footwear, the ubiquitous nylon training shoe.

I was with the young and poor, armed with paperback novels and a moneybelt containing the essentials: passport, travellers cheques and the all-important Interrail pass, which gives the freedom of Europe's railways at an economical price. I had eight days and planned to head for the Alps, then Italy, before swinging back through Southern Germany and Holland. In the following days, I was to travel 3,000 miles, spending four out of seven nights on the move. Twice, the demands of this schedule were to make me fork out extra money for a couchette, something that hard core backpackers generally begrudge. 'We try,' explained Patricia, from Canada, squatting on deck with her two companions, 'not to go above $20 a day. Budgeting is a state of mind ... you don't use restaurants but grocery stores.'

Patricia and her friends had already been travelling for nine weeks, including five days in Britain. There, alas, their passes were invalid. 'We wanted to visit friends in Leeds but the fare was too expensive.' What had been the highlight so far? 'Munich' they chorused in unison. 'We found our first MacDonalds. We ran so fast! You know the food is basically good there – it's kind of regulated.' Europe, they added, had many attractions. In Munich again, they had found themselves inadvertently taking part in an American TV series.

Alison, a student from Manchester was making her sixth consecutive trip. 'I've seen every country in Europe except Romania. I've never spent more than three nights in a row on the train, even though it saves you such a lot in accommodation bills.' 'Sometimes', she added, 'Interrail holidays could seem more fun in retrospect'. Some of those I met might have agreed, like the three lads I met on the train from Salzburg to Trieste. They were hoping to make their passes really pay by taking part in a competition to record the highest mileage. Unmistakeably in need of a bath, they explained, 'If we get to the end and we haven't got quite enough, we'll take a train to the North of Norway, and then catch another one straight back.'

Most travel in twos and threes, but some can be found on their own. The trains and stations of Europe are buzzing with strangers meeting each other and exchanging information. Off the boat, the youthful human stream headed for the train to Paris. Holly and Paula, 17, stood sharply out from the crowd – each had scarlet-painted fingernails and hair that had clearly been done very recently in a top London salon. The cash for the trip had been raised by long hours after school in a pizza restaurant. In the autumn they would be going to university in Los Angeles. 'What we've enjoyed most,' said Holly, 'is the British Grand Prix'.

Then the Paris Metro and the Gare du Lyon, with Kate, Mark and Paul, deeply depressed at finishing their studies at Cambridge, now heading for the Mediterranean. 'We don't want to go everywhere,' said Mark, as the humble pizzas – actually very humble indeed – arrived. It is supposed to be a holiday.' Kate described the sad end to Cambridge that they would remember for the rest of their lives. 'It was a wonderful party. We fed each other jelly, blindfolded.'

Making my way to the Chamonix train I noticed that the first unlucky station sleepers were already bedding down for the night, having arrived too late to find a bed anywhere. With any luck they would fare better than travellers in Venice, where as several Interrailers told me, the police are in the habit of arriving at four in the morning and blowing whistles until everyone gets up. I looked again at the Interrail pass, divided into thirty sections. Thirty journeys in a month: that would not be bad going. At the end of the last space, the pass informed me: 'To obtain a booklet of additional pages, please apply to the nearest station.' Somehow, I didn't think I would be doing that.

B Choose the best answer, A, B, C or D.

1 According to the writer, what is similar about the two groups on the boat?

A They are eating.
B They are on deck.
C They are wearing similar shoes.
D They are going on holiday.

2 How many nights did the writer spend on the train?

A seven
B four
C two
D eight

3 Where did he talk to Patricia?

A On the boat.
B On the train.

C At the station.
D In Britain.

4 What are the 'three lads' trying to do?

A To find somewhere to have a bath.
B To travel as far north as possible.
C To get to Trieste.
D To travel as many miles as possible.

5 What does the writer think of Interrailers?

A He admires their spirit of adventure.
B He thinks their experiences are shallow.
C He is impressed by their physical stamina.
D He thinks that travel helps them develop their ideas.

41

Reading

 A Discuss in pairs.

What do people wear when they go walking in the hills and mountains?
What do they take with them?
Why do some people enjoy this kind of walking?
What are the possible dangers?

TAKING THE WRONG PATH

I am very keen on hill walking and often spend weekends walking and sometimes camping in remote parts of the country. I thought I was quite experienced and skilful but a few months ago something happened which made me feel a lot
5 less confident. One Friday evening after finishing work I drove with three friends to a town about two hundred miles away. It was in the middle of an area which is famous for walking and climbing. We stayed the night in a bed-and-breakfast and set off early next morning. We drove a few miles and then parked
10 the car and got ready. We were wearing walking boots, and anoraks and carried rucksacks in which we had waterproof clothing, food, flasks of hot coffee and things that we might need in an emergency such as a torch, whistle and first-aid kit. Obviously, we had a map but we didn't have the one thing
15 which, as it turned out, we should have had – a compass.

We set off along a well-defined track, feeling cheerful, confident and looking forward to a good day's walking. The sun was up and as we walked along we soon began to sweat. It was hotter than we had expected. According to the map, there was
20 a farm after about four kilometres, and sure enough, there it was, although the path went to the left of it rather than to the right, as indicated on the map. Confident that we were going the right way, we ignored this discrepancy. Soon the path forked and, following the map, we took the left fork. The path
25 became less well-defined and soon petered out altogether. According to the map, the path continued for several more kilometres, but we ignored this discrepancy too. Things must have changed, we thought, since the map had been printed. The slope became steeper, the day hotter, our shirts stickier
30 and we were bothered by flies but we trudged on.

After about three hours we reached the summit of the hill and had a clear view of the countryside all around. We tried to compare what we could see with where we thought we were on the map, but we just couldn't make sense of it. We were confident
35 that we had taken the right path but finally we had to admit that we had gone wrong somewhere and were hopelessly lost. We decided to return to the car but it took a long time to work out the best way and we got lost again. We soon became fed up and anxious and started to quarrel and blame each other for what had
40 happened. It was getting dark before we reached the car and we were panicking about the prospect of still being lost when night fell. It was only when we arrived at the car park that we realised that we had, right from the beginning, been heading in precisely the opposite direction from the one we should have taken.

B Find the word or phrase in the text which in context is similar in meaning to:

Paragraph 1
1 enthusiastic about
2 faraway

Paragraph 2
3 clearly visible
4 perspire
5 as we expected
6 split
7 side of the hill
8 annoyed
9 walked in a tired way
10 argue

C Explain the meaning of these phrasal verbs as used in the text.

Paragraph 1
1 set off
2 turned out

Paragraph 2
3 petered out

Paragraph 3
4 work out

D Work in pairs. Ask and answer these questions.

1 On what day of the week did the walk begin?

2 What did they carry with them?

3 Were they suitably dressed?

4 At what point did the map indicate a possible problem?

5 Why were they worried when they got to the top of the hill?

6 How did the mood of the walkers change during the day?

7 What were they most worried about?

8 How long did the walk last?

9 When did they first take the wrong path?

10 Why does the writer mention that they had no compass?

Talking Points

Section 1

Read the poem and with a partner discuss the
questions below.

The Subway Piranhas

Did anyone tell you
that in each subway train
there is one special seat
with a small hole in it
and underneath the seat
is a tank of piranha fish
which have not been fed
for quite some time.
The fish become agitated
by the shoogling of the train
and jump up through the seat.
The resulting skeletons
of unlucky passengers
turn an honest penny
for the transport executive
hanging far and wide
in medical schools

Edwin Morgan (b.1920)

Where do the piranhas live?
What do they feed on?
What happens to the things they feed on?
Who benefits from this?

Section 2

Discuss with a partner:

What different ways of travelling by public transport
are there?
Which forms of public transport do you use yourself?
What do you think is the best way of travelling in a city?
What's your opinion of cars being allowed in the city?
When you're shopping, do you prefer pedestrian areas
to areas where cars are allowed?

Section 3

Discuss in groups of three:

When you travel to unfamiliar places, do you prefer to
travel independently or to go on a package tour?

What are the advantages and disadvantages of these
different ways of travelling?

Useful expressions:

The good/bad points are ....

What I like/dislike about .... is ....

I'd rather .... than

Listening

Planning a journey

Listen to the instructions on the tape about how to get to someone's house. Complete the notes. Write *one* or *two* words in each gap.

Leave the motorway at junction .... (1).

Go past the .... (2) in Bedford.

Turn .... (3) at the .... (4) roundabout.

Go .... (5) for about .... (6) kilometres.

Turn .... (7) after a pub called 'The Compasses'.

Turn .... (8) opposite a .... (9).

Go straight on to the .... (10) and turn .... (11) into Manor Road.

Turn .... (12) into Grangeway.

The house is just after the .... (13) on the left.

It's number .... (14).

The garage has a .... (15).

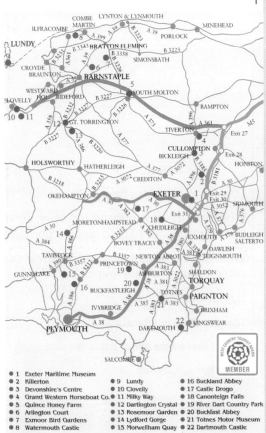

Writing

A letter of advice

Some friends of yours, Mr and Mrs Muller and their daughters, Petra, 16, and Sybille, 10, are planning to come to England for a holiday. They want to spend one day in the West Country, starting in Exeter and travelling by car. Use the map and the information given to write them a letter of advice, suggesting how they can best spend their day. You know that Mr Muller is a teacher and likes sailing at weekends and that his wife teaches horse-riding. Sybille intends to be a vet when she grows up and Petra wants to be a fashion designer. Don't forget how long they will spend at each place and how long it will take to get to the next place. Remember that they will need to eat and may want to buy souvenirs. Write between 120 and 150 words.

EXETER MARITIME MUSEUM
Explore 100 boats from all over the world. Boat trips on the historic Exeter canal. Rain or shine, a great day out for all ages. Reduced prices for families. Charming restaurant and tearoom. Gift, souvenir and book shop. Free parking. Open all year, every day from 10 a.m. to 6 p.m.

KILLERTON
There are fifteen acres of beautiful hillside gardens which sweep down to wide lawns and herbaceous borders. The garden and park offer delightful walks through rare trees and shrubs. The Pauline de Bush collection of costume is displayed in the house in a series of rooms furnished in different periods ranging from the eighteenth century to the present day.
Restaurant and shop. Open March to October, daily except Tuesday 11 a.m. to 6 p.m.

THE MILKY WAY
A warm welcome awaits you at this working dairy farm. Watch the milking of 130 cows from our viewing gallery. Many baby animals for children to cuddle. Tractor rides. Adventure playground. Shop. Café. Picnic area. You will need 3-6 hours to see everything. Free parking. Located on the A29 between Clovelly and Bideford.

ARLINGTON COURT
Arlington Court is famous for its collection of carriages and horse-drawn vehicles. Carriage rides are a speciality. In the park there are ponies and sheep. Traditional Victorian garden and lakeside walks. The house, built in 1822, contains a fascinating collection of model ships, costume and furniture. Restaurant and picnic site. Open March to October, daily except Saturday. Near Barnstaple on the A29.

GRAND WESTERN HORSEBOAT
A 2½ hour horsedrawn barge trip along the beautiful Grand Western Canal. Open Wednesday and Sunday in May. Departure times 11 a.m. and 2.30 p.m. Reservations strongly recommended. Free parking. Near Tiverton.

English in Use

 1 Phrasal Verbs

Travelling and meeting people

Complete these sentences. Use the verb in the correct form.

see off	make for	pull up	check in
pick up	get away	drop in	call for

1 I'll .... you at 8 p.m. and we'll go to a restaurant.

2 At 10 a.m. exactly the taxi .... outside my house.

3 Phone me as soon as you arrive and I'll .... you .... at the airport.

4 Peter and Sarah are planning to .... for a few days at the end of May.

5 When he lost power in one engine, the pilot decided to .... the nearest airfield.

6 You must .... two hours before your flight.

7 Mary doesn't like even close friends .... without phoning first.

8 On Saturday I have to go to the airport to .... my sister .... She's going back to Canada.

2 **A** So, neither

Agree with these statements. Begin with *so* or *neither*. (Grammar Notes **4.4**)

EXAMPLES: I love sunbathing on the beach. *So do* I.
            I never drink water from the tap. *Neither do* I.

1 Peter won a prize in last week's lottery.

2 I always get up early.

3 I had finished writing before the invigilator told us to stop.

4 Sally hasn't got a ticket for the concert.

5 We won't be able to go to Julia's party.

6 I used to live in Madrid.

Now disagree with the six sentences.

EXAMPLES: I love sunbathing on the beach. I *don't*.
            I never drink water from the tap. I *do*.

B Re-write the second sentence using *so* or *neither* and two other words.

1 Janet hasn't completed her course yet. Sarah hasn't completed hers either.

2 Michael would like a job in advertising. Christopher would also like an advertising job.

3 Professor Watt couldn't read the inscription. Nicholas couldn't read it either.

4 Elizabeth is going to sing at the concert next week. Maria is going to sing as well.

5 I'd rather wait for the express train. Peter prefers to wait as well.

6 Bill climbed Mount Snowdon last summer. Jenny climbed it too.

3 Word-formation

Complete the sentences with the correct form of the word in capitals.

EXAMPLES: Because of recent medical advances this disease is now ..*curable*.. .   CURE

            The village is so ..*attractive*.. it's no surprise many people want to live there.   ATTRACT

1 It's not a good idea to send .... objects through the post.   BREAK

2 The new management team aims to make the factory more ....   PRODUCE

3 Chris never stops talking – he's the most .... person I know.   TALK

4 The weather over the past week has been very ....   CHANGE

5 Army officers need to be ....   DECIDE

6 It's .... to carry some foreign currency when you travel abroad.   ADVISE

7 Last year the island suffered the .... force of a major hurricane.   DESTROY

8 The type of clothing she was wearing was not at all .... for the tropical conditions.   SUIT

9 The whole group spent an .... evening singing and dancing.   ENJOY

10 All the children enjoyed .... activities such as music and painting.   CREATE

unit 5 CAKES AND ALE

Lead-in **1** What is happening in the pictures?
What kinds of food do you like?
Do you like different types of food in
summer or winter?
Is the food you like good for you?
What kind of food do you eat on
special occasions?

2 Choose the correct word for each gap.

> tough   tasty   balanced   tender
> take-away   root   lean   bun   pie
> raw   staple   tart   fast food
> instant   beans

1   If you want to be healthy you should be sure to eat a .... diet.

2   Kevin enjoys eating the fat on the meat, but his wife says it's better to eat only .... meat.

3   A number of nutritionists point out the value of eating uncooked food, such as salad and .... vegetables.

4   I sent back my steak because it was ....

5   .... vegetables, such as carrots, parsnips and turnips taste very good when made into thick winter soups.

6   Potatoes, rice and pasta are examples of .... foods.

7   The lamb Sara cooked was so .... it seemed to melt in the mouth.

8   When Richard and Kate turned up unexpectedly, Sam dashed out and got a .... from the Chinese restaurant.

9   Most children love the sort of .... they serve in places like burger restaurants.

10   Mary doesn't like .... coffee. She prefers to buy the .... and grind them herself.

11   Jane manages to prepare really .... dishes from the simplest ingredients.

12   Tom's favourite dish is steak and kidney ....

13   Anna made a lovely jam ....

14   A .... is a sweet bread roll which often contains currants or spices.

3   Choose the correct word or phrase for each gap.

> main   cereal   heavy   dinner
> go out   mugs   bar   green   hot
> fillings   flavour   pudding   courses
> slice   fruit   vegetables

ucy, aged fourteen, describes the sort of food she eats.

'Well, when I get up in the morning the most I can face is a .... (1) of toast and two big .... (2) of tea. My brothers head straight for the cornflakes, but I'm not into .... (3) At least this means we don't argue. During break in the morning, I have a biscuit. It keeps me going till lunchtime. Usually I eat in the canteen, and it's not bad, we have a bit of choice. If I'm being sensible, I avoid the chips and go for a baked potato. There are usually three .... (4) to choose from, and baked beans are my favourite. I always take some .... (5) with me, so that's when I eat it. It's usually an apple, an orange or a banana. On the way home from school, I usually stop at the sweet shop and get a .... (6) of chocolate. It raises my spirits a bit when I think about all the homework I've got to get done in the evening.

Mum always cooks .... (7) for us in the evening, and she tries to make sure we are all there to eat it together. It's a proper meal and we usually have two .... (8). The .... (9) course will be either meat or fish, usually meat, and Mum likes us to eat lots of vegetables, especially .... ones. My favourites are broccoli and spinach. Sometimes she cooks us a casserole, and I think this is quite a good way of combining meat and .... (11). You can also vary casseroles quite a lot by changing the .... (12) of the sauce. After that, we have a .... (13), and my mother often cooks fruit in different ways. It's not too .... (14), which is good for me because I have to get on with my homework.

Occasionally, on special occasions, we .... (15) to eat in a restaurant. I like trying different sorts of cooking, and I really like anything that is .... (16), like curry. I don't think I'd like to eat this every day but it's really good for a change.'

Reading

A What kind of food do you like to have when you want to entertain people?
Do you make the preparations in advance, or on the day?
How do you make your guests feel really at home?
Read the text and see what happened to Sally the day she had invited people to dinner.

A Dinner Party

After finishing work, Sally rushed to the supermarket to buy the things she needed for the dinner party she was giving for
5 three friends. The first disaster occurred on the train home. It was so crowded and there was such a crush that the tomatoes were squashed and the pot of
10 cream burst open in the bag. As soon as she got home she took out the chicken, rubbed it with salt, put butter under its skin and then put the chicken in the oven.
15 She started to slice the carrots and chop the onion but the knife slipped and she cut her finger. She ran cold water over it to stop the bleeding, then put on a
20 plaster. She couldn't be bothered to peel the mushrooms so she cut

them in half and threw them in the pan with the other vegetables. She started to wash
25 the lettuce and was disgusted when two beetles crawled out. A strange smell seemed to be coming from the oven and she opened the door to have a look.
30 The chicken looked all right – it wasn't burnt. Then she realised with horror that she had left some plastic wrapping under the chicken and it was melting. She
35 swiftly removed it and hoped the smell would go away before the chicken finished cooking.

She turned her attention to the salad again and salvaged as many
40 squashed tomatoes as she could. On looking in the cupboard for the rice, she was appalled to find she

had run out. She threw on her coat and rushed to the corner shop to
45 buy some more – at an exorbitant price. She got back just in time to prevent the vegetables from burning. She remembered that the strawberries were still in her bag
50 and got them out. She was horrified to find, as she rinsed them, that the ones at the bottom of the box were mostly squashed and couldn't be used.
55 When everything was more or less all right, she dashed upstairs to get herself ready. She was in the middle of having a quick shower when her friends rang to
60 apologise for telling her at such short notice that they could not come after all, but could they come at the same time next week?

B Find a word or phrase in the passage which in context, is similar in meaning to:

Paragraph 1
1 crushed
2 cut
3 didn't want to make the effort
4 take the skin off
5 quickly

Paragraph 2
6 rescued
7 very expensive
8 washed gently

Paragraph 3
9 hurried
10 without very much warning

C Make a list of the things that went wrong on the evening Sally had invited her friends to dinner. Compare your list with a partner's.

Grammar: *Sentences with if*

This unit looks at writing sentences with *if*. All of these sentences will refer to the present and future.(Grammar Notes **5.1**).

A Look at these examples of sentences about things which are *likely* to happen, in the view of the speaker.

EXAMPLES:

<u>If you buy</u> a television this month, <u>we will give you</u> a free video recorder.

<u>You will not have to pay</u> a fine <u>if you bring</u> your library books back tomorrow.

<u>If the car isn't</u> suitable, <u>will you take it back</u> ?

Now complete these sentences.

1 ...., we will miss the train.

2 ...., I will arrive about 10 am.

3 ...., you will not catch malaria.

4 .... he will have a good chance of winning the race.

5 If you lift weights regularly, ...

6 If you follow this diet, ...

7 What .... if I sign an exclusive contract with you?

8 If I drive your children to school today, ... ?

9 What .... if we press this button?

B Look at these sentences which refer to things which are *unlikely* or *impossible*.

If I trained very hard, I would be able to complete a marathon.
If I had wings, I would be able to fly

Look closely at the verb forms. What forms are used?

a If I knew the answer, I would tell you.

b I would telephone her if I knew her number.

c If we touched the electric fence, we would get a shock.

d John wouldn't give money to beggars even if he were a millionaire.

C Match the two halves of the sentences.

1 If the rent goes up,

2 If we don't repair it now,

3 If she doesn't qualify as a doctor,

4 If you don't hurry up,

5 If we refused to obey these orders,

6 If he had the money,

7 If you don't let them rest,

8 If I had £100,000,

9 If we didn't protect it,

10 If I lied to Terry,

a I would feel guilty.

b I would invest the money in shares.

c Martin would repay the loan.

d the horses will become exhausted.

e John will leave his flat.

f we'll leave without you.

g birds would eat the fruit on the tree.

h what would happen to us?

i what job will Sarah do?

j the roof will leak next winter.

D Complete these sentences.

1 ...., I would buy my own personal jet.

2 ...., I would grow my own vegetables.

3 ...., there would be crocodiles in English rivers.

4 ...., we would get stuck in the morning traffic jams.

5 If we bought this house and redecorated it ....

6 If I had enough time, ...

7 If I understood Russian, ...

8 If John knew who the thief was, ... ?

9 .... if I told you the secret?

10 .... if someone stole your passport?

Listening

Being a vegetarian

 Listen to these two young women, Helen and Katherine, talking about being a vegetarian.

Look at these statements and say which of the women each statement refers to. You may find that a statement refers to both speakers. Helen speaks first, Katherine second. Tick the appropriate box.

	Helen	Katherine
1 states the age when she became a vegetarian		
2 still eats fish		
3 lost weight when she changed her diet		
4 continued to eat some meat after first becoming a vegetarian		
5 feels it is wrong to kill animals for meat		
6 admits her eating style is now a matter of habit		
7 mentions the kind of food she now prepares		
8 isn't concerned about other people's eating habits		
9 felt healthier when not eating meat		
10 refers to the exact moment she became a vegetarian		

English in Use

For questions 1–15, read the text below and look carefully at each line. Five lines are correct, and ten have a word which should not be there. Tick the correct lines and underline the wrong words in the incorrect lines.

EXAMPLES: 0 ✓

00 <u>is</u>

Soup

0 Soup is one the world's most popular dishes. There are

00 various types of thin soup, the first is being clear soup

1 made from meat, poultry, fish or vegetables. Semi-clear soup

2 has added in meat, vegetables or rice. Thick soups include

3 those with starchy ingredients, such as like flour, pulses or

4 potatoes. Cream soups are thickened with either butter, cream

5 or egg yolks. The thickening agents produce a richer

6 texture than for the soup as well as changing its colour.

7 Soups are often improved by the addition of such a garnish,

8 which improves the flavour or provides a contrasting

9 texture. Pasta is used to garnish many of thin soups, while

10 cheese goes on well with vegetable soups. To add colour to

11 plain cream soup, a vegetable garnish is appropriate. Celery

12 leaves, watercress or parsley look good on the top surface

13 of the soup. Cucumber makes an attractive garnish

14 for chilled soups. Soup provides you a tasty and nutritious

15 dish with little of preparation.

Reading

A What are the basic foods in the diet of most people in your country?

Do people in different parts of your country eat differently?

A Tale of Two Diets

IT IS 1pm outside Coatbridge High School. Two vans are parked by the gates, a group of children at each window clamouring for burgers, sweets and crisps. For many, this
5 is the menu for lunch every day. They don't like school food: 'It stinks.' They don't like this food much either, but it's cheaper and it isn't school.

Ian Danvers, 14, has finished his meal:
10 a sausage in a white roll and a Coke. Ian Hutton, 15, has eaten a bit more: a roll, a potato scone, a Coke, a Mars Bar icecream and a Toffee Crisp. Both boys' parents know their sons eat from the van and
15 don't mind.

John Forsyth, the head teacher, points out that pupils are taught about diet in their lessons on home economics. 'But we have to break down the habit of years and years in
20 western Scotland of chips, chips, chips,' he says. 'It's their money and their decision. There is wholesome food in the canteen, but if we stopped serving chips, a lot of youngsters would simply go to the chip shop
25 across the road.'

Coatbridge is a predominantly working-class town nine miles outside Glasgow in Monklands, an area where about 75 per cent of the population lives in council
30 accommodation, the highest level in Britain. It also has the highest death rate from heart disease in Europe.

Outside Coatbridge's Asda supermarket on a busy weekday, nearly every trolley
35 contains cereal, white bread, sugar, Coke, biscuits, sausages, eggs, crisps and cakes. Janet Rayner has just spent about £30 on these for her family of four. Her son, William, 15, comes home for lunch. 'He has
40 four rolls, two cream rings, a Kit Kat and a big glass of Diet Coke,' she says. A typical evening meal is steak pie with potatoes and peas, apple tart and icecream. She sometimes cooks a fry-up for lunch.

45 Kim McKay, a part-time clerk, spends about £55 a week on herself, her husband and their small daughter. About £6 of that goes on fruit and vegetables. She has also bought lasagne, and spare ribs from the
50 freezer shop. Another shopper says she spends £4.50 a week on fruit and vegetables for a family of four.

Finding a fresh brown sandwich in Coatbridge is difficult. The bakery windows
55 sparkle with cakes covered in bright icing sugar. In one, the cafe serves chips, sausage rolls and beefburgers. In another, the assistant says they sell more than twice as much white bread as brown. The butcher
60 makes six different kinds of pies and sells about 50 of each a day. 'We Scots are guilty of eating a lot of fat,' the manager remarks. 'I love it.'

Peter Orchard, acting fresh-food manager
65 at Asda, has recently moved from Edinburgh. In Coatbridge, he says, Asda has a lot more customers but takes less money. 'People in

Scotland are getting on to the healthy-eating train, but not in areas like this. Here they're
70 sticking to traditional ways.'

Were Coatbridge residents to shop at Waitrose in London's Kings Road, they might feel they were in a foreign land. Locating the cream cakes is tricky, and
75 when you do they turn out to be 'mandarin, kiwi and almond slices.' Shoppers push trolleys loaded with skimmed milk, wholemeal bread, mineral water and fresh soups such as 'green pea
80 with yoghurt and mint'. There are ready-made salads like 'endive and radicchio' and 'broccoli and peanut'. The selection of pies is negligible.

Pamela Dale, a school secretary, spends
85 about £100 a week on food for four adults. She says she never fries food. They would eat grilled steak or fish with a green vegetable and potatoes, perhaps a home-made trifle, more likely some fresh fruit. Penny Girling, a
90 librarian, says she spends about £80 a week for two adults and two children, about a third of it on fruit and vegetables.

Back in Scotland, Monklands District Council is alarmed and has decided to act. It
95 is planning a health strategy to re-educate its residents. A council spokesman says: 'If you talk to people here about diet, they'll assume you mean slimming. This is an old-fashioned society, but the time has come to
100 change people's approach. If you can afford to buy cream buns and Coke, you can afford to buy fresh fruit and veg.'

B Look at the following questions and choose the best answers, A, B, C or D.

1 What kind of food is most popular with the schoolchildren?

  A The food served in the canteen.
  B The food they can buy in the chip shop.
  C The food they bring from home each day.
  D The food sold from a van outside school.

2 Schoolchildren in Coatbridge like to eat

  A fruit.
  B fish fingers.
  C rolls.
  D fried potatoes.

3 What particular problem makes Coatbridge worth studying?

  A what people die of
  B unemployment

  C crime
  D the kind of housing people live in

4 Which kind of food is not considered as being very important by shoppers in Coatbridge?

  A white bread
  B fruit
  C chips
  D cakes

5 How does the King's Road supermarket differ from the one in Coatbridge?

  A People buy more cream cakes.
  B The pies have different fillings.
  C The emphasis is on fresh food.
  D Frozen food is very popular.

Reading

A Are you careful about what you eat? Are you the weight you want to be? If you feel you are overweight, what do you do to lose weight?

B Now read the introduction to a book on diet, and find three ways to:
a eat in a healthy way
b lose weight

Eating the Healthy Way

If you feel fat, your body is trying to tell you something: lose weight.

I want to assure you that you can get to your ideal weight and stay at your ideal weight – and be and feel healthy – and enjoy food. In fact, you can enjoy as much food as you're eating now: you just need to swap some
5 less-fattening food for some of the fattening food you're eating. Perhaps you're a diet expert, you've tried every one going and your weight has gone up and down like a yo-yo. Or maybe you've never been on a diet before, know you need to lose some weight but are confused by the conflicting advice when you flick through diet books and magazines. Or perhaps you're
10 interested in your family's health and their weight and you want to understand about healthy food as well as slimming food.

Whoever you are, if you let it, this book could change your life. A big claim? A tall story? How do you know I'm not a quack? Well, I am a doctor, but being medically qualified doesn't absolve one from being wrong. There
15 are diet books on sale which are written by doctors and are mistaken; in fact they are sometimes shocking in the outdated and incorrect advice they offer.

But the main views expressed in this book are not only my own: they are also held by the overwhelming majority of medical and nutritional experts around the world. There is now a medical consensus on the sort of diet we
20 should follow to lose weight – which is also the most healthy diet we can eat.

No one can claim we know all there is to know about nutrition, obesity and healthy eating as there are still gaps in our knowledge. But what we can now confidently assert is that the healthiest diet – the one which most reduces the risk of a wide range of diseases – is also the safest and most
25 effective one to return you to your ideal weight and keep you there. This is good news after all, everyone wants to be slim and healthy, not thin and ill. This book gives you the knowledge you need to take control of your own

body and your own life. Don't be fatalistic about being fat: it may be harder for you than for others, but if you want to be slim, and commit yourself to it, then you will succeed.

You need to understand why you are fat. Being overweight can be
30 explained in one sentence. If you take in more energy (calories) in your food than your body needs for your particular lifestyle, then your body will lay down that surplus energy as fat. The only way to lose weight is to take in less energy or to use more. Please, please don't let anyone tell you any different. So many people want to believe in a magic 'something' which will
35 help them lose weight but it doesn't exist. If you want to believe in something, why not believe in fact rather than fiction?

If you cut down the amount of fat you eat, you will take in fewer calories.

If you cut down the amount of sugar you eat, you will take in fewer calories.

If you increase the amount of fibre you eat, you will be able to cut down fat
40 and sugar without feeling hungry.

If you increase your amount of physical activity, you will burn up more calories.

If you follow these principles, you will lose weight.

This book explains why those facts are true and how to put those principles
45 into practice in your own life. After you've read it, you'll understand why we get fat and how to get slim. You won't have to carry a diet plan or calorie chart around for ever. You will be in charge of your own body, your own health, your own life.

If you feel fat, your body is trying to tell you something: lose weight.
50 Here's how …

C Choose the best answer according to the text.

1 swap

  A exchange
  B eat
  C cook

2 conflicting

  A difficult to understand
  B of different kinds
  C disagreeing

3 flick

  A look through quickly
  B study
  C consult

4 surplus

  A extra
  B sufficient
  C little

D Now answer these questions.

1 Who does the writer think should read his book?

2 How can people lose weight while eating as much food as they are eating now?

3 Why does this doctor claim the authority to write this book?

4 What kind of diet is the most healthy, according to the book?

5 How can being overweight be explained?

6 What is the author's view of 'magic' diets?

7 What two ways are indicated of cutting down on calories?

8 Why is fibre useful in a diet?

Talking Points

Section 1

Work in groups of three. Think of your favourite fruit, and without saying what it is, find three ways of describing it, as it appeals to you. Tell the members of your group your words, and see if they can guess the fruit you are describing.

With a partner, write down three words to describe plums.

Now read this poem:

I have eaten
the plums
that were in
the icebox

and which
you were probably
saving
for breakfast

Forgive me
they were delicious
so sweet
and so cold

William Carlos Williams
(1883–1963)

Section 2

Describe your favourite meal.

Work in groups of three.
Try to agree on the perfect meal and together write down the menu.

Discuss in groups of three:

What does the poem make you think of, apart from plums?

53

Listening

In a restaurant

Listen to these people who have just had a meal in a restaurant and answer the questions.

1 What do the customers in the restaurant want?

2 What does the waiter say about the bill?

3 Why does he need the table?

4 Are the customers willing to leave?

5 Did they enjoy the meal?

6 Does the waiter give them what they want?

7 What happens in the end?

Writing

Letter to a friend

 A Look at the two recipes in the next column that have got mixed up. With a partner, decide which sentences belong to each recipe. Give each recipe a title.

B When you have separated the recipes, look at how instructions are given. What form of the verb is used? What must you do to make sure that people will understand your instructions?

C A penfriend is coming to visit you in your country and has written to ask you about what kind of food he/she can expect to eat. Write to your friend, explaining what people normally eat and what the usual mealtimes are. You should include a recipe for a typical dish, and could also talk about what people eat on special occasions.

Before you write the letter, look back to page 24 in Unit 2, to remind yourself of what a letter to a friend should look like.

1 First line a cake tin.

2 Add the chicken pieces a few at a time and brown on all sides.

3 Beat the eggs into creamed mixture a little at a time.

4 Wash and dry currants, sultanas and raisins. Halve the cherries. Stir into fruit with peel.

5 Stir the onion and herbs into the pan. Add the flour, followed by the stock and the beans.

6 In separate bowls, sift flour and spices, then cream together butter, sugar and rind.

7 Add the bay leaf and the seasoning to the chicken. Cover and cook at 180°C for about an hour. Serve with boiled new potatoes.

8 Fold in half the flour then add the dried fruit and almonds.

9 Spoon into a tin. Cook on a baking sheet in an oven pre-heated to 150°C.

10 Check if it is ready by inserting a skewer into the centre. When the skewer comes out clean, the cake is ready.

11 First, finely chop the onion and cut the beans into thirds.

12 Then heat the olive oil and add the crushed garlic.

13 Remove from the pan. Drain off the fat and reserve a small quantity of the liquid.

14 Bring to the boil and pour over the chicken.

English in Use

1 Complete the sentences with a preposition.

1 The monkeys lived .... a diet consisting .... fruit and nuts.

2 Mary fried the fish .... olive oil.

3 What are the ingredients .... this recipe?

4 This avocado mix can be used .... its own or .... a dip.

5 The soup is made .... vegetables from our garden.

6 This meal is low .... calories.

7 The chicken has been cooked .... the oven.

8 She put the saucepan .... the hot plate.

9 Brown for five minutes .... a hot grill.

10 This delicious drink is made .... apples.

11 Beat the eggs and add .... the pan .... the seasoning.

12 Cut the meat .... small chunks.

13 Cook the beans .... tender.

14 These tomatoes have been dried .... the sun.

15 The athlete needed a diet that was high .... carbohydrates.

16 Place all the ingredients .... the pan and bring .... the boil.

17 He expertly separated the white of the egg .... the yolk.

18 The waitress put all the dishes .... the tray.

2 Phrasal Verbs

Complete the sentences with a phrasal verb based on *bring*.

EXAMPLE: The shop assistant said I could *bring* the jumper *back* if it didn't fit.

1 The taste of the biscuit .... memories of his childhood.

2 I'll .... the presents some time before Christmas.

3 Mary's mother .... her old photograph albums to show to Mary's boyfriend.

4 The accountant .... the subject of late payment.

5 He got soaked in the storm and this .... a bad cold.

6 She had the dress for her wedding .... from Paris.

7 What .... your change of mind?

8 Many shopkeepers found it necessary to .... their prices to attract customers.

9 The skier .... a completely unexpected victory.

10 This director always manages to .... the best in the actors.

3 Word-formation

Complete the sentences with the correct form of the word given in capitals.

EXAMPLES: The company has a ...*removal*... service, that you may find useful when you move house. REMOVE

For many years people doubted the ...*existence*... of this animal, but then one was discovered in the jungle. EXIST

He didn't know what to do and asked his teacher for ...*guidance*... . GUIDE

1 The council has received a .... for a new restaurant to be built on the site. PROPOSE

2 We serve a varied menu, and adapt our dishes according to the .... of our guests. PREFER

3 Sarah expressed her .... by stamping her foot. ANNOY

4 The cook is not allowed to change the menu without the .... of the owner of the restaurant. APPROVE

5 It is compulsory to have car .... INSURE

6 It's an .... for a restaurant to have a dirty kitchen. OFFEND

7 The police had to deal with a number of .... caused by people celebrating their team's victory. DISTURB

8 Mike's .... to eat the main course upset Mary. REFUSE

9 What .... did you notice between the food you usually eat and what you ate in New York? DIFFER

10 Joan's catering business has grown so fast she has had to take on another secretary to deal with the .... CORRESPOND

Exam Practice 1

1 (Exam Hints: Paper 1)

You are going to read a magazine interview with a dress designer. Choose the most suitable heading from the list A–I for each part (1–7) of the interview. There is one extra heading which you do not need to use. There is an example at the beginning (0).

A First Time My Name Was On A Shop
B First Impression I Gave
C First Influence
D First Priority In Life
E First Born
F First Time In Britain
G First Sale
H First Priority At Work
I First Ambition

First Person: Designer **Catherine Walker**

The dress designer to the Princess of Wales was born in France.
She came to England 25 years ago and married an English lawyer.

(0) ....I.......

I wanted to be a physiotherapist. Of course, at sixteen you don't know anything about anything – it's the last thing I'd have been able to do. I got cold feet the week before I was due to start. The only thing I could move to was philosophy. Even though I was nervous in exams, I got a distinction.

(1) ....

I was in Aix-en-Provence finishing my degree and the father of one of my English friends gave a really posh dinner party. He was a very nice gentleman and I realised I couldn't even say thank you to him. I felt really silly. I decided to come here to learn English. I arrived with a very big suitcase at Victoria Station and found a place to live at the end of the District Line. That's how I began life in England, in a little place, feeling lost. I think I was quite brave.

(2) ....

When I arrived here, not speaking English at all, the most irritating thing was that everyone thought I was terribly sweet. I hated it.

(3) ....

My French background had pushed me towards being academic. But when I had Naomi I became more aware of my sense of touch, my visual sense – all of my senses developed. I adored having the babies and I would never have been a fashion designer if I hadn't experienced those changes.

(4) ....

My husband died in 1975 and I started making things as a therapy to get over his death. I made some children's clothes and went to a shop on the King's Road called 'Small Wonder' with a basketful to sell. I was so shy I dropped the whole lot, but they still bought some. I wasn't selling to make money, you have to get rid of what you make so you can make some more. It's still the same principle. The kick for me is always to try something new.

(5) ....

This was only about a year ago. Before this I had kept the name as the Chelsea Design Company Ltd. When I put 'Catherine Walker' there too, it was a statement. In Paris if you open a shop and put your name on the door, people will laugh at you unless you have the talent to back it up.

(6) ....

It's too easy to be pushed to the business side and try to make money. I try to stick as much as possible to designing and doing what I really want to do. Of course, it is only a garment and shouldn't be taken too seriously. On the other hand, if you don't give it such personal consideration, you should be doing mass production.

(7) ....

I learned when my husband died to live every day as fully as I can, to take it seriously and the moment it's over to forget about it. Life is too short to do anything else.

2 (Exam Hints: Paper 3, Part 2)

For questions 1–15, read the text below and think of the word which best fits each space. Use only **one** word in each space. There is an example at the beginning (0).

Airships

In 1852, Henri Giffard, a French engineer, designed a gas-filled balloon powered (0) ......**by**...... a steam engine. Unlike earlier balloons, Giffard's balloon did not go (1) .... the wind took it. The pilot used the power of the engine to (2) .... the balloon go in the direction he wanted. Giffard had built the first airship.

By the 1890s, airships had long rigid bodies and petrol engines. They were filled with hydrogen, a gas (3) .... is lighter than air but explodes easily. In the 1920s and 1930s, large airships carried passengers across the Atlantic and over the North Pole. However, (4) .... were several disastrous accidents. In 1930, a British airship, the R101, which was on (5) .... way to India, crashed in flames near Paris. In 1937, a German airship, the Hindenberg, burst into flames soon after arriving (6) .... the United States. After (7) ...., the development of airships was abandoned.

Nowadays, small airships are used (8) .... scientific or publicity purposes. They are filled with helium, (9) .... safe gas. Airships cannot travel as fast as aeroplanes but they use (10) .... fuel. They can carry enormous loads and (11) ....not need large areas in which (12) ....take off. Compared (13) .... aeroplanes, they are spacious and comfortable. Large airships, carrying passengers and cargo, could be built and (14) .... be perfectly safe but (15) .... such development is taking place.

3 (Exam Hints: Paper 3, Part 3)

For questions 1–10, complete the second sentence so that it has a similar meaning to the first sentence, using the word given. **Do not change the word given.** You must use between two and five words, including the word given.

EXAMPLE: I don't want to go out tonight.
rather
I _'d rather not_ go out tonight.

1 Elizabeth and Susan were both born on 5 March.
the
Elizabeth and Susan both .... birthday.

2 He told me almost nothing about his research project.
hardly
He gave .... about his research project.

3 Can you advise me on the legal aspects of this matter?
some
Please .... on the legal aspects of this matter.

4 'How much do you earn per month?' said the manager.
salary
The manager asked me .... was.

5 Jack spent his winnings on a new car.
money
Jack spent the .... on a new car.

6 I don't think anyone is to blame for the accident.
was
The accident ...., in my opinion.

7 Sheila's parents really didn't like the way she behaved at the party.
of
Sheila's parents strongly .... at the party.

8 The only thing Roland could see was the dark tower.
except
Roland could .... the dark tower.

9 John has stopped being scared of spiders.
no
John is .... scared of spiders.

10 'There was a significant rise in temperature yesterday,' said the weatherman.
the
'Yesterday ....,' said the weatherman.

4 (Exam Hints: Paper 3, Part 1)

For questions 1–15, read the text below and decide which answer A, B, C or D best fits each space. There is an example at the beginning (0).

Tea

Without (0) ....B.............., tea is one of the world's great drinks and has become an integral part of many cultures. (1) ...., tea is drunk in more than 150 countries, and the world produces an annual (2) .... of 2.5 million tons, of which 80 per cent is black tea. However, the tea drinking habit is (3) .... new to many parts of the world even where tea seems inseparable from daily life. For instance, tea is first referred to in English only in 1615. This was in a letter sent from an agent of the English East India Company (4) .... in Japan. A London coffee house first sold tea to the (5) .... in 1657 but at that time coffee was the most popular drink in Britain. Tea gradually (6) .... popularity, however, and the first (7) .... for it appeared in a London newspaper in 1658, but the habit of 'afternoon tea' did not become (8) .... until the 1840s.

The habit of drinking tea is believed to have (9) .... in China. The (10) .... of tea as a beverage started around five thousand years ago, (11) .... to a Chinese legend. The habit of tea drinking came to Japan about a thousand years ago when many officials went to China and returned home with a (12) .... of tea cultivation. At about the same time, the Arab world also knew about tea through (13) .... with China. However, tea was (14) .... to Europeans until 1559 when it was (15) .... by a Venetian author, Gian Battista Ramusio.

0	A hesitation	B doubt	C contradiction	D denial
1	A Actually	B Temporarily	C Momentarily	D Currently
2	A total	B amount	C sum	D number
3	A shockingly	B amazingly	C remarkably	D surprisingly
4	A made	B positioned	C stationed	D occupied
5	A customers	B people	C public	D citizens
6	A found	B gained	C got	D enjoyed
7	A notice	B commercial	C announcement	D advertisement
8	A settled	B established	C fixed	D set
9	A originated	B initiated	C launched	D practised
10	A introduction	B arrival	C beginning	D welcoming
11	A according	B referring	C recording	D stating
12	A secret	B skill	C knowledge	D way
13	A dealings	B communications	C associations	D contacts
14	A unconscious	B obscure	C unknown	D ignored
15	A written	B described	C accounted	D told

Listening

5 (Exam Hints: Paper 4, Part 1)

You will hear people talking in eight different situations. For questions 1–8, choose the best answer, A, B or C. You will hear each piece twice.

1 You are waiting to use a public telephone and you overhear what the caller is saying. What does she want to pay for?

A a hotel room
B a theatre ticket
C a train ticket

2 In a shop, you overhear an assistant talking to a customer. What does the customer want to buy?

A a jacket
B a pair of trousers
C a rucksack

3 A friend tells you about something he bought. What did he buy?

A a book
B a model aircraft kit
C a magazine

4 A friend tells you about a fascinating story. Where did she first find out about this story?

A in a newspaper
B in a book
C on television

5 A friend tells you about a personal experience. What did he do?

A He arrived late for a meeting.
B He didn't read his invitation.
C He made a mistake.

6 You have been invited to a friend's house and hear your friend talking to another visitor. What is your friend doing?

A criticising in a gentle way
B saying thank you
C asking for information

7 You hear someone ask a question and the answer to that question. Where are these people?

A at a university
B at a political meeting
C in a television studio

8 You overhear two people discussing a problem. Who is asking the questions?

A a doctor
B a builder
C a mechanic

6 (Exam Hints: Paper 4, Part 2)

You will hear a woman talking about the place where she grew up. For questions 1–10, complete the sentences which summarise what the speaker says. You will need to write a word or a short phrase in each space.

Mandy grew up in a (1) ....

Her house was next to the (2) ....

Parts of the house were at least (3) .... old.

From her bedroom window, Mandy could see the (4) ....

At the river the children sometimes saw (5) ....

If they didn't return along the Drove, they explored the (6) ....

There Mandy remembers the many (7) ....

She also appreciated the (8) ....

She felt the whole area was beautiful and (9) ....

She thinks that nowadays people would use such an area for (10) ....

unit 6 HOW THINGS WORK

Lead-in **1** How is technology used in this house?
How is the temperature controlled?
How does the water come in?
How is the water heated?

What electrical appliances, such as TV,
CD player, video recorder, satellite dish
do you have in your house?

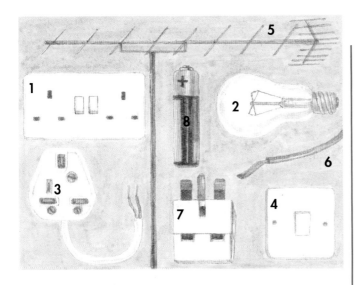

2 Match the words to the parts of the diagram.

a plug   e aerial
b socket   f adaptor
c lead   g battery
d light-bulb   h switch

3 Choose the correct word or phrase for each gap.

line   collect call   phonecard   engaged
extension number   hold   hang up
connecting   make   receiver   buttons
ringing   put through
switchboard operator   dial   coins   call

*T*o .... (1) a phone call from a pay phone in Britain, the first thing you have to do is to pick up the .... (2) You then have to pay for the .... (3), usually by inserting some .... (4), if you are using cash, or by inserting a .... (5) you have previously bought. There are other ways of calling too, such as paying by credit card or making a .... (6), which means that the person at the other end is going to pay for the call. Once you have decided how you are going to pay, you .... (7) the number you require, by pressing the .... (8) on the telephone. You will hear a .... (9) tone, which means the call has got through, or an .... (10) tone, which means the .... (11) is busy. If you are phoning a company, then the person who answers is usually the .... (12). You ask to be .... (13) to the person you want to talk to, and it is quicker if you can tell the operator the .... (14) of the person you need. If the line is engaged the operator will ask you if you wish to '.................... (15)', and when the line is free, the operator will say 'Putting you through' before .... (16) you to the person you want to speak to. When your conversation is over, you .... (17) by putting the receiver back in position on the telephone.

4 Choose the correct word for each gap.

shutter   load   developed   rewind
prints   slides   photograph   film
automatic   flash   projector   record
camera   exposure   screen   album
store   image

*T*here can be few people these days who haven't taken a .... (1) at some time in their lives and many people can't imagine going on holiday without their .... (2) They want to come back with a permanent .... (3) of the people and places they have encountered while they've been away. There's a great variety of cameras to choose from (single lens reflex, compact, autofocus, polaroid) and these days most are quite easy to use. Some people like to buy cameras where you can adjust the focus, ... (4) speed and exposure, but others prefer .... (5) cameras that make all the necessary adjustments for them. A number of cameras come with a built-in .... (6) so there is no need to add an extra attachment if you are taking pictures in poor light conditions.

The first thing to decide is whether you want to end up with prints or .... (7) This determines the kind of .... (8) you need to buy. You .... (9) the film into your camera and you're ready to start taking pictures. When you have finished the film, you ....(10), unload it and take it to be .... (11). .... (12) are easy to handle and to show to other people but if you prefer slides, then you need a .... (13) in order to be able to view them properly. It's possible to buy small hand viewers, but you can study your slides more carefully if you have one that projects the .... (14) onto a .... (15).

Many people like to .... (16) their prints and slides in an .... (17) which protects them from the damaging effects of .... (18) to light and dust.

Reading

A When did you last see a film?
Which film was it?
What kind of films do you like?
Is cinema the best form of entertainment?

THE MAGIC OF THE SILVER SCREEN

On 28 December 1895, in a café in Paris, the Lumiere brothers, Louis and Auguste, gave the first public showing of a motion picture. This event, hardly noticed at the time, marks the beginning of one of the world's major
5 entertainment industries. The earliest films were very short, just snippets in fact, and the audiences were easily impressed. One film by the Lumiere brothers showed a train arriving at a station. It caused some of the audience to flee in terror, believing that they were about to be run over. Another film,
10 by Thomas Edison, lasted one minute and showed a man sneezing. Early film makers were very keen on shots of wild animals charging towards the audience and of cowboys shooting straight at them.

Technical development was very rapid. By 1914 feature
15 films were up to two hours long and most of the techniques used by modern film makers had been discovered. Colour films were made as early as 1906, although they did not become common until the 1940s. Experiments with sound began as early as 1896 but the first film with sychronised
20 sound was 'The Jazz Singer' (1927). Until that time, performances of silent films were accompanied by live piano music. One of the disadvantages of 'talkies' is that if you can't understand the language, you can't understand the film, unless it is sub-titled or dubbed. Back projection was being
25 used by 1913 and is still used very effectively in modern films such as 'Superman' (1978). Back projection involves shooting a background scene, projecting that scene onto a screen and then filming the actors in front of the screen. In this way, we get the impression that Superman is flying over a landscape,
30 which has, of course, previously been filmed from an aircraft. Special effects of various kinds, including the use of models, were used by Georges Méliès in his fantasy film 'Voyage to the Moon' (1902). Another film that used models effectively was 'King Kong' (1933). What seemed to be a gorilla as a tall as a
35 house was in fact a 40 cm model. By using the technique, first used by Méliès, of stop action, (in which the film is stopped, the model is moved and the film is started again), King Kong was made to move fairly realistically. Sometimes models are life-size, like the shark in 'Jaws' (1975), which could only be
40 shot from one side because the controls that enabled it to move realistically were on the side that was not filmed.

During the first half of this century, going to the cinema was a very popular activity and audiences were huge. From the 1950s onwards audiences declined and many cinemas
45 were forced to close as more and more people bought television sets. Several technological innovations were introduced to counter the threat from television, such as ultra-wide screens, stereophonic sound and, less successfully, films that could be seen in three dimensions if special glasses
50 were worn. Nowadays, films are so technically advanced and so well made that they provide an experience that television cannot match.

B Explain the meaning of these words and phrases, as used in the text.

Paragraph 1
1 snippets

Paragraph 2
2 feature films
3 synchronised sound
4 live piano music
5 'talkies'
6 sub-titled
7 dubbed
8 back projection
9 special effects
10 stop action

Paragraph 3
11 ultra-wide screens
12 three dimensions

C These sentences contain incorrect information. Re-write them using the correct information in the text.

1 The Lumiere brothers opened the first cinema in Paris in 1895.

2 Audiences were terrified by one of Thomas Edison's films.

3 Early film makers tried not to frighten the audience too much.

4 Georges Méliès was the first film maker to use back projection.

5 Colour films lasting two hours were being made by 1914.

6 At first 'The Jazz Singer' was accompanied by live music.

7 A life-size model of a gorilla was used very effectively in 'King Kong'.

8 In 'King Kong' the technique of stop-action was used for the first time.

9 The model shark in 'Jaws' looked the same as a real shark.

10 Nowadays, going to the cinema is more popular than it was in the first half of the century.

Grammar

 Passives

A Complete each sentence using a passive form in an appropriate tense. Use the verbs in brackets. (Grammar Notes **6.1**)

EXAMPLE: Passengers cannot get on the train now because .... (clean)
Passengers cannot get on the train now because _it is being cleaned_ .

1 People think he committed suicide but Miss Marple believes .... (murder)

2 The candidates .... still .... (interview)

3 I came by bus because my car .... yet. (repair)

4 Deliveries .... every Tuesday. (make)

5 'As far as I can see, nothing .... from the office,' said the manager. (steal)

6 The car .... still .... when I arrived to collect it. (clean)

7 The captain told me that the island .... for ten years. (not inhabit)

8 'Everything possible .... to save the patient – we are still hopeful,' said the doctor. (do)

9 We expect that all the paintings in the exhibition .... by the last day. (sell)

10 When I went to the shop, I .... that the photos .... yet .... (tell, not develop)

11 All employees .... to talk to the press, but many did so. (forbid)

12 As soon as he looked at her face, Tom realised .... (not forgive)

B Complete each sentence using a passive form in an appropriate tense. Use the verbs in brackets.

EXAMPLE: .... the missing document .... yet? (find)
Has the missing document _been found_ yet?

1 .... the painting .... by next Friday? (not finish)

2 .... the new procedures .... to you yet? (explain)

3 .... Mr Jones .... to the airport or did he go by train? (drive)

4 How many times a week .... the offices .... (clean)

5 How much .... Professor Sweet .... for his lecture last month? (pay)

6 .... the new swimming pool .... next week? (open)

7 .... you .... how to use the camera before you bought it? (not show)

8 How many times .... the grass .... this month? (cut)

9 Do you know how the jewels .... ? (lose)

10 Do you realise how many people tomorrow's programme .... by? (watch)

C Complete the sentences using the modal verb and the verb in brackets. Use a passive form. Some sentences are negative.

EXAMPLE: Students .... to apply before April. (should, advise)
Students _should be advised_ to apply before April.

1 Photos .... unless a stamped addressed envelope is enclosed. (will, return)

2 You .... a bonus in December if sales are high. (may, offer)

3 He is a good runner but he .... in the final. (might, beat)

4 The painting .... from the museum last Saturday night. (must, steal)

5 You .... earlier than this. (should, tell)

6 .... it .... before you can eat it? (have to, cook)

7 Do you think the signature .... during the artist's lifetime? (could, forge)

8 The children .... like that. (ought, treat)

9 In my opinion, this information .... to the enemy at least six weeks ago. (must, give)

10 This equipment .... There is nothing wrong with it. (need, replace)

2 Anything, something, nothing

Read the following sentences and answer the question that follows each sentence.
(Grammar Notes **6.2**)

EXAMPLE: You can wear anything for the party.

QUESTION: *What kind of party is it?*
ANSWER: It is a very informal party and it doesn't matter what you wear – but you must wear something.

1 Anyone can become a member of the club.
   (Is it difficult to join?)
2 John would do anything to get revenge.
   (Is he dangerous?)
3 There is nothing John wouldn't do to get revenge.
   (Is this the same as 2?)
4 He does hardly any work.   *(Is he lazy?)*
5 Hardly anyone knew the answer.
   (How many people knew?)
6 What kind of present shall I give them? Anything?
   (Is it necessary to give a present? What kind?)
7 I like any music by Bach.
   (Do I like Bach's music? How much of it?)
8 Any flight on Tuesday will do. *(Can I fly on Tuesday?)*

Listening 🔊

Surviving air crashes

Deborah Smith talks to Professor George Brown about how to improve survivability in air crashes.

1 List the *five* safety measures that Professor Brown recommends.

2 What *two* safety measures have airlines already introduced?

3 What *four* pieces of advice does Professor Brown give to passengers?

English in Use

1 A Must be, could be

Complete the text with *must* or *could*.
(Grammar Notes **6.3**)

EXAMPLE: It ___must be___ the same person – the handwriting is identical.

It ___could be___ the same man but it is difficult to say after all these years.

'The man we are looking for .... (1) have black hair,' said Inspector Collins,' because we have found some strands of black hair at the scene of both crimes. He .... (2) be extremely strong because he carried the safe down the stairs and out of the building. He .... (3) be the same man we were looking for last year because there are similarities in his technique, but we are not sure yet. If the fingerprints match then it .... (4) be the same man. There .... (5) be more than one man involved but we have no evidence concerning a possible accomplice.'

B Comment on these sentences using *must* or *could*.

EXAMPLE: He paid for a new Rolls Royce in cash.
   ___He must be rich___ .

6 John is in a hurry to get to work – he's almost running.

7 Although it looks like a Leonardo da Vinci drawing, the paper was made in the early twentieth century.

8 These diaries look genuine, but we don't know where they have been all these years.

9 There are five cars travelling together but which one is the President in?

10 I can hear voices inside the house.

2 Invent, discover, find

Complete the sentences with these words. Use the word in its correct form.

invent	discover	find out	find
	found	establish	

1 Professor Green has .... a machine that will iron clothes automatically.

2 In a remote desert area, geologists .... rich deposits of iron ore.

3 Sometimes amateur astronomers have become famous for .... new stars.

4 I .... a £20 note on the floor of the supermarket.

5 The shop was .... by the present owner's grandfather in 1920.

6 Have the police .... why the murder was committed?

7 Wadham College, Oxford was .... in 1610.

8 Michael Faraday's work on electro-magnetism led to many modern ....

Reading

A Would you like to spend a holiday on the moon or in an orbiting space station? What new experiences would such a holiday offer?

B Read the following article about holidays in space. Seven sentences have been removed from the article. Choose from sentences A–H the one which fits each gap (1–7). There is one extra sentence that you do not need to use.

HOLIDAY IN SPACE

IN 1957 THE FIRST SATELLITE, Sputnik, orbited the Earth. In 1969, Neil Armstrong was the first man to set foot on the moon. (1) .... Major industrial companies are now carrying out serious research in the use of space for recreational purposes with a view to building hotels both in space and on the Moon. Such hotels will be constructed by robots controlled by computers based on Earth. Much of the material used in construction will be taken from the Moon, which has all the minerals and metals which are needed. It would not be necessary to launch all the building material into space from Earth. (2) ....

Hotels which orbit the Earth will be shaped like a wheel, which will spin in order to create artificial gravity. Almost certainly the guest rooms will have artificial gravity, as well as all the facilities you would expect to find in a hotel room on Earth. (3) .... As well as just floating about, guests will be able to take part in sports, such as tennis or pole-vaulting, which will be very different in a low-gravity environment. (4) .... Gravity can be controlled to enable guests to float or slide from one level to another. One of the great attractions of a space hotel will be the absolutely stunning views of Earth, especially of sunrises and sunsets.

Undoubtedly, many people are looking forward to spending a few days in space or on the Moon, but there are some drawbacks. (5) .... Doctors who have examined astronauts have found that they have lost calcium from their bodies, which means that their bones have become brittle and can break more easily. (6) .... Potential guests at the Orbit Hotel or the Hotel Lunar may not be put off by these drawbacks because they will be in space for only a few days, and it seems to be long-term exposure to weightlessness that causes the problems. (7) .... Perhaps they will all be robots.

A Space hotels are a great step forward for mankind despite possible health risks.

B But how will the hotel staff cope with the hazards of working in space?

C There will be no need for lifts or stairs in a space hotel.

D Other parts of the hotel will have lower gravity or zero gravity so that guests can enjoy the sensations of weightlessness.

E Muscles, including the heart, also become weaker and some evidence suggests that after long periods in space people lose a couple of centimetres in height.

F In the near future, perhaps you will be one of the first tourists to stay at an orbiting space station or at a hotel on the surface of the Moon.

G We can confidently predict that such hotels will exist sometime in the first half of the twenty-first century.

H Astronauts have complained that weightlessness gives them a sensation of nausea and they feel great physical discomfort in many ways.

Reading

A Have you played any computer games that were extremely realistic?
How will people use computers in twenty years' time?

ENTER A NEW WORLD

Virtual Reality (VR) is the term used to describe computer simulations of reality which are very similar to real-life
5 experience. To enter VR, you put on a special headset, or head-mounted display (HMD) which allows you to see three-dimensional, computer-
10 generated images. You also hear sound effects and wear a special glove, which, like the HMD, is connected to the computer. This glove allows you
15 to manipulate the objects that you see and to have some sense of touch. What you see exists only inside the computer, but while wearing the HMD you
20 cannot see anything except the computer-generated image. Consequently, you have the sensation of entering a different world, and this sensation is
25 enhanced by the sound effects and by the glove. When you turn your head, the computer adjusts the images.
Virtual reality is close
30 enough to the real world to be both useful and enjoyable. It has obvious practical uses. It can be used to train pilots without any risk of destroying
35 valuable aeroplanes. It can be used to enable surgeons to practise carrying out operations without any risk to a patient. It can also be used to help people
40 overcome irrational fears. For example, people who are scared of spiders can be exposed to them in the virtually real world in the hope that they will stop
45 being scared of them.
Students can learn foreign languages by entering a computer simulation of another country without the
50 inconvenience of actually going there. There are also many industrial applications of VR. Robots working in environments that are
55 dangerous to humans, such as deep under the sea, in fires or in nuclear reactors, can be remotely controlled by human operators who, by using VR,
60 have the sensation of being exactly where the robot is. Above all, Virtual Reality has great entertainment value. Users can have all kinds of
65 experiences that they could not have in real life. They can take part in motor-races, become astronauts and fighter pilots without any risk to themselves
70 or others. These VR experiences are far more intense and exciting than the experiences of watching films and television, especially since VR can involve,
75 to some extent, the senses of touch and smell as well as sight and hearing. In the future, it will be possible for people to create, in their own homes, any
80 kind of fantasy world they wish.
However, many people are alarmed by the potential dangers of VR. According to Professor George Brown,
85 people may confuse the real world with the computer simulated world and someone used to crashing cars in VR car races may do the same, with
90 serious consequences, when driving a real car. 'Moreover,' he says, 'it is possible that some people may begin to enjoy committing serious crimes in
95 VR. These crimes could be committed without guilt and without consequences, but it is impossible to say what effect such activities would have on
100 real-life behaviour. We don't even know whether prolonged use of the headset damages the user's eyesight. VR is ready to be sold in shops before any
105 research has been done on its psychological effects.'

B Find a word or phrase which, in context, is similar in meaning to:

Paragraph 1
1 move with the hand
2 feeling
3 made better
4 alters

Paragraph 2
5 danger
6 frightened

Paragraph 3
7 bother
8 from a distance

Paragraph 4
9 accustomed
10 long-term

C Work in pairs. Ask and answer the following questions.

1 What do people wear in order to experience VR?

2 What do people see and hear in VR?

3 Name five useful applications of VR.

4 How can VR be used for entertainment?

5 Why could VR be much more entertaining than television or films?

6 Why is Professor Brown worried about VR?

7 Do you think that Professor Brown's fears are justified?

Talking Points

Section 1

Describe what you can see in the pictures.
How does the computer in these pictures
relate to work, study and entertainment?

Section 2

Discuss in groups of five:

How important are computers in your life?
What do you use them for?
How difficult is it to learn to use them?
What happens if they go wrong?
What role do they play in language learning?
Can computers affect your health?

Listening

Supermarket checkouts

 Listen to the talk about supermarket checkouts. Complete each sentence by writing in the required word/s.

customer	bar code	retailer	till
receipt	scanner	computer	

1 A .... reads information attached to the product.

2 A .... gives an individual details of all the goods bought.

3 A .... is able to use up-to-the-minute information.

4 A .... provides information about each product.

5 A .... records information about how payment has been made.

6 A .... receives information on a piece of paper.

Writing

Describing a process

1 When you describe how to do something, it is important to make it clear exactly what you do and in what order, especially if someone else is going to read your instructions so as to be able to carry out the task themselves.

A Look at this description of how to use an automatic cash dispenser. Some of the words have been left blank. When you have read the piece, look at the words given below, and put them in the correct position.

finally	first	for example	by
next	then	before	once

.... (1), insert your bank card into the machine. The machine will .... (2) ask you to key in your personal number.
.... (3) you have done this, the machine will ask you to choose the service you require. You make your choice .... (4) selecting from a list and pressing the appropriate button.

.... (5), if you wish to get some money, you press one of the two keys that says 'Cash'. There are two keys because you can either have cash with a receipt or cash without a receipt.
.... (6), the machine will ask you whether you require another service. If you do not want anything else, you press the 'No' button, and .... (7) producing the money the machine tells you to take your card.

You take your card and .... (8) your cash arrives. The transaction has been concluded.

B Now choose one of the following tasks.

1 You have asked a cleaning service to send someone to clean your house, but you can't be there to tell the cleaner what to do. Leave a set of instructions about what you want done in each particular room. Use about 100 words.

2 You work as a trainer in a sports centre. Some of the clients who use the centre have not previously had experience of exercise and the centre equipment. You cannot always be there to give advice. Write a set of instructions, including information about how to warm-up and how to use specific pieces of equipment. Use about 100 words.

English in Use

1 Too, enough

Complete the sentences using *too* or *enough*. (Grammar Notes **6.4**.)

1 These shoes don't fit me. They are hurting my feet.
They are _____ .

2 We need ten tickets but we only have six.
We haven't _____ .

3 The meal has been on the table for ten minutes.
It won't be _____ .

4 John has had two years experience overseas but he needs five.
He hasn't had _____ .

5 The word-processor weighs 60 kilograms. One person can't carry it.
It is _____ .

6 The oasis is 80 kilometres away. We can't walk there in a day.
The oasis is _____ .

7 He lacks the experience to do this job.
He isn't experienced _____ .

8 Mr Baxter is still sick. He cannot travel yet.
Mr Baxter is _____ .

2 A Rise, raise, arise

What is the difference between *rise*, *raise* and *arise*? Look at the table.

Infinitive	Past	Past Participle	Present Participle	(In)transitive
rise	rose	risen	rising	intransitive
EXAMPLE: The sun *rose* at 5 am.				
raise	raised	raised	raising	transitive
EXAMPLE: He *raised* his arm.				
arise	arose	arisen	arising	intransitive
EXAMPLE: A problem has *arisen* concerning your application.				

B Complete the sentence with the correct form of *rise*, *raise* or *arise*.

1 Our hopes _____ as we saw the rescuers approaching.

2 We need to _____ £1,000,000 for this project.

3 Prices have _____ by 10% this year.

4 The shopkeeper decided to _____ his prices.

5 An opportunity has _____ in our Singapore office. Are you interested?

6 Some difficulties have _____ with the new computers.

7 I'll _____ this matter at the next meeting.

8 His temperature has _____ by two degrees.

3 Phrasal Verbs

Answer the questions using the phrasal verb in brackets. Work in pairs.

EXAMPLE:

Your house is in very bad condition. What are you going to do about it? (do up)
I'm going to do it up.

1 When the thief grabbed Sarah's handbag, what did he do next? (make off with)
2 Will the meeting take place as planned? (call off)
3 Shall we stop now? (carry on)
4 Do you think this style will become popular? (catch on)
5 Where did you find that necklace? (come across)
6 Why did the research project stop? (run out of)
7 I'm afraid there is no milk or sugar. (do without)
8 I know John has been ill. Has he returned to work yet? (get over)

4 Word-formation

Complete the sentences with the correct form of the word in capitals.

EXAMPLES: Jane loves telling __humorous__ stories. HUMOUR

Stephen is a __thoughtful__ boy – he always considers other people. THOUGHT

1 The inventor was very _____ when he was asked detailed questions about his latest ideas. SUSPICION

2 You must be very _____ when handling this equipment. CARE

3 The fumes given off in the metal making process were _____ . POISON

4 The student got _____ advice from his science teacher. HELP

5 He's such an _____ designer that he will use anyone who can help him in his career. AMBITION

6 Mike's decision to leave the company was _____ . DISASTER

7 He's a _____ man and has never given up despite many setbacks. COURAGE

THE FAMILY

Lead-in 1 Describe the people in the picture. What relationship do the people have to each other?

Do you think they get on well with each other?
What is the usual family size in your country?

2 Choose the correct word to fill the gap in each sentence.

> step-brothers   single   in-laws
> bachelor   orphans   adoption   elderly
> widow   toddler   great-grandparents

1 Richard was a .... until his marriage at age of forty-two.

2 Mary changed her job in order to be closer to her .... parents.

3 .... agencies changed the rules regarding children from overseas.

4 When John's mother remarried, he found he had three ....

5 The war left many children ....

6 When Harry married Sally he didn't realise what an important part his new .... would play in his life.

7 All the family are long-lived, in fact three of my .... are now in their nineties.

8 Frances has two children, a .... of three and a baby of six months.

9 Barbara remained .... until the age of thirty-five.

10 At the age of twenty-five Jenny's husband died and she was left a .... with two small children to bring up.

3 Complete the text with a word or phrase from the list.

> depended   home   wedding
> introduced   fiancé   engaged   running
> close   support   work out   pregnant
> give up   intention   split up
> bringing up   plan   benefit
> independent   career   nanny

Granddaughters often have good relationships with their grandmothers. Sandy has always been .... (1) to her grandmother, Nancy, who's now in her eighties. Nancy was thrilled when Sandy got .... (2) to her boyfriend Paul and the two of them talked about the differences in their attitude to marriage.

Nancy was twenty when she got married in 1935. Her .... (3), David, was an engineer and they had been .... (4) at a party given by members of David's family. They were engaged for two years before the actual .... (5). Nancy was working in a dress shop when they met and she had to .... (6) her job when she got married. She stayed at .... (7) in the house she and David rented. She had no money of her own and so she .... (8) on her husband for necessities. Soon she was .... (9), and her first child, Sandy's mother, was born in 1937. Nancy had her second child a year later. Her life revolved around .... (10) the house and .... (1) the two children. David was busy with his job and worked long hours to .... (12) the family.

Sandy doesn't see her married life being like this. She's got a good job and has no .... (13) of giving it up. She's told her grandmother that her .... (14) is as important to her as being Paul's wife. She is twenty-seven now, and she and Paul don't .... (15) to have any children until she is in her thirties. Even then she intends to continue working. She will be able to pay for a .... (16) to look after the children. She thinks that her children will .... (17) from having a mother who has her own interests and career, and who is financially .... (18). Looking on the dark side, if things don't .... (19) in the marriage, both she and Paul agree that it's better to .... (20) than to stay together unhappily for the sake of the children.

Nancy says, 'It was all so different in my day.'

Reading

A
Do you expect members of a family to behave in a particular kind of way? What makes families different?

Anita Roddick

a millionaire businesswoman talks about her family.

MY MOTHER, Gilda Perella, came to Britain from a village in Italy when she was fifteen to be a nanny. She still lives in the terraced house in Littlehampton, Sussex, where I was born in 1942. It is called Atina after her village and
5 has bright red window frames. It was always understood that when she reached England, she would marry a boy from her home village called Donny.

My mother made us, my two sisters, my brother and me, understand that love and work are the only
10 important things in life. She also made me feel special, which gave me great confidence. She loved my sisters, but they were no trouble to her, whereas I was maddening but entertaining. As a teenager, she allowed me extraordinary freedom. But because she trusted me, I
15 developed a strong sense of responsibility.

The greatest thing she gave me was my work ethic. After my father died, she ran our café and we had to help. I don't remember playtimes from my childhood; it was always summer and we were always working. Sometimes
20 we'd complain about never getting to the beach, and then she'd rush us down there for an hour – she was always one for the big gesture. Then it was back to work.

Not that she's perfect: my mother has the greatest capacity to embarrass of anyone I've ever met. When
25 she came to collect me from college while I was training to be a teacher, I'd ask her to arrive after everyone had left, because she was so dreadful. She does have the most appalling taste; she'd win any bad taste award going. The presents she buys are legendary in our
30 family. She only once bought me something nice – a copper frying pan – I was so excited I rang to thank her immediately. She said: 'What do you mean? It's a clock.' And I turned it over, and it was. A clock. Hideous.

I taught for a bit, then went off travelling for a couple
35 of years. I got back to find my mother too excited to listen to my stories. She couldn't wait to tell me about this man who came to the nightclub she was running then. His name was Gordon Roddick. The minute I set eyes on him, I knew this was the man I wanted to be the
40 father of my children. He says when he saw me he knew instantly that I was his fate. I think I just felt an immense relief.

B
Find a word or phrase in the passage which in context is similar in meaning to:

Paragraph 1
1 someone who looks after other people's children
2 the village where a person grows up

Paragraph 2
3 a strong belief in yourself
4 irritating

Paragraph 3
5 belief in the value of work

Paragraph 4
6 very ugly

C
Choose the best answer, A, B, C or D according to the information in the text:

1 When Gilda Perella came to Britain she

   A was already married.
   B was hoping to find a husband.
   C was in love with someone in her village in Italy.
   D was planning to marry Donny.

2 How does Anita think she developed a sense of responsibility?

   A She was given a job to do.
   B She had to look after her sisters and brothers.
   C She was free to do what she wanted.
   D She wanted to copy her mother.

3 Anita admires her mother most for

   A her hard work.
   B her romantic spirit.
   C her loyalty to the family.
   D her ability to be alone.

4 One negative aspect about Anita's mother, according to the text is that:

   A She interferes in her children's lives.
   B She deliberately tries to embarrass her children.
   C She never relaxes.
   D She does things that shame her children in public.

5 When Anita met her future husband she

   A was looking for a partner for her travels.
   B was in a nightclub.
   C was planning another trip.
   D knew her mother's feelings were correct.

Grammar: *present perfect*

A Look at these examples. All the sentences are examples of the *present perfect*. (Grammar Notes **7.1**)

a I have just cut my finger!   *What is happening now?*

b These dinosaur bones have lain in this cave for 200 million years.   *Where are they now?*

c Jane has lived in three different countries.
    Do we know when?

d Paul has baked a cake.   *Is the baking finished?*

e I have known Mary since 1970.   *Do I still know her?*

In the light of these examples, decide whether the following statements about the *present perfect* are true or false.

1 The present perfect is used only for recent past events.

2 The present perfect always describes completed actions.

3 The present perfect tells us when something happened.

B Put one of these words in each statement, in the correct position.

already   just   yet   ever   never

1 We have sold two hundred tickets and there is still a month to go before the concert.

2 I have visited New York. I'm looking forward to going.

3 Have you thought of learning to fly?

4 I have received my exam result. It came ten minutes ago.

5 Janet hasn't finished with the camera. She needs it tomorrow.

C Complete the following sentences using the *present perfect*. There are **two** sentences where it is impossible to use this tense. Identify these sentences and complete them.

EXAMPLE: *I've learned five hundred Russian words* so far.

1 ....
so far.

2 ....
for ten years.

3 ....
since I left school.

4 ....
since 1990.

5 ....
for as long as I can remember.

6 ....
in 1990.

7 ....
three days ago.

D Answer the following questions using the *present perfect*.

EXAMPLE:

Can we use your car? <u>No, I've taken it to the garage</u> .

1 Is your brother at home? No,
....

2 Does Bill know what happened? Yes,
....

3 Is there any soup left? No,
....

4 Do the Browns still live there? No,
....

5 Do you know what happens at the end of *Macbeth*? No,
....

E Complete these sentences using the verbs given in the *present perfect* or *past simple* tense.

1 Although Sarah .... the competition many times, she .... (never) before. (enter, win)

2 During the last ten years, I .... the work that Professor Sweet .... (continue, start)

3 I'm sorry I'm late. The bus .... so I .... a taxi.   (come, take)

4 Where (you) .... ? We .... you an hour ago.   (be, expect)

5 We (first) .... to Cornwall in 1980 and we .... back every year since then.   (go, be)

6 All my life I .... for this moment and at last it ....   (wait, arrive)

Listening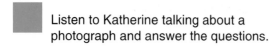

A family photo

Listen to Katherine talking about a photograph and answer the questions.

1 What is it a photograph of?

2 Is the photograph in colour?

3 Where are they standing?

4 What is the woman wearing?

5 What is the man wearing?

6 What is the woman carrying?

7 What article of jewellery does Katherine mention?

8 How did she get it?

9 How was it lost?

10 How did she feel when it was lost?

11 What did she do to try and get it back?

12 What was its value?

English in Use

1 Prepositions

1 Martin was attracted .... Mary, but it was a long time before he managed to ask her ....

2 Tom fell .... love .... Anna the moment he met her.

3 Frank's engaged .... Veronica.

4 Charles has been married .... Henrietta for ten years.

5 James's parents don't approve .... his relationship with Caroline.

6 Andrew and Jean are related .... marriage.

7 Sally broke .... her engagement .... Arthur.

8 Tim and Eileen have split ....

9 Alison is very fond .... all her children.

10 Barbara and Joe are related .... each other.

2

For questions 1–15, read the text below and look carefully at each line. Some of the lines are correct, and some have a word which should not be there. Tick the correct lines and underline the wrong words in the incorrect lines.

EXAMPLES: 0 ✓
00 <u>years</u>

The Roberts Family

0   For the last five years, Alex Roberts has brought up her

00 daughters Kim, who's twelve years, and Tina, aged 10, on

1   her own. She says: 'In the beginning, it was very

2   difficult for all us but that's the past and we are really

3   happy now. We spend a lot of time talking together.

4   The girls like to talk about clothes, how they've spent

5   the day, what they're going to watch out on TV. We feel

6   very much close but we all have our own opinions so

7   there is the occasional row.' 'If you love with people,'

8   says Kim, 'of course you are disagree. No-one is to

9   blame for, and Mum makes sure that afterwards we kiss

10 and make up.' The family doesn't have much of money,

11 so they must to save up for special treats. What they like

12 best is giving up supper parties for friends. They go

13 shopping for a special food and then prepare everything

14 together. Alex worries about her children but says: 'We're

15 OK, I think.' Tina and Kim would agree that.

Reading

A What are weddings like in your country? Do people have a choice about where and how to get married?

Look at the different way these people decided to get married.

Weddings

A Church of England Wedding

When Jonathan and Sarah Gibbs were married, the couple never considered anything other than a church wedding. 'Getting married in a register office just
5 wouldn't have had the same sense of occasion.' Neither is a regular church-goer. Sarah, who wore a lace and silk dress, agrees that pleasing her parents was a big factor in opting for a traditional do. The 20-minute
10 ceremony at the church was followed by champagne on the lawn of an Elizabethan manor, a receiving line, and a three-course sit-down meal for 100, followed by dancing into the night. The couple were waved off to a
15 honeymoon on safari in Kenya and Tanzania. Most of the cost was borne by Sarah's father. 'It was an awful lot of money but worth it,' she says. 'I mean, you only get one chance to have a really big do like that, don't you?'

20 ### A Muslim Wedding

Five hundred guests and four days of festivities marked the marriage of Naila and Rizwan Minhas. Theirs was a winter wedding, last December: Naila veiled in the
25 traditional Punjabi wedding outfit of beaded red lace, remembers shivering in the snow as she was taken from one venue to the next. 'An Asian wedding is a really big deal and people travel miles to go to them – we had
30 guests from Hong Kong, Pakistan and the United States at ours,' says Naila. Naila and Rizwan both grew up in Glasgow where their parents have been friends for years. 'It wasn't exactly an arranged marriage,' says
35 Rizwan, 'but you could say there was a fair amount of parental persuasion. We wouldn't have done it if we hadn't both been very happy with one another, though.'

The wedding celebrations started when
40 250 guests gathered to welcome Naila and mark her hands with henna, the traditional greeting for a bride. The following evening there was a similar ceremony for Rizwan. The actual marriage took place at
45 Eastwood Hall in Glasgow and the couple arrived separately to the serenade of a kilted piper. 'I feel very Scottish as well as Asian,' explains Rizwan. During the ceremony itself, the couple were in different
50 rooms – the priest went first to the bridegroom and then to the bride to ask whether they had consented to the marriage. A ring ceremony followed, in which Rizwan's mother placed a gold ring
55 on Naila's finger and Naila's mother placed one on Rizwan's. 'Wearing rings is a western custom which we've started following too,' says Rizwan. A sit-down meal of traditional Pakistani dishes was
60 followed by speeches. Naila, now officially part of Rizwan's family, left with him for his family home where music and dancing continued into the night. The newly-weds stayed with Rizwan's parents for a few days before leaving for a honeymoon in Tunisia.

65 ### A Modern Wedding in Las Vegas

Bryony Mander married Jake Peck in Las Vegas last January part-way through a touring holiday of the States. On arrival in Vegas the couple spent an afternoon
70 checking out the numerous wedding chapels and eventually decided on the Little White Chapel. Bryony had brought her own dress with her, emerald green and shocking pink taffeta, but Jake hired a western-style tuxedo
75 with flared nylon trousers. They were collected from their hotel in the complimentary limo and driven to the County Court House to obtain their licence, then on to the chapel itself. 'The ceremony
80 was actually quite pleasant,' said Bryony. 'We had a female minister and we chose to have the civil ceremony.' After the ceremony, the real business started. 'The lady behind the counter tried to sell us the video that
85 we'd said we didn't want in the first place, a cassette recording of our vows and a white leather-bound photo album. Under pressure we gave way on the latter.' There were more extras to come. Bryony and Jake were
90 handed an envelope which read 'Minister's donation: between $40 and $100' and in the limo a sign stated that the driver worked only for gratuities and would accept tips over $25. 'Looking back, it was a great laugh,'
95 says Bryony. 'A big church wedding seemed too much and a register office not enough, so this was the perfect alternative.'

A Humanist Wedding

'We'd been coming to Lulworth Cove for
100 years and thought it would be a brilliant place to get married,' says Debbie. 'Neither of us had been brought up with any formal religious belief and we felt it would be hypocritical to go to church just to get
105 married. A friend told us about humanist ceremonies.' Humanist ceremonies have no standing in law, so Debbie and Nick had to go along to Hammersmith register office the previous day to be legally wed. For the
110 ceremony at Lulworth, the bride wore an ankle-length white dress and a veil and walked the quarter of a mile up the hill from the car park on her father's arm. A hundred friends had gathered on top of the
115 hill to hear Nick and Debbie recite vows they had written themselves, in which they promised to recognise each other as equals and to 'love, honour and tenderly care' for each other in the years ahead.

120 After the formalities, everyone walked the mile back into the village for an afternoon of festivities, followed by dancing to the sound of a Cajun band. Hiring the hall cost just £6 and the overall costs were
125 split between both sets of parents and the bridal couple themselves. 'We were a bit worried about whether our parents would approve,' says Debbie. 'But they loved it. I think they were quite proud of us for being
130 creative and doing something else.'

B Match the details of the wedding to the couple.

A Jonathan and Sarah
B Naila and Rizwan
C Bryony and Jake
D Debbie and Nick

1 went abroad for the ceremony

2 had guests from around the world

3 say they didn't think a register office was the appropriate place for the ceremony

4 got married in the open air

5 had dancing after the ceremony

6 were encouraged after the ceremony to spend more

7 took account of what their parents might think

8 left for a trip abroad shortly after the ceremony

Reading

A What difficulties do wives and children face when a man is sent to prison?

Read the text and see what this wife says.

I'M SERVING A SENTENCE TOO

While Sakina Fitzpatrick knows her husband deserves to pay for his crime, she's also suffering. So often, it's prisoners' families who become innocent victims.

5 She thought he'd gone to borrow some money from a friend. The hours passed and he didn't return. Then the police knocked at the door. She stood there while they said her husband, Patrick, had been arrested and would be charged with armed robbery. 'It's hard to explain what goes through your head at a time like that. I knew my husband had been in
10 trouble in the past, before I met him, but he'd been so good with me and he loved our children. But he was out of work and I think he just got desperate.'

Patrick was sentenced to eight years and nine months. Sakina has remained loyal to him, visiting him regularly with
15 their three children, Gemma, James and Paul. Like many prisoners' wives, Sakina is a typical loving, law-abiding mother and housewife. Far from moaning about the sentence, she says: 'In a way, Patrick was lucky not to get longer. He did wrong and he's paying for it.'

20 Sakina is now 26 and her life revolves around her family. Money is very short and her council flat is tidy but threadbare. She has a dog for protection but says: I do feel defenceless, especially in the middle of the night, but I must be strong and cope because of the children. Gemma's always
25 been a daddy's girl. Patrick watched her being born and they've got this very close bond. Now Gemma only sees her dad twice a month, in jail. I always take the kids.' Sakina can spend up to 90 minutes with Patrick in a large visiting room. They're allowed to hold hands during the visit and the
25 children can sit on his lap. 'We're all excited when we go and miserable when we leave,' she says.

One of Sakina's biggest problems is money. She admits: 'I'm in a lot of debt because I put bills off in order to feed the children properly. Patrick's always saying I should go out
30 more but you get used to being alone and I don't want to mix. I can't afford to go out anyway. I can't really afford to live.'

'Being a prisoner's wife is worse than being a widow because then you have to accept your husband has gone and get on with your life.' Of course, people ask why she stays
35 with Patrick. 'They don't usually come straight out with it. Most people say they don't know how I cope after all he's done. You've got to have a very strong relationship to stick it out but I've told him I won't put up with it or put the children through it again.'

40 She often wonders what the future will hold for her family. A prison record inevitably means finding work is harder. 'We've both changed a lot too. I've got to cope with the bills and children while he doesn't have to worry where he lives or what he earns. I really can't wait for him to come out but I
45 know we'll both have to adjust a lot.'

B Which of the following provides the best explanation of these words and phrases that appear in the text?

1 to pay for his crime

   A to pay a sum of money to a court
   B to be punished
   C to give help to those he injured

2 arrested

   A stopped by the police
   B put in prison
   C noticed

3 law-abiding

   A breaking the law
   B consulting lawyers
   C respecting the law

4 moaning

   A making a noise
   B being angry
   C complaining

5 They've got this very close bond

   A they depend on each other
   B they feel great affection for each other
   C they have a tense relationship

6 a prison record

   A the maximum time spent in prison
   B a song describing life in prison
   C being known as a person who's been in prison

C Answer the following questions.

1 When the police knocked on Sakina's door, did she have any reason to suspect her husband?

2 How does Sakina justify her husband's action?

3 Does she agree with what he did?

4 Why does Sakina keep a dog?

5 How often do the children see their father?

6 What is Sakina's financial situation like?

7 What do most people think about Sakina staying with Patrick?

8 What is Sakina's view if Patrick breaks the law again?

9 Does Sakina anticipate any difficulties when her husband gets out of prison?

Speaking

Section 1

Work in pairs: one student describes one picture, and the other student identifies which photo is being described.

Then compare the two photos together.
What are the differences between the people in the photographs?

Section 2

Discuss in groups.

Do you have any elderly relatives?
What problems do old people face?
Who should pay the costs involved in looking after the old?
What do you think it's like to be old?

Section 3

An English friend of yours has told you about a problem that her family has to deal with. What advice would you give your friend? Discuss the problem in groups of three.

The problem is that my grandmother, on my father's side, is too old to be able to live on her own any more. My father wants her to live with us permanently but my mother thinks that grandmother should spend some of her time at her daughter's house, that is, my father's sister, my aunty, and some of the time at our house. My aunty isn't keen on having grandma because she says her house is too small. But our house isn't that big, and if grandma stays with us I'll have to give up my own room and share with my sister. I don't fancy that at all. Also, I know that mum and grandma don't really get on, although they pretend that they do, and there might be a horrible atmosphere, which I really dread. What should we do?

Listening

Childhood memories

Listen to the cassette and answer these questions.

1 In what year was the picture taken?
2 What is the person in the picture wearing?
3 How old is he?
4 What is significant about his age?
5 What happened to him?
6 What does the speaker seem to regret?
7 In what way is the speaker similar to his grandfather?
8 What incident does the speaker remember vividly?

Writing

A Letter of advice

Mark Fraser has just left university with a degree in engineering. He has received a number of job offers but is not sure which one to accept. He has written to you, asking for your advice. Read Mark's letter and write a letter of advice to him. Use between 120 and 180 words.

---

15 July

Dear . . . . . .

I hope you are well and have had some luck in finding a job. I'm in the 'fortunate' position of having several job offers to choose from. The trouble is I don't know which one to go for. I'd appreciate your advice. I've got a definite offer of a job with a company in Birmingham at a salary of £20,000. Actually, that's with Amanda's father's company. Do you remember Amanda? She's my fiancée – and she's very keen to fix a date for the wedding. It seems that there is a house available if I take that job. The trouble is that, according to what I've read in the newspapers, Birmingham Engineering isn't doing very well. It has made a big loss this year and there are rumours of an American take-over. It might not be a secure job. I haven't mentioned this to Amanda but I've got an interview with Channel Engineering on 1 August. If I got that job, I'd be paid £30,000 (plus bonus) and be based in Dover.

I've also got a definite offer of a job in Australia at an annual salary of £40,000 plus free accommodation and meals. It's a two-year contract. Amanda is very much against me taking that job because it's for single men only – it's in a remote desert location – and she has read in the newspaper that MIMC's Tennant Creek mine (that's where I would be) has a poor safety record, with several deaths recently. If I take that job I have to let them know by 1 August and fly to Australia on 31 August.

Well, I've got a lot of choices. What do you think I should do?
Best wishes

Mark

English in Use

1 Look at the word *like* in these questions.

1 What does she look *like*?
2 What is she *like*?
3 What does she *like*?

A Match the question with the answer:

a She's tall with long black hair.
b She likes chocolate.
c She's reliable and efficient.

B What is the difference between the first question and the second?
What is the difference between the first two questions and the third?

C Look at the following answers to questions and supply a suitable question using the word *like*.

EXAMPLE: He likes ice cream.
<u>What does he like</u> ?

1 Alice is kind and helpful.
2 Anna looks like her mother, but Helen looks more like her father.
3 Strawberries, plums and tangerines.
4 It's quite a big house, with a front door that is painted red.
5 Yes, I quite like lettuce, but I prefer tomatoes.
6 Patrick's tall and thin, with curly red hair.
7 He's always untidy.
8 Shirley always gives in excellent work.
9 It'll be warm and sunny in the morning and then the afternoon will be cloudy.
10 No, it's the worst film I've ever seen.

2 Phrasal Verbs

Complete the sentences with a phrasal verb based on *take*.

EXAMPLE: The trousers were too long so I had to
<u>take</u> them <u>up</u> .

1 Sarah wanted to devote herself to studying but she found that earning her living .... most of her time.

2 The detective opened the drawer and .... a gun.

3 The police .... all the items that could be used as evidence.

4 Because of the fog, the plane is unlikely to .... for another hour or so.

5 Helen .... her grandfather – they both adore mountain climbing.

6 I know you are fed up with your job but don't .... me.

7 There was so much new information in the lecture that I found it difficult to .... it all ....

8 John needs the money – that's why he .... all the work he is offered.

9 Arthur was so tired he could hardly manage to .... his clothes before falling into bed.

10 The waistband on this skirt is too big, I'll have to .... it ....

3 Word-formation

Complete the sentences with the correct form of the word in capitals.

EXAMPLES: All the players in the match were angry with the <u>referee</u> .   REFER
The <u>violinist</u> missed the first few notes.   VIOLIN
All Tom's children are talented <u>musicians</u> .   MUSIC

1 The .... made a remarkable discovery.   PHYSICS

2 Shirley left school last year and is now a .... in an insurance company.   TRAIN

3 The .... pointed out that the film was not based on what had actually happened.   HISTORY

4 My brother is an excellent ....   PIANO

5 .... are frequently talking about family values.   POLITICS

6 Each .... in the company is entitled to time off when a baby is expected.   EMPLOY

7 The educational .... reported that a number of children in the school had learning difficulties.   PSYCHOLOGY

8 This .... gets a lot of work performing at children's birthday parties.   MAGIC

9 Two .... working on the project were murdered.   SCIENCE

10 My goddaugher has decided she wants to train to be a ....   BEAUTY

unit 8 GOOD COMPANIONS

Lead-in **1** What relationship is there between the people in the pictures?
What makes people feel they are members of a particular group?

2 Choose the correct word for the gap in each sentence.

penpals   acquaintances   colleagues
schoolfriends   outsiders

1 It was a sad day when Paul left the company and had to say goodbye to all his ....

2 People who move into the village from the cities are treated like ....

3 We know quite a few people in the town, but they are .... rather than friends.

4 It was David's eighth birthday and he invited all his .... to the party.

5 Susie loves writing letters and has .... in five different countries.

3 Choose the correct word for the gap in each sentence.

spectators   gang   crew   staff
team   mob   audience   fans
congregation   crowd

1 There are two new players in the football .... for the match on Saturday.

2 The .... of the private jet consisted of the pilot, co-pilot, one steward and two stewardesses.

3 All members of .... working in this company must undergo regular health checks.

4 A large .... had turned out to watch the arrival of the princess.

5 A .... of angry protesters shouted at the police.

6 Three men were arrested in connection with the robbery but the leader of the .... has not been caught.

7 The .... at the school concert was made up of parents and teachers.

8 Improvements in the stadium meant that none of the .... had to stand to watch the match.

9 After the performance the star of the show was surrounded by .... waiting at the stage door.

10 When an estate was built on the edge of the village, the .... at the local church doubled in size.

4 Choose the correct word for the gap in each sentence.

praised   congratulate   make
encouraged   motivate
support   boosted   betrayed   trust
criticized   keep

1 William was .... by the teacher for not doing his homework.

2 Everyone was eager to .... Anita on winning the race.

3 The trainer knew exactly how to .... his players so that they would give their best.

4 The teachers .... all the students to work harder.

5 The emergency services were .... for their speed and efficiency in dealing with the accident.

6 Jane and Harriet are good friends and always .... each other.

7 You can .... Celia – she'll never tell anyone your secrets.

8 Mary felt she had been .... when she heard her sister telling a schoolfriend about their family problems.

9 Don't .... promises you can't ....

10 Stephen's success in the competition .... his confidence.

Reading

   A   Why do people like dolphins so much? How can contact with animals help to keep people healthy?

DOLPHIN'S MYSTERY POWERS CURE SLIM-MAD JEMIMA

In the cold, hostile waters of the North Sea, Jemima Biggs is undergoing an astonishing course of treatment. She is
5 swimming with Freddie, a 4-metre long, 275- kilogram dolphin who seems to possess almost magical powers to cure human illnesses. He is
10 not a tame, aquarium dolphin. He is a wild creature who lives in the sea outside the harbour at Amble, on the north-west coast of England.
15 Jemima, 25, is not an athletic superwoman. In fact, she has suffered from anorexia nervosa – the 'slimmers' disease' – for nine years. At
20 her lowest point last summer her 162 cm frame weighed little more than 31 kilograms. Thanks to her swimming sessions with
25 Freddie, she is finally making progress. 'The way I think and feel about food has changed,' she said. 'I can now eat with other people in a
30 way that I couldn't before. I don't weigh myself – it's a policy of mine – but I think I am about 41 kilograms.'
Jemima, a postgraduate
35 student at Exeter University, is taking part in a unique scheme for people with depressive illnesses, pioneered by Dr Horace Dobbs. She
40 wrote to him after her mother saw a TV programme about his work with dolphins. Soon afterwards she began making the 1300-kilometre round
45 trips from Exeter to Amble. For her latest session just last week she set out in a boat and Freddie broke surface only minutes out of
50 the harbour. Jemima plunged over the side to play with him

for ten minutes until the cold became unbearable. When she was hauled back on
55 board, she was exhilarated. 'Brilliant,' she said. 'Absolutely brilliant – the best ten minutes of my life. It was better than the other five
60 or six times. I stroked him from under his chin to his tail. He just loved it. He was so big that I could not get my arms around him, but I was
65 not intimidated' Later she said, 'I have no doubt that the dolphin has saved me. They are absolutely marvellous creatures. They are real
70 friends. They welcome you and make you feel wanted. I feel I am transported into another world. When you are low, you avoid eye-contact
75 with people but when a dolphin looks you in the eye, you feel he is not judging you. With anorexia, you get into a state of paralysis. A dolphin
80 helps you open your mind and become alive again.'
Dr Dobbs, director of International Dolphin Watch, said, 'Wild dolphins
85 have a mysterious way of reassuring you that somebody loves you. They generate an enormous sense of well-being in people. I
90 can't tell you how they do it. Their brain is as big as a human's, but they must be doing something with it that we don't understand.'
95 Freddie appears all year round at Amble and enjoys the company of swimmers. 'Not everyone can visit, so we have devised a tape of
100 music and dolphin sounds that may help some people,' said Dr Dobbs.

B   Find words in the text to help you complete these sentences. Use *one* word in each space. You must *change* the word in the text to fit the grammar of the sentence.

EXAMPLE:

Many people are .... by Jemima's course of treatment.
Text: '*an astonishing course of treatment*'
Many people   *are astonished* .... by Jemima's course of treatment.

1   Jemima has decided to .... treatment for anorexia nervosa.

2   Dr Dobbs believes the dolphin is .... human illnesses.

3   The dolphin is wild – it has not been ....

4   Jemima has been .... from anorexia nervosa for several years.

5   She doesn't know what her .... is but thinks she is putting on a few kilos.

6   Dr Dobb's scheme is for people whose illnesses make them ....

7   Dr Dobbs is a .... of this new treatment.

8   The people in the boat watched Jemima .... over the side of the boat into the water.

9   After ten minutes, they had to .... her back into the boat.

10   Swimming with Freddie gave her a feeling of ....

11   She enjoyed .... the dolphin from his chin to his tail.

12   In a curious way, people feel .... by dolphins.

C   Read this summary of the text. It contains a number of errors. Re-write it, correcting the errors.

In the sea off the west coast of Britain, Jenny Bicks, 21, has been swimming with Fred, a 3-metre long, 275 lb dolphin who used to be in a dolphinarium. Swimming with this dolphin is helping Jenny to overcome an unknown disease which is making her lose weight – she currently weighs 31 kilograms. She is making progress but she cannot yet eat with other people although she does weigh herself now, which she used to be too nervous to do. Jenny is a student at Exeter University and travels a short distance every weekend to swim with Fred. The treatment is supervised by Professor Horatio Dobbs who was contacted by Jenny's grandmother after she heard a radio programme about his work. Jenny has had six sessions with Fred and plays with him for up to half an hour and touches him a lot. Professor Dobbs has made a video of his dolphins to help people who are unable to swim.

Grammar: *present perfect (simple and continuous)*

 A (Grammar Notes **8.1**)
Respond to the following remarks using a sentence with a *present perfect continuous* verb.

EXAMPLE:
Why are your hands covered in flour?
.... *I've been baking* .... bread.

1   You seem to be out of breath.
2   Your hands are sticky with paint.
3   You look exhausted.
4   Your shoes are very muddy.
5   There's a delicious smell in your kitchen.
6   Why is your hair wet?

B Complete the following sentences, using a verb in the *present perfect continuous* form.

EXAMPLES:
How long .... *have you been reading 'Clarissa'?* ....
.... *Have you been living* .... here since you got married?

1   How long ....
    for the results?
2   How long ....
    tennis?
3   How many years ....
    Latin?
4   How many weeks ....
    for this company?
5   How long ....
    these pills?
6   ....
    from headaches since the accident?
7   ....
    to ring him since 9 am?

C There is sometimes little difference between the *present perfect simple* and the *present perfect continuous*. This happens because of the meaning of the particular verb in the sentence.
For example, there is little difference between

I have lived in Manchester for ten years.
and
I have been living in Manchester for ten years.

The reason that there is little difference is that the verb *live* means something continuous. Verbs such as *live*, *work* and *study* do not make clear the difference between the simple and continuous tenses.

Is the difference clear in these sentences?
a   I've cut my finger.
b   I've been cutting my finger.

One of these sentences is impossible. Which one?
c   He has shot himself in the heart.
d   He has been shooting himself in the heart.

One of these sentences is highly unlikely. Which one?
e   She has murdered her husband.
f   She has been murdering her husband.

D Complete these sentences using either the *present perfect simple* or *the present perfect continuous*.

1   'I .... gold at last!' said the old prospector.   (find)
2   The police .... for the stolen money but
    they .... yet.   (search, find)
3   'Our tests show that you .... calcium from
    your body for several years,' said the doctor.   (lose)
4   'I'm afraid we .... your file,' said the
    manager.   (lose)
5   'The champion .... out of the ring,' said the
    commentator.   (fall)
6   Someone .... my car!   (steal)
7   I am afraid I .... accidentally ....
    the page.   (tear)
8   Peter .... the apple pie – there's only one
    piece left.   (eat)
9   The birds .... the strawberries. We need a
    net to protect them.   (peck)
10 Scientists .... the data for several days
    now but they .... nothing unusual so far.
                                                (analyse, find)

E Complete these sentences with one verb in the past simple and one verb in the *present perfect* (simple or continuous as appropriate). Sometimes you will have to make the verbs negative.

EXAMPLE:
The solicitor .... *wrote* .... to him a fortnight ago but
.... *hasn't received a reply* .... yet.

1   I first .... my driving test three
    years ago. I .... ten times
    since then.   (take, fail)
2   Jonathan .... his first piece of
    music when he was 12. He ....
    five symphonies so far.   (compose).
3   I .... a model aircraft kit last
    year but I .... it yet. (buy, build)
4   Mr and Mrs Myers .... to
    Dorchester in 1949. They ....
    there ever since.   (move, live)
5   When I lived in Australia I never ....
    a kangaroo but since returning to England I
    .... them in zoos.   (see, see).

6 Last year we .... a holiday at
  all but this year we .... three
  already and it's only June. (have)
7 Edward .... for ages although
  he .... his pilot's licence
  twenty years ago. (fly, get)
8 We .... him since last April
  although we .... his wife only
  yesterday. (see)
9 Peter .... in prison from 1988
  to 1992 but he .... back
  behind bars since then. (be)
10 Lucy and Emily .... on their first
  day at university and they ....
  good friends ever since. (meet, be)

Listening

Listen to the cassette and complete the text.
Use *one* or *two* words in each gap.

PETS AS THERAPY

In the 1970s doctors discovered that
patients recovering from .... (1)
survived longer if they owned pets. In fact,
only .... (2) of pet owners died in
the first year after leaving hospital
compared with .... (3) of patients
who did not own pets. Many doctors now
believe that owning a pet speeds up
.... (4). Giving .... (5)
lessons to physically-handicapped children
is one of the most successful schemes
involving animals. Another interesting
scheme involves using .... (6) to
assist disabled people. In order to control his
nimble assistant the disabled owner is able
to give it .... (7) when necessary.

English in Use

Definite article
(Grammar Notes **8.2**)
Look at how *the* is used or not used in these
sentences. Divide them into ten correct
sentences and ten incorrect sentences. Write
out the incorrect sentences correctly.

1 He lived in United States for ten years.
2 John has cut the leg and needs the stitches.
3 The camera I bought yesterday doesn't work.
4 William Wordsworth is famous for his poems about nature.
5 It was first time I had crossed Equator.
6 This is only one left but you can have it.
7 Frank does a lot of work for the disabled.
8 I will be visiting the Netherlands next month.
9 Society doesn't care enough for old people.
10 This is the same film I saw last week.
11 The worst thing was not knowing exactly what had happened.
12 Harder we work, more money we make.
13 Smiths are coming round to dinner tonight.
14 The aeroplane is one of the greatest inventions of the twentieth century.
15 It's very disappointing news but that's the life.
16 Eating the chocolate always gives me pimples on my face.
17 What is on radio this afternoon?
18 John plays the football very well.
19 The furniture was sold at auction.
20 He was sent to prison for life.

Reading

A Before you read the text, discuss these questions:

What organisations can young people join in your country?

What skills do they learn in these organisations?

Do young girls join different organisations from young boys?

Are there differences in the skills that are taught to young people of different sexes?

B Now read the following article about a girls' school. Four paragraphs have been removed from the article. Choose from the paragraphs A–E the one which fits each gap (1–4). There is one extra paragraph that you do not need to use.

LITTLE GIRLS DRESSED TO KILL

Fifteen-year-old Jessica Blake looked as tough as a girl can get. Dressed to kill in a blue beret, combat suit and army boots, she barked out an order. At her command fourteen pairs of feet crunched to attention on the gravel. And they were all girls. St Michael's, Burton Park, a private girls' boarding school in the South of England, is thought to be the only school in the country with an all-girl army cadet force.

(1) ....

The girls' commander, Lieutenant Miss Hilary Law, normally a maths and physics teacher, greeted us in front of the school wearing her olive-green uniform. Miss Law brought her military enthusiasm with her two years ago when she transferred from another school, where she was second-in-command of a mixed cadet force.

(2) ....

And then there were the girls. Henrietta, Bernadette, Anna and Louise settled down to cook beans and steak and kidney pie, while the others timed each other's progress over the assault course, jumping over fences, leaping ditches and swinging from car tyres. All the girls handle guns and learn to shoot. They learn fieldcraft. 'Things like how to cross an open field without being shot, that sort of thing,' said Jessica. 'You never know, it might come in useful one day.'

(3) ....

And talking to Miss Law, it was the photographer who put the question that had to be asked. 'Just to play devil's advocate for a moment,' he said, 'aren't you, in fact, encouraging *girls to kill* ?' Miss Law kept her sang-froid under fire. 'I would say no. It's entirely the opposite of that. It's training them to be safe with weapons. A lot of them have shotguns at home. They need to know about gun safety. The cadet force is a youth organisation on military lines to teach responsibility, co-operation and expertise.'

(4) ....

None of them thought they were particularly aggressive, though girls were more assertive these days. They enjoyed the competition and discipline. 'It's fun,' was the single most popular reason for getting into uniform. Will it catch on? Perhaps it's unlikely but meanwhile if you are thinking of poaching rabbits in Burton Park on Thursday night, forget it. The girls of St Michael's might get you.

A The girls of St Michael's are not a squad to give up easily. Ordered by Jessica to march at the photographer, the girls kept on going. It was the photographer who turned and fled, taking pictures as he went.

B Every Thursday evening, for two hours, the well-groomed and well-heeled young ladies of St Michael's shed their school clothes for army uniform, polish their boots and head for the woods to tackle the assault course (an obstacle course for training soldiers) and cook meals over a camp-fire. The squad of up to sixteen girls drills in front of the school's neo-classical facade.

C Are girls, then, becoming more aggressive? Miss Law did not think so. 'I think of myself as feminine,' she said, 'but that doesn't prevent me from being in the cadet force.' As for the girls, most wanted to prove that they could be the equal of boys or men at shooting, map reading and fighting their way through bushes.

'I'm a tomboy,' said thirteen-year-old Bernadette. 'I just like the idea of doing assault courses and getting muddy,' said thirteen-year-old Henrietta. 'Girls have as much right to do this as boys.'

D Couldn't they be learning these skills just as well on the sports field? The school has a strong tradition in this area, but Anna and Louise insisted they preferred the chance to tackle the assault course and camp. 'We are learning to work together,' they said, 'not just learning how to win.' Miss Law clearly agreed.

E Since she started at St Michael's she has been training girls over twelve in military skills. 'The girls were really keen to join,' she said. 'These are marvellous grounds,' she added as we walked across the school's 50-hectare estate in search of the assault course. 'You could land helicopters here. Plenty of space for playing war games and that sort of thing.' We found the assault course in the wood next to the hockey pitch.

Reading

A What advantages or disadvantages are there in sharing a flat with other people?

AN EXTRAORDINARY FLATMATE

We met next day as he had arranged, and inspected the rooms at No. 221B Baker Street, of which he had spoken at our meeting. They consisted of a couple of comfortable bedrooms and a single large airy sitting-
5 room, cheerfully furnished and illuminated by two broad windows. So desirable in every way were the apartments, and so moderate did the terms seem when divided between us, that the bargain was concluded upon the spot, and we at once entered into possession.
10 That very evening I moved my things round from the hotel, and on the following morning Sherlock Holmes followed me with several boxes and portmanteaus. For a day or two we were busily employed in unpacking and laying out our property to the best advantage.
15 That done, we gradually began to settle down and to accommodate ourselves to our new surroundings.

Holmes was certainly not a difficult man to live with. He was quiet in his ways, and his habits were regular. It was rare for him to be up after ten at night,
20 and he had invariably breakfasted and gone out before I rose in the morning. Sometimes he spent his day at the chemical laboratory, sometimes in the dissecting rooms, and occasionally in long walks, which appeared to take him into the poorest parts of the city. Nothing
25 could exceed his energy when the working fit was upon him; but now and again a reaction would seize him, and for days on end he would lie on the sofa in the sitting-room, hardly uttering a word or moving a muscle from morning to night.
30 As the weeks went by, my interest in him and my curiosity as to his aims in life gradually deepened and increased. His very person and appearance were such as to strike the attention of the most casual observer. In height he was rather over six feet, and so
35 excessively lean that he seemed to be considerably taller. His eyes were sharp and piercing, except during those intervals of torpor to which I have alluded; and his thin hawk-like nose gave his whole expression an air of alertness and decision. His chin,
40 too, had the prominence and squareness which mark the man of determination. His hands were invariably blotted with ink and stained with chemicals, yet he was possessed of extraordinary delicacy of touch, as I frequently had occasion to observe when I watched
45 him manipulating his fragile scientific instruments.

B Explain the meaning of these phrases as used in the text.

Paragraph 1
1 cheerfully furnished
2 we at once entered into possession

Paragraph 2
3 the dissecting rooms
4 for days on end
5 hardly uttering a word

Paragraph 3
6 so excessively lean
7 the most casual observer
8 hawk-like nose
9 blotted with ink

C Are the following statements *true* or *false*?

1 Holmes heard about the flat first.

2 The flat had three rooms.

3 The rent was quite high.

4 They were glad to provide their own furniture.

5 They agreed to rent the flat as soon as they saw it.

6 Holmes moved in the day after he saw the flat.

7 Holmes was talkative most of the time.

8 Holmes was the first to leave the flat in the morning.

9 There were three different ways in which Holmes might spend his day.

10 Holmes was always full of energy.

11 Holmes was very slim.

12 Holmes was rather clumsy.

Talking Points

Section 1

What do you think of each of these activities as a way to relax?
When you relax, do you prefer to be alone or to be with other people?

Section 2

Work in groups of four:
Find out what each person likes.
For each person put a tick in the appropriate column

Find out which activities are most popular in your group, and report to the class. Do all the groups agree? If no, how is each group different.

Do you enjoy:	enjoy	quite like	don't like
1 taking exercise			
2 team sports			
3 getting away from other people			
4 being in the fresh air			
5 listening to pop music			
6 listening to classical music			
7 practising a sport			
8 playing a musical instrument			
9 dancing			
10 going shopping			
11 watching films			
12 playing board games			
13 going to the theatre			
14 wearing the latest fashions			

Listening

Losing a friend

You will hear four people talking about friends that they used to have but don't have now. They speak in the order given below. Match the statement with the speaker. Two statements do not go with any of the speakers.

	how long the friendship lasted	how it ended
James		
Kate		
David		
Mandy		

1 lasted a very long time.

2 lasted from nought to thirteen or fourteen.

3 ended when the friend stole some money from his mother's purse.

4 lasted for five years.

5 ended when the friend wrote her an unpleasant letter.

6 ended when the speaker went abroad.

7 ended because the friend didn't like children.

8 lasted from five to thirteen.

9 lasted from university days until soon after marriage.

10 ended when the friend began to 'fancy' the speaker's brother.

Writing

A letter requesting information

You have seen the following advertisement and are interested in learning new skills. Read the advertisement and the notes you have made on it. Write to the centre and ask for more information and an application form. Use the ideas in the notes and ask about any other points that you think are important.

The Centre for Adventure Skills Training

- Learn mountaineering, sailing, scuba-diving, canoeing, survival techniques
- Open all year
- Accommodation and meals provided
- Minimum age 16
- For further information and an application form write to: The Director, TCFAST, Blair Atholl, Scotland.

Notes:

Cost? Different for different times of year?

Courses for beginners?

Equipment provided or bring own?

Certificates at end of course?

How to get there?

English in Use

1 Phrasal Verbs

Complete the sentences. Use the correct form of the phrasal verb.

> fall in   break up   snuggle up
> drift apart   fall out   make up
> get on with   let down   bring up

1 The twins like nothing better than to
.... to their mother on the sofa.

2 Charles .... love with Emma
as soon as he saw her.

3 John and Mike were good friends at university but
later they just .... and now
hardly ever see each other.

4 Surprising though it may seem, all the step-children
.... each other very well.

5 Sally and her sister often .... over silly
things, but they soon .... it ....

6 After years of terrible rows, their marriage finally
....

7 Although Angela is fun to be with, she is not very
reliable and often .... her
friends ....

8 Mrs Lee .... four children of
her own and two adopted children.

2 Word-formation

Complete the sentences with the correct form of the word in capitals.

EXAMPLES: A soldier should not ....*disobey*.... orders.
　　　　　　　　　　　　　　　　　　　　OBEY

I ....*mistook*.... that man for someone
I knew.　　　　　　　TAKE

1 He's such a naughty boy – he's always ....
　　　　　　　　　　　　　　　　　　　BEHAVE

2 The politician did not have the correct information –
he had obviously been ....　INFORM

3 You may not agree with the theory but it is very
difficult to ....　　　　PROVE

4 John and Mary have a .... son.　ABLE

5 'No, you're quite wrong. I completely ....
with what you have said.'　　　　AGREE

6 It's impossible to please my boss, because he
.... of everything I do.　APPROVE

7 The farmer was accused of .... his
animals.　　　　　　　　　　　TREAT

8 My grandmother says she's going to do exactly what
she wants, she's too old to do things she ....
any more.　　　　　　　　　　LIKE

9 The suspect gave the wrong information to the police
in order to .... them.　　LEAD

10 I took my eyes off the little boy for one moment and
when I looked around he had ....　APPEAR

unit 9 EMOTIONS AND FEELINGS

Lead-in **1** How do the people in the photo feel? What shows how they feel?

What do you think has happened?

2 Choose the correct word or phrase for the gap in each sentence.

> bury their differences   gets on
> burst out   eye to eye   break off
> burst into tears   loses his temper
> enjoys her company   raise your voice

1 The joke was so funny all the students .... laughing.

2 Things are difficult in the office because no-one .... with the new sales manager.

3 Tammy was so upset she ....

4 Tom says he's not in love with Harriet, he just ....

5 Sally and her husband have a lot of similar ideas, but on this subject they just don't see ....

6 Michael and Joanne have decided to .... their engagement.

7 I know you're angry but there's no need to ....

8 John is under so much stress that he often ....

9 Colin and his brother refused to speak to each other for many years but finally they agreed to ....

3 Choose the correct word or phrase for the gap in each sentence.

> blush   argument   nervous   furious
> tension   quarrel   sympathetic
> butterflies   kiss   embarrassed

1 Interviews make most people feel quite ....

2 Everyone was very .... when Claire told them the bad news she had just received.

3 Sarah felt everyone was looking at her make-up and knew she was going to ....

4 Before the performance all the singers felt they had .... in their stomachs.

5 There was a sense of .... in the air as the students waited to receive their examination results.

6 Jane and Mary were best friends for years, then one day they had an .... and fell out with each other.

7 The best thing to do if you have a fight with someone you are close to is to .... and make up.

8 Jamie was so .... that he rushed out, slamming the door behind him.

9 The boys' mother doesn't like leaving them alone because they always .... with each other.

10 Karen felt .... when she was asked to sing in front of the whole class.

Reading

A Discuss with a partner:

When you have problems, who do you ask for advice?
Have you ever written for advice to someone who writes
in a newspaper or magazine?
What is your opinion of the advice these people give?

Look at these two letters sent to a magazine.
Would you give the same advice?

1

I'M DEPRESSED ABOUT LEAVING COLLEGE

I will be leaving college next year to get a job and most of my
friends are going to university. I'm very close to a boy in my
year and I'm going to miss him and my friends like mad. I
have made some very good friends at college and get so
depressed when I think of them going away that it makes
me cry. Please help as I have nothing to look forward to.

*Actually, you have your whole life to look forward to –
it's just that you are experiencing a major landmark in
your life and entering the big, wide world, which can be
scary and depressing as well as exciting. You may lose
touch with some of your college friends, but there is no
reason your closest friends shouldn't stay in touch. Why
not make an effort by writing or calling them regularly?
There's also no reason why you shouldn't stay in touch
with this boy, and even see him on occasional weekends
and holidays. It is true that university life is hectic, and
many of your present friends may get caught up in the
social whirl and slowly drift away – but what about your
life? What about the new job that you will start, and the
new friends that you are bound to make there? Think of
all the new experiences you will soon have: it isn't just
your college friends who will have all the fun. So by all
means feel nostalgic about your college days, but don't let
it prevent you from looking forward to the future.*

2

I DON'T HAVE ANY CONFIDENCE

I feel life is not worth living. I am at university and enjoy
the course but have not made that many friends. I seem
to be inhibited by confident, outgoing people. They make
me feel so inadequate. I am a shy person but I can talk
freely with people I know well. If my friends cannot make
it to a lecture and I have to sit on my own, I feel like the
ground should open and swallow me up. Other students
seem to have a wonderful social life, and to be making
lots of friends. I realise I may be paranoid and lack self-
confidence but this is ruining my life.

*First, realise that it is quite normal in your teens and
early twenties to feel as you do – I remember this time
acutely, and shared your feelings about sitting alone.
Most people are shy with strangers, but many are
good at hiding it. So-called confident, outgoing types
have just developed a particularly good way of
coping. The next time you are with friends, take the
attention away from yourself by asking about them,
their studies and interests. The trick is to stop
thinking of yourself as the centre of attention, by
making someone else the centre of attention. Believe
me, this phase of yours will pass as you gain more
insight and experience through daily interaction with
others. So don't be so hard on yourself!*

B Find words or phrases in the text which in
context are similar in meaning to:

letter 1
1 fond of
2 at the same stage of study

reply 1
3 an important point in your life
4 frightening
5 maintain contact
6 odd
7 very busy
8 certain

letter 2
9 unable to express yourself
10 not good enough
11 come
12 spoiling

reply 2
13 clearly
14 way of managing

C According to the text, are the following
statements *true* or *false*? Justify your answer.

problem 1
1 The student has been lonely at college.
2 The student has been left by her boyfriend.
3 The student dreads starting her job.
4 The advice is that the student should change her
   attitude.
5 The person writing the advice is critical of the student.

problem 2
6 The student feels her studies are not going well.
7 The student feels other people are making fun of her.
8 The advice is that the student should recognise how
   other people feel.
9 The adviser is sympathetic.
10 The adviser says things will improve with time.

Grammar: *who, which, that*

 A Join the sentences with *who* or *which*. (Grammar Notes **9.1**)

EXAMPLES:

The man had ticket No.158. He won the prize.
The man who had ticket No.158 won the prize.
The painting was damaged by fire. It is now being repaired.
The painting which was damaged by fire is now being repaired.

1 The man found some gold coins. He took them to a museum.

2 The stream has dried up. It runs through the village.

3 The girls had university degrees. They were interviewed by the bank.

4 The firefighters rescued two children. They got a reward.

5 The hinges squeaked. They have been oiled.

All of these sentences can be written with *that* instead of *who* and *which*.

B In which sentences can we remove *that*, *which* or *who*?

EXAMPLES:

He is the man *who* Jennifer intends to marry.
(She intends to marry *him* so *the man* is the object and *who* is not essential in this sentence).
He is the man *who* intends to marry Jennifer.
(*He* intends to marry *her* so *the man* is the subject and we cannot omit *who*).

1 The horse that I bet £10 on won the race.

2 The official that I spoke to gave me all the forms I needed.

3 John is not the same person that I knew years ago.

4 I told the detectives all the details that I could remember.

5 Mr Roberts is the only man who knows the answer.

6 I couldn't find a carpet that I liked.

7 The computer that broke down was six years old.

C Join these sentences together to make one sentence. You must decide whether it is necessary to use *who*, *that* or *which* or not.

1 The man committed the robbery. He was never identified.

2 Here is a cake. I made it earlier.

3 I recognised all the names. They were on a list.

4 Michael spent all the money. His grandfather gave him it.

5 The treasure was buried. Captain Kydd buried it. It has never been discovered.

6 The horse broke its leg in the race. It had to be shot.

7 The paintings had been stolen. Two of them were recovered in less than a week.

8 Maria helped me with the question. I couldn't answer it.

D Add the extra information in brackets to the sentence. Remember to include the commas – they are essential because the information between the commas is only extra information and does not identify the subject of the sentence.

EXAMPLES:

I met the Duke of Cumberland and had a long argument with him.   (*he is a leading supporter of fox-hunting*)
I met the Duke of Cumberland, who is a leading supporter of fox-hunting, and had a long argument with him.

Sally Browne is likely to win the race this year.
                    (*she has won three years in a row*)
Sally Browne, who has won three years in a row, is likely to win the race this year.

1 General Campbell has now fully recovered from his wounds.   (*he was shot in the leg*)

2 The President has returned to his palace.
        (*he narrowly escaped an assassination attempt*)

3 The new supermarket opened last Saturday.
            (*it is built on the site of an old school*)

4 The exhibition at the Royal Academy will close on Saturday.   (*it has been visited by 100,000 people*)

5 *Robinson Crusoe* is Daniel Defoe's most famous novel.   (*it is based on a true story*)

6 Professor Green died yesterday.
            (*he won the Nobel prize in 1990*)

7 The Goodwin lighthouse is now controlled automatically.   (*it was built in 1806*)

Listening

Embarrassing moments

A Listen to the speakers talking about embarrassing moments.

For the story about the taxi, answer the questions.

1 How was the woman travelling?

2 What was the traffic like that day?

3 What time of day was it?

4 How did the woman feel?

5 Why couldn't she move?

6 How did she find out what was wrong?

7 How did she feel then?

B For the story about the man and his father, say whether the statement is *true* or *false*.

1 James invited his father out to celebrate his birthday.

2 James's father is still quite a young man.

3 James's father often goes to watch cricket matches.

4 James's father usually gets excited when watching cricket.

5 The other members of the audience reacted in an excited way.

6 James's father enjoyed the evening out.

7 James enjoyed the evening too.

English in Use

For questions 1–15, read the text below and look carefully at each line. Some of the lines are correct, and some have a word which should not be there. Tick the correct lines and underline the wrong words in the incorrect lines.

EXAMPLES: 0 <u>come</u>

00 ✓

Declining an invitation

0	Thank you for your invitation to come your
00	party. I am very pleased that you thought of
1	asking to me. After giving the matter a lot of
2	thought because I have decided that I cannot
3	accept. I could have give you a tactful reason
4	for why I cannot come. I might have a previous
5	appointment. I might be visiting by my mother
6	in the hospital. But I have decided to tell you
7	the truth. I cannot come because you have
8	invited Stephen and I cannot bear myself to
9	be in the same room with him either. You may
10	not know but we had a big row three weeks
11	ago during which any terrible things were said,
12	by both of us I must be admit. I have not yet
13	got over it. Perhaps I never will. Please do
14	not make any such changes in your plans. I
15	will try explain when I next see you.

Reading

A What is bullying?
Why does it happen?
What can be done to stop it?

BEATING THE BULLIES

Finally Lucy decided that she could not stand another day of it. She went up to the bathroom, swallowed every aspirin she could find, and then sat down to dinner with her family. She didn't tell anyone what she
5 had done. There was no point. Her life was not worth living and though they loved her they could do nothing to help. She was within a hair's breadth of death by bullying. Fortunately, her sister, recognising the signs of a drug overdose, called an ambulance. Lucy lived.

10   Perhaps the thing that makes Lucy's story so frightening is its very ordinariness. She is an attractive, intelligent fifteen-year-old from a concerned and affectionate family. There is nothing about her which singles her out, nothing obvious which might make her a target. And yet her whole
15 school life has been spoiled by bullying.

The circumstances which almost ended her life appear particularly banal from a distance. Lucy had befriended a girl who was being ostracised. The result was that she, too, became the target of insults and threats. She had
20 tried to involve teachers without naming names and had asked to be moved to a different maths class to avoid her torturers, but the teacher refused. She could see no way out and no way of going on.

When bullying hits the headlines, we usually think of
25 physical attacks. The image of a bully is of a big strong boy who hits someone. But what Lucy experienced is just as common, though less obvious. Children discover very early in life that the need to be liked is the most powerful means of controlling others. Little girls are particularly
30 adept at using the fear of rejection to control their peers.

In the past there has been a tendency to dismiss bullying simply as a part of growing up, to assume that it is good for a child to come to terms with life in the real world. But anyone watching their own child go through
35 this 'learning experience' will testify that the lessons learned are rarely positive ones. If there is a common characteristic of those children most likely to be bullied, it is that they are more vulnerable. Children may also be taunted because of the colour of their skin or because of a
40 physical disability. A couple of 12-year-olds told me that kids in their school are bullied 'because they are thick.'

According to Phillipa Linklater of the Anti-bullying Campaign, a self-help network for parents, bullying often happens when a child is under stress. But it is not
45 only the victims who would benefit from a reduction in bullying. Bullies don't do too well, either. They are less likely to make satisfactory relationships and considerably more likely than other children to use violence in adult life and get into trouble with the police.
50 Bullies are not born, but made. Children who are bullies at school are often bullied at home. They have learned that the way to get someone to do what you want is not to reason with them, but to threaten them. The children who witness violence also learn something – that
55 bullying behaviour is very powerful.

B Choose the best explanation for the words and phrases from the text:

Paragraph 1
1 there was no point
   A There was no justification
   B There was no explanation
   C There was no hope

Paragraph 2
2 singles her out
   A makes her feel lonely
   B makes her different
   C makes people look at her

Paragraph 3
3 banal
   A uncommon
   B unoriginal
   C unlikely

Paragraph 4
4 hits the headlines
   A is advertised
   B is a subject for TV and newspapers
   C is discussed by parents and pupils
5 adept
   A familiar with a situation
   B encouraged
   C skilled

Paragraph 5
6 dismiss
   A send away
   B consider as not serious
   C tell someone to leave their job
7 come to terms with
   A agree
   B support
   C accept
8 taunted
   A praised
   B made to feel stupid
   C surprised

Paragraph 6
9 witness
   A observe
   B take part in
   C enjoy

C Work in pairs. Discuss these questions.

1 How was Lucy saved?
2 Why did Lucy act the way she did?
3 What did Lucy ask her teacher?
4 How did the teacher react?
5 What different examples of bullying are there in the text?
6 Why are children bullied?
7 What effect does bullying have on the person who is the bully?

Reading

A Before you read the text, discuss this question:

Where do you go when you want to meet new people?

B Now read the text and see how this couple, now married, got to know each other. Seven sentences have been removed from the article. Choose from sentences A–H the one which fits each gap (1–7). There is one extra sentence that you do not need to use.

How We Met

THE RIGHT HONOURABLE William Waldegrave, a government minister, won a scholarship to Eton, gained an excellent degree at Oxford, became President of the University Union and a Fellow of All Souls College. His wife, Caroline, a professional cook, is the co-principal and managing director of Leith's School of Food and Wine. She has written and collaborated on seven books. They live in Kensington, and at their small house on the Waldegrave estate near Bristol, with their four children, aged between three and eleven.

WILLIAM WALDEGRAVE

I was living in a flat in London and my first memory of Caroline is of seeing her dressed exactly as she is now, in T-shirt and jeans, sitting in somebody else's flat. I was 29 and Caroline six years younger. It was difficult not to be struck by her quality of straightness and openness. Like most pretty girls, she didn't think she was pretty; now she is even prettier, she has bloomed wonderfully with children. I was already a parliamentary candidate when Caroline and I met. It never occurred to me to ask her to give up her work. You'd go mad as a political wife if you didn't have some sort of other activity, though four children is enough activity for most people. (1) .... It's all right now I'm a government minister, but when I was just an ordinary Member of Parliament,

Caroline was earning more than I was.

She works incredibly hard, runs an efficient business, writes books, is a political wife and has four small children. (2) .... Anything she undertakes she does properly, like her tennis. She plays serious tennis, is very good at it and wins prizes.

We both have a very strong feeling that happy relationships don't happen by luck. (3) .... She has an absolutely unclouded clear sense of the right actions, both in terms of right and wrong and the necessity of doing things: she always manages to make space for things that really matter.

We never have rows, but I do tend to get depressed – I'm a total pessimist. (4) .... Caroline, in contrast, always looks on the bright side and is optimistic about everything.

CAROLINE WALDEGRAVE

My best friend from school ended up being William's secretary, but I'd have met him anyway; we both had the same crowd of friends. I knew quite quickly I was going to marry William. I was so busy that I only took Friday and Monday off to get married, and I was back at work on Tuesday. (5) .... I started doing only three mornings a week when I had

Harriet, because I felt tired and had faint feelings of guilt. Now I've worked out that if you feel guilty you shouldn't be working at all. I enjoy my children when I'm with them, if one of them is ill I go off work, but without my job I'd go mad.

I have someone I like and trust to look after the children in London; I couldn't manage without her, but we don't have any help at all at weekends. Last thing at night I write down, in order, exactly what I'm going to do the next day. You have to be organised with small children. We do have people to dinner. I do the food and wine and William sets the table and makes the house look nice and glamorous; he's tremendously interested in style. (6) .... I think shopping is absolutely ghastly; my poor children wear hand-me-downs because I so hate going into a shop. William buys things for me; he has terribly good taste. People say: 'Gosh, that's a nice dress,' and I've never heard of the designer, which must be quite depressing for him.

If something goes wrong in any of my three lives, it affects the rest. But on the whole I'm a natural optimist. And William is always, always there at the right time. In fact, William is terribly dependent. (7) .... We have become, apart from anything else, real best friends.

A I always assume the worst and am pleasantly surprised when it doesn't happen.

B I'm totally uninterested in clothes.

C I don't know how she does it all.

D We admire each other's qualities, and although we do not always share the same opinions, we respect the other's right to hold them.

E He does like to talk things over with me, he needs a real friend he can trust.

F Besides, the money is useful.

G I wanted to have children straight away.

H There are skills about living happily together which Caroline has much more than me.

Talking Points

Section 1

When you meet people, how do you form your first impressions of them?

How do you decide what kind of people they are? What makes you like someone?

'Look. Don't judge me by the clothes I wear, the car I drive, the books I read, the food I eat, the music I like, the friends I see, the money I earn, the place I live, the job I have, the things I say or the way I act. OK?'

Section 2

Things go better when you're feeling confident.
Look at this extract from a magazine.

How to improve your self confidence
Here are five ways:

1 Make a list of positive points about yourself and read them aloud to yourself every morning.

2 Stop apologising – for the way you look, your opinions, your character.

3 Look after your body and appearance and make sure you eat well and exercise regularly.

4 Stretch your mind by learning or developing a skill.

5 Be honest in your personal relationships – if you don't like what a friend says or does, say so.

Do you agree with them?
Can you think of any more?

Listening

Difficult situations

1 Listen to the two people, James and Mandy, talking in an office and say whether the statements are *true* or *false*.

1 This is the first time the problem of James being away from work has been discussed.

2 James says he has had to travel long distances in connection with work.

3 Mandy doesn't agree with what James says.

4 She says his contract requires him to work every day, Monday to Friday, from 9 to 5 p.m.

5 Mandy criticises his work.

6 James gets on well with members of his team.

7 Mandy wants James to get the right form from her secretary.

8 Mandy says she will sign the form.

2 Listen to the person describing how she made a complaint. Put the events in the correct order.

A The customer spoke to an assistant in the shop.

B The newspaper did not arrive.

C The manager said all the papers had been sold.

D The newspaper was finally delivered.

E The manager blamed the delivery boy.

F The customer went to the shop.

G The customer spoke to the manager.

H The customer phoned the shop.

Writing

A letter of apology

 You stayed in a house belonging to David and Anne, two friends of yours, while they were away. A number of things went wrong:

– the washing machine didn't work properly and flooded the kitchen

– you accidently knocked over a china ornament which broke when it fell on the floor

– you had a party and the neighbours complained to the police

– you spilled coffee on the new light-coloured carpet which made a bad stain

Write to your friends explaining what went wrong, and what action you took.

Remember: you will need the correct layout for a personal letter (see page 24)

give all the details of exactly what happened and what you did to try and put things right

be extra polite and apologetic

Useful phrases:

I'm very sorry to have to tell you ....
Unfortunately, ...
Although I was trying to be very careful ....
It was my fault entirely ....
I admit I was to blame ....
I accept full responsibility for ....
It wouldn't have happened if ....
Of course, I'll pay for ....
Apart from all this, everything is all right.

English in Use

1 Complete the text with one correct word in each gap.

All their friends thought Elizabeth and James made a perfect couple. They were both lively and attractive and got a lot .... (1) of life. They shared many interests and managed to keep in .... (2) with a wide circle of friends. They had met when they were students in Manchester – Elizabeth was in her second year studying music and James was enrolled .... (3) a computer course. After graduation they moved to London and .... (4) friends expected them to get married. But things started to go .... (5). Elizabeth was a talented pianist, and she .... (6) asked to do a number of concerts. These usually took .... (7) in the evening. James had found a good job, which he enjoyed very much even .... (8) it was tiring. He worked long hours but when he wanted to relax in the evening he found that Elizabeth was often out, ... (9) a concert. Elizabeth had to practise .... (10) the day and accept work whenever it was offered to her. They didn't seem to have any time to .... (11) together.

James was the one .... (12) was most upset. Elizabeth thought it was natural that they would have to .... (13) sacrifices if they both wanted to .... (14) on. James wanted Elizabeth to be there when he was free. They tried to .... (15) things over. Elizabeth said she couldn't refuse offers at .... (16) stage in her career and James thought she was being unreasonable. After a particularly unpleasant row, Elizabeth said she had had .... (17). She thought they should .... (18) up. Reluctantly, James .... (19). It was a sad ending to a happy relationship. The people who .... (20) most surprised were their friends.

2 Phrasal Verbs

Complete the sentences with a phrasal verb based on *get*.

EXAMPLE: What time do you ....*get up*.... in the morning?

1 It was raining, so when John opened the car door I .... as fast as I could.

2 If you want to go to the Royal Academy you should .... the bus at Piccadilly Circus.

3 How do I .... the station from here?

4 You look tired. Why don't you try to .... for a short break?

5 ....! I don't want to see you here again.

6 All it ever does is rain! This weather is .... me ....

7 It's always easier to .... serious work when you are refreshed after a holiday.

8 He was such a clever crook that he managed to .... several serious crimes.

9 I have to do this work. There's just no way I can .... it.

10 He manages to .... three hours' practice a day.

3 Word-formation

Complete the sentences with the correct form of the word in capitals.

EXAMPLES: Her face was so white that she looked quite ....*ghostly*.... .   GHOST

He's an excellent ....*dramatic*.... actor but not so good at comedy.   DRAMA

1 The soup was too .... for me to eat.   SALT

2 When he began his teaching career, he was very ....   IDEAL

3 Tom has a .... account with the shop. MONTH

4 I consider this to be the best .... magazine on the market.   PHOTOGRAPH

5 In times of trouble we all need a .... ear.   SYMPATHY

6 The weather here has been just horrible, ... and cold.   RAIN

7 It always amazes parents how young children can be so ....   ENERGY

8 This magazine provides information about the latest .... discoveries.   SCIENCE

9 Everyone likes Mr Smith because he's so ....   FRIEND

10 She's a very .... girl.   ARTIST

MAKING THE MOST OF YOURSELF

Lead-in **1** What are the people doing?
Why do you think they are doing
these things?
What are they trying to achieve?

2 Complete the passage using the following words:

> search   salary   conditions
> prospects   impression   agency
> image   anxious   experience
> stressful   interview   post   vacancy
> qualifications   applicants   notified

Getting a job is not an easy business. First there's the difficulty of deciding what you want to do and getting the right .... (1) and training. Then you have to find out where there is a .... (2), and apply for a particular .... (3). Some people look at advertisements in a newspaper, others use an employment .... (4). There is usually an application form to complete with all the details about your previous .... (5).

The company selects the .... (6) it is interested in and invites them to attend an .... (7) This is often a .... (8) experience, not least because most people have to find something suitable to wear, and then get very .... (9) about what sort of questions they should ask and what kind of .... (10) they should present. You are more likely to make a good .... (11) at the interview if you have found out something about the organisation you want to work for. Most applicants for jobs want to know about the working .... (12), the .... (13) of promotion and the .... (14). Unsuccessful applicants are usually .... (15) by post and then their .... (16) for a job starts all over again.

3 Choose the correct word or phrase for the gap in each sentence.

> high earner   risks   aspire   improve
> challenge   skills   achieve   goal
> potential   sacrifices

1   Sarah's .... in life is to be a research scientist.

2   Mary was keen to develop her photography .... and took a course at the local college.

3   The whole family was prepared to make .... so that their mother could return to study.

4   What do you hope to .... as a result of gaining this qualification?

5   My father was an intelligent man but he was never able to realise his ....

6   John decided early that his main aim in life was to be a ....

7   Tom is successful because he has never failed to accept a ....

8   Most politicians don't just want to be members of parliament – they all .... to high office.

9   Tony is a good enough worker but he is not prepared to take any ....

10   Shirley went on an intensive course to .... her driving.

Reading

A Before reading the text, discuss:

What qualities do you think a fashion model needs?

Are the same qualities required of male and female models?

B Now read the text where two models speak about their experiences. Seven sentences have been removed from the article. Choose from sentences A–H the one which fits each gap (1–7). There is one extra sentence that you do not need to use.

Being a fashion model

Claire Adams, 16, describes what it's like being a fashion model.

Last summer I was walking through Covent Garden and a woman from a modelling agency came up to me. I had little spectacles on, huge Doc Marten boots and my hair was pulled back in a bun. She asked if I'd ever thought of modelling, and I said, 'No, never.' But I was signed up and started modelling in the school holidays. I decided to go into it full-time this year. My parents supported the decision, though they would rather I'd stayed on at school and gone to university. But they're fairly keen on show business themselves. (1) .... I think I've grown up a lot. You have to be very self-disciplined: eating the right things, exercising, looking your best when you get up in the morning. It sounds easy but it's hard work. But I hate being typecast as the innocent redhead. Sometimes you want to be wild and wicked but I'm usually the English rose.

It's a very competitive profession. When you go on castings all the models look you up and down; but a lot of them are very friendly. I would say male models are more vain: all the ones I've met seem terribly in love with themselves. (2) .... I spend most of my time with my boyfriend, who's a computer programmer, or with old friends. Modelling's a lot of fun but it's not something I want to do as my career. (3) .... I know people say models always go on to acting and singing and can't do it, but if I'm making the money I don't really care what they say.

Matt Jones, 20, describes what it's like being a male model.

About two years ago, when I was living in a small town, one of my ex-girlfriends took me to a fashion show in London, and straightaway modelling scouts came up to me. I was in complete confusion; I'd never thought of modelling. (4) .... At the end of the show, they had a competition for the best-looking guy in the place, and I won. I was going to walk out, I was so embarrassed, I was saying, 'No, no, no. I don't want to get into modelling.' I wanted to do the same thing I still want to do – technical illustration – which is what I was studying. (5) .... I was a naughty boy. After all these compliments and stuff, I just thought: why not have a go? There's a bit of money to be made here and I'm not going to lose out. So I went down to London and joined an agency.

People think that if you are a model, you love yourself and you're dumb. That's all down to the Press, isn't it? (6) .... I know that for a fact. Most models are doing the job because it's silly money. Most of my friends are models, not because I only want to hang around with models, but five days of the week I'm with them and we talk and say 'How's it going?' and 'What clubs do you go to?' – that sort of thing. (7) .... If you do a job with a girl who is a big model and you're trying to be nice, she says, 'Huh, who do you think you are?'

A I mean, people had said at school and college, 'Oh, he looks like a model,' but I took it as an insult, really.

B It's always been my ambition to be rich and famous, but what I really want to do is to be a singer.

C The money is the main justification for doing the job – you get a chance to put something behind you so in a few years' time you've got the money to do what you want.

D My mum used to be an actress and my dad was also an actor and now writes film scripts.

E I'm not thick.

F But I didn't finish my studies.

G With male models we're all friends, we help each other out; women are more competitive.

H They're not the people I see at weekends.

Grammar

 Mixed modals

Rewrite the following sentences, keeping the meaning the same. Use the words in the box. Write one sentence for each answer. (Grammar Notes **10.1**)

> should   could   might   must   should have
> could have   must have   might have

EXAMPLE: It wasn't necessary for John to take a taxi. There is a cheap and convenient train service.
John could have taken a train instead of a taxi.

1 This is the wrong way. We made a mistake in turning right instead of left.

2 I think Jack stole the radio. There is no other reasonable explanation.

3 You have a number of choices. Taking the course again is one possibility.

4 Is it possible that there is a tenth planet?

5 He wants to sell his bicycle for £100 but it is possible he will accept £80.

6 It was obvious it would break. Why didn't you realise that?

7 It's possible that Jane was at the party. I really don't remember.

8 You are likely to win the race if you train hard.

9 I'm sure that's Professor Smith. He always wears that kind of coat.

10 A week after we bought the computer, the price went down by £200. We didn't know that was going to happen.

11 I have no idea what knocked the plant pots over. Was it the wind, perhaps?

12 When Peter woke up in hospital, he realised that he had no memory of the accident.

 Any-, some-, no-, every-

Complete the text with the words in the box. You may use some words more than once. (Grammar Notes **10.2**)

> any anywhere everywhere somewhere nothing
> everyone/body anyone/body someone/body
> everyone/body anything no-one/nobody

'Is .... (1) here?' said Mrs Thomas to the students on the coach. 'Is .... (2) missing?'
'I think .... (3) is missing,' replied one student. 'It's Peter.'
'Does .... (4) know where he is?' asked Mrs Thomas. .... (5) answered.
Mrs Thomas asked Mr Smith to go back into the museum to look for Peter. Ten minutes later Mr Smith returned alone. 'I can't find him .... (6),' he said. 'I looked .... (7).'
'Did Peter say .... (8) to .... (9)?' said Mrs Thomas to the students.
'No, ... (10) at all,' muttered several students.
'.................... (11) suggestions?' said Mrs Thomas.
'I think .... (12) should go and look for him. One of us is bound to find him.' suggested another student. 'He must be .... (13).'
'But where?' said Mrs Thomas. 'He could be .... (14).'
So .... (15) got off the coach, went back to the museum and spread out to search for Peter. After a few minutes, ... (16) found him, still engrossed by the museum's fascinating exhibits.

 Whose

A Join the sentences using the word *whose*. (Grammar Notes **9.1**)

EXAMPLE: The man was arrested. His car was involved in an accident.
The man whose car was involved in an accident was arrested.

1 The girl reported the incident to the police. Her handbag was snatched.

2 The children were given £10 each. Their paintings won a prize.

3 The people received compensation. Their houses had been destroyed.

4 The shopkeeper chased the youths down the street. His window had been smashed.

5 People must pay a fine of 5p per book per day. Their library books are overdue.

B Join the sentences using the word *whose*.

EXAMPLE: James Clark will be present at the dinner.
His new play opens at the National Theatre on Tuesday.
James Clark, whose new play opens at the National Theatre on Tuesday, will be present at the dinner.

Remember to use commas to enclose the extra information – this is essential.

1 John Forrest died last week. His portrait of the Queen caused so much controversy.

2 Sally and Sarah will be looked after by their grandparents. Their parents are on tour with a theatre company.

3 The Prime Minister spoke about controlling inflation. His speech was broadcast live.

4 Mrs Lawson will welcome guests to the exhibition. Her son has just won two gold medals.

5 Martin Brook will appear on the programme next week. We discussed his novel last week.

4 Used to

Complete the gaps. (Grammar Notes **10.3**)

1 You used to fly with British Airways, ... you? Yes, I .... , but I don't work as a pilot any more.

2 Didn't you .... to be on television? Yes, but it was ten years ago.

3 I didn't .... to like opera, but I'm beginning to enjoy it now.

4 John .... to cycle to work but he's given up now.

5 People .... to use coal or wood to heat their house but nowadays they mostly use gas or electricity.

Can *used to* refer to things you do regularly now? What is the difference between these two sentences?

I used to get up at 5 a.m. when I was a postman.
Being a postman, I usually get up at 5 a.m.

Listening

Talking about interviews

What interviews have you had?
Did they go well?
How did you prepare yourself for them?

Listen to the cassette and complete the following text. Use *one* to *three* words in each gap.

Dr Campbell carried out her research by .... (1) candidates during the interviews and by .... (2) before and after the interviews. She discovered that successful male candidates usually wore a .... (3) suit and successful female candidates wore clothes that were slightly .... (4) and avoided .... (5). During the interview, successful candidates did three things more than unsuccessful ones: they .... (6) heads more, ... (7) a lot, and made .... (8) with the interviewers. Successful candidates always managed to give a .... (9) to even the most critical questions and had often arranged .... (10) with their friends.

English in Use

1 Like, as, as if, alike

Complete the sentences with *like*, *as*, *as if* or *alike*. (Grammar Notes **10.4**)

EXAMPLES: Sarah looks ....*like*.... her great-grandmother when she was young.
Those brothers look very much ....
Bob plans to get a job ....*as*.... a lorry-driver.
You look ....*as if*.... you've just run a marathon.

1 Lucy works .... a receptionist in a dentist's surgery.

2 This film stars Roger Moore .... James Bond.

3 You look .... you've seen a ghost!

4 I hate to be rude, but William really does look .... a horse.

5 .... his father before him, Neil entered the legal profession.

6 .... headmaster, Mr Myers is responsible for the health and safety of all the children in the school.

7 The little cottage was just .... I had expected it to be.

8 We decorated our new house exactly .... our old one.

9 Jill and her sister look ....

10 The students looked .... they knew the answer – but they didn't.

Reading

A How do people's lives change when they become famous?
What are some of the disadvantages of being famous?
Is it possible to give up fame and return to being anonymous?

What have I done?

A man sits alone in a corner of a crowded bar. No one seems to notice Albert Eccles, a middle-aged carpenter, as he sits staring at his whiskey glass. Nobody sees the pain on his face as the jukebox begins to play the unmistakable first bars of *Nights in White Satin*. That song plagues him. Wherever he goes it seems to get played. And there is no let-up from the memories it brings back. Albert Eccles was once Clint Warwick, bass guitarist with one of the world's most successful groups – The Moody Blues. Now in their 27th year, the Moodies are on another sell-out world tour and record sales have topped £30 million. That song is just one of many hits that have made each member of the band a millionaire, with private jets and luxury homes. And Albert, sitting nursing a drink in a scruffy pub, knows that he's the man who threw it all away. And he can only blame himself.

In the early sixties, Albert had been a founder member of the group, and their first years were exciting. From being a local band, they had become one of the hottest new groups around. Albert's life moved into the fast lane. When the Moodies went on tour with the Beatles, it seemed that he was never in the same place for more than a few hours. The band would land in London in the middle of the night, grab forty minutes' sleep and then spend twelve hours preparing for a TV show. It was hard for all of them, but Albert found it almost impossible. The trouble was he was the only married member of the band. He also had a son, Lee, and he'd fly back from abroad to be with his family if only for a couple of hours. Then he'd be back on the road, to that unreal, glittering life of a rock star. Trying to live in two different worlds at once became a real strain. Things came to a head when the band recorded a version of a blues number called *Go Now*. It became an instant hit. Christine had just given birth to

another boy – named Paul after their Beatle friend. But the hit song meant more recording and more touring, and yet more time away from his family. Albert began to agonise about his future – surely it was best to get out now, while they were still at the top? Surely the only way now could be down? Christine was the other factor. She was stuck at home reading stories about the band's wild parties – most of which were true – and it was getting to her. Cynthia Lennon (John's wife) used to compare notes with her and Christine would then give Albert a bad time. Finally, sitting in his London flat one day, listening to *Go Now*, Albert made the decision he's regretted ever since. To quit the band. The next day he said goodbye to the guys and walked out of the London recording studios an ex-rock star.

For the first few months afterwards, life was great. Albert had a chance to enjoy his family for the first time. Money was no problem. With the Moody Blues he had been drawing £100 a week just as pocket money – a fortune in those days. He had a nice place. His troubles were over. But in under twelve months, the money had run out. Bills began to mount up and they moved to a smaller flat, but that wasn't enough. Finally, Albert realised he'd have to go back to work. He couldn't re-enter the music world. His place in the band had been filled, and, besides, he'd been out of the limelight for a year – an eternity in the fast-moving sixties pop scene. In desperation, he turned to a skill he learnt when he left

school at fifteen: carpentry. The day he started back at work as a carpenter was the blackest of his life. His brother had fixed Albert up with a job renovating a pub. At the end of the day, he trudged half a mile down the road in the pouring rain to the bus stop. Standing there, soaked, it seemed impossible to him that he had ever been with the band. 'My God, what have I done?' he thought. 'To think a year ago I was playing to 60,000 fans at Wembley ...'. Albert's misery was compounded the following year (1967), when he and Christine split up. The boys, Lee and Paul, stayed with him while he struggled to make ends meet.

And the band did not fade into obscurity as Albert had forecast. Instead, the Moodies went from strength to strength with a succession of hits and albums. Today, Albert earns about £200 a week and lives with his elderly mother in Kingstanding, near Birmingham. He finds it hard to forget that they could so easily be living in a Hollywood mansion. 'Every day I hear something we did on the radio,' he admits. 'And every time I ask myself: "What if?"' There's some consolation for him in the way his boys have turned out – Lee, 27, is managing director of a successful graphic design company, and Paul, 25, runs his own meat company. Says Albert: 'I suppose having an old man who turned his back on fortune must have spurred them on.'

The group haven't forgotten about him; Albert sees them whenever they play in Britain. 'I'm always invited backstage and there's lots of hugging and pats on the back,' he says. 'We get on so well. In some ways nothing's changed because we really are the same people. The biggest difference,' he adds with a sad smile, 'is that afterwards they fly back to Florida in private jets, and I catch the bus back to Kingstanding.'

B Choose the best answer to the questions, A, B, C or D.

1 Why doesn't Albert like to hear *Nights in White Satin*?

  A It makes him feel ill.
  B It is played too frequently.
  C Nobody realises he played on the record.
  D It brings back painful memories.

2 Why did Albert find touring especially difficult?

  A He became exhausted.
  B He hated the travelling.
  C He wasn't used to the fast pace of life.
  D He missed his family.

3 Which of these was not a reason for Albert leaving the band?

  A His wife had just had a baby.
  B He thought the band had reached its peak.
  C His wife criticised him a lot.
  D Cynthia Lennon advised him to.

4 Despite his regrets, what is Albert pleased about?

  A His success as a carpenter.
  B The fact that his records are still played.
  C The success of the band.
  D The fact that his sons have become successful.

Reading

A Do you know anyone who has suddenly changed their lifestyle? What did they do? What happened to them?

People who made the break

In the third of our series on 'People Who Made The Break', Sally Hoskins went to meet Jim Frobisher, chief instructor at Surrey Sailing Club.

When I arrived, Jim was instructing a group of teenagers who were preparing for a round-Britain voyage. He left his crew and greeted me warmly. He was lean, fit, suntanned and had the relaxed and confident manner of a man who is
5 doing exactly the job he wants to do.

But it wasn't always like this. Jim told me of a decision he made five years ago which transformed his life. He used to work as a civil servant and one cold, wet, November evening he left his office, where he had been sitting at a
10 desk all day, and walked, tired and bored, through the bleak streets of South London to the small flat where he had lived alone since his divorce two years previously. A sudden heavy shower caused him to dart into a café to seek shelter. Sitting morosely in the corner, sipping his coffee, he picked
15 up, just to while away the time, a newspaper that another customer had left behind. An advertisement in that newspaper would change his life forever.

> **Crew wanted for three-year round the world voyage. No experience necessary. Sense of humour and £50,000 essential.**

'When I look back,' said Jim, 'I realise it was pure chance that I saw the advertisement. I might never have known
20 about it. But I knew I had to go – I just had to. My friends told me I was being rash. I had to sell my flat to raise the money and everybody said, 'When you come back in three years – if you come back – you'll have no money, no job and nowhere to live.' But I wanted to do something with my life.
25 Jim applied and was selected as a crew member. Before the voyage began, he had to undergo an intensive training programme in which he learned how to sail, how to navigate, how to give first aid, how to operate a radio and many other skills. 'I was able to improve all these skills
30 during the voyage and learn some new ones. I learned a lot of things that might not seem very important but I'm glad I know them. For example, I can now identify all the constellations in both hemispheres which I certainly couldn't do before.' Jim also got married again after the
35 voyage – to Sarah, another member of the crew.
What advice does Jim have for people who might be considering doing something similar? 'I'd advise people to seize the opportunity to do something adventurous. It isn't always a good idea to play safe and choose a comfortable
40 life. It was very uncomfortable on the boat and sometimes dangerous – a couple of times we were in extreme danger – but I wouldn't have missed it for the world. In fact, in a few years' time, when we've got our own boat, we're going to do it again. It isn't just a matter of learning new skills, it's
45 gaining a sense of fulfilment, a feeling that you've made the most of yourself, that you've stretched yourself and lived life to the full.'

B Find words in the text which, in context, are similar in meaning to:

Paragraph 1
1 people who work on a ship
2 slim and muscular

Paragraph 2
3 someone who works in a government office
4 depressing
5 move quickly
6 in a bad-tempered and unhappy way
7 drinking small amounts

Paragraph 4
8 foolish and impulsive

Paragraph 5
9 patterns of stars

Paragraph 6
10 avoid taking risks

C Work in pairs. Ask and answer these questions.

1 What does Jim Frobisher do now?
2 What job did he do five years ago?
3 What happened to Jim seven years ago?
4 What did Jim's friends say?
5 How did he find the money to pay for the voyage?
6 How did Jim get to see the advertisement?
7 What did Jim have to do before the voyage?
8 What did Jim do after the voyage?
9 What advice does Jim give?
10 What are his plans for the future?

Talking Points

Section 1

Describe the person in the pictures.
What similarities and differences are there
between the two photos?

Section 2

Work in groups of three. Each of you wishes to
make an improvement in one aspect of your
life. Decide which of the three self-improvement
ideas would be best for each of you.

gymnasium:

Stay Fit at the Garden Gymnasium
Personal Fitness Trainers
Diet Advice
Sauna

career guidance:

What's the Best Way to Maximise Your Potential?
Executive Careers has over thirty years' experience in
helping people to find the career that is best for THEM.
Send curriculum vitae and we will provide a computer
analysis of the best career for you.

distance learning course:

The University of the Air provides you with the chance for
professional development. Over 140 courses and study
packs. Study for the degrees or diploma you have
always wanted.

Section 3

Look at the poem. How does the poet feel?

Some More Light Verse

You have to try. You see a shrink.*
You learn a lot. You read. You think.
You struggle to improve your looks.
You meet some men. You write some books.
You eat good food. You give up junk.
You do not smoke. You don't get drunk.
You take up yoga, walk and swim.
And nothing works. The outlook's grim.
You don't know what to do. You cry.
You're running out of things to try.

You blow your nose. You see the shrink.
You walk. You give up food and drink.
You fall in love. You make a plan.
You struggle to improve your man.
And nothing works. The outlook's grim.
You go to yoga, cry and swim.
You eat and drink. You give up looks.
You struggle to improve your books.
You cannot see the point. You sigh.
You do not smoke. You have to try.

Wendy Cope (b. 1945)

*shrink is a colloquial word for psychiatrist.

Writing

A leaflet

 Write a leaflet giving information about your school or college to new students. This should not be an official prospectus issued by the college authorities but should contain the kind of information that existing students think that new students need to know. Therefore, the language can be fairly informal. Write about 150 words.

Style:

1 Remember that this is a leaflet, not a composition.

2 Use headlines in CAPITAL LETTERS.

3 Use sub-headings, either in capitals or <u>underlined</u>.

4 Use question-marks (? or even ???), exclamation marks (! or if necessary !!!) to emphasise the points you are making.

5 Use numbers, (brackets) – and dashes, if appropriate.

6 Keep the paragraphs fairly short.

7 It's a good idea to use contractions and question-tags, isn't it?

8 You should address the reader directly – as *you*.

9 Consider the use of rhetorical questions (i.e. questions that you ask and then answer).

10 Consider carefully the order of your points. Start with something that attracts the reader's attention.

11 Look at some magazine articles and real leaflets to see what techniques they use.

Content:

In your leaflet, you may wish to say something about:

• the building

• the courses

• the administration

• sports facilities and clubs

• the library

• refreshments

• social activities

• important dates

• warnings!!!

Listening

How to study

 A Listen to the advice given to students by educational advisor, Emily Harrison.

What *three* pieces of advice does she give to students specifically about revising for exams?

B Emily makes some general points about study skills. List the *five* general points she makes.

English in Use

1 About to

Comment on these sentences using *about to*. (Grammar Notes **10.5**)

EXAMPLE: The parachutist is standing in the open doorway of the aircraft.
He is about to jump.

1 John is standing right on the edge of the diving board.

2 The President has taken the microphone in his hand.

3 The racing drivers are revving up their engines.

4 The election is over and all the votes have been counted.

5 The patient has rolled up his sleeve and the doctor has the syringe ready.

2 Bound to

Comment on these sentences using *bound to*. (Grammar Notes **10.6**)

EXAMPLE: All four engines of the aircraft are on fire.
It's bound to crash.

1 Marjorie is 50 metres ahead of all the other runners.

2 The burglar left his fingerprints everywhere.

3 Mrs Richards is driving the wrong way down the motorway.

4 Peter has eaten a kilo of strawberries and a plate of hot curry.

5 The yacht has a large hole below the water-line.

3   A little, little, a few, few

Complete the sentences with these words.
(Grammar Notes **10.7**)

a little	little	a few	few

EXAMPLES: We have   <u>a few</u>   eggs left so we can make a cake.

The shop had   <u>few</u>   customers and soon closed.

This glue is very strong so you only need to use   <u>a little</u>   .

We have   <u>little</u>   time left so hurry up!

1   Patricia made .... friends at university and felt rather lonely.

2   John felt .... embarrassed when he had to stand up and make a speech.

3   .... people have returned their questionnaires, so we may have to abandon the research project.

4   .... research has been done in this area – there is much to be discovered.

5   .... people have already paid in full so I am sure the trip will go ahead.

6   The police had .... information to give us, so we must just wait for something to turn up.

7   Dr Martin gave me .... advice which I found most useful.

8   The climbers had eaten .... during their ascent of the mountain and were very hungry.

9   'There is .... to report,' said Inspector Collins. '................... progress has been made since our last meeting. We are no further forward.'

10   .... daffodils have already appeared and it's beginning to look like spring.

4   Phrasal Verbs

Many phrasal verbs have a noun form.

EXAMPLE: The aeroplane will take off at 2.30 p.m.
The aeroplane crashed on <u>take-off</u> .

Complete the sentences with the words given.

kick-off	check-up	mix-up	telling-off
stand-in	lie-in	break-in	send-off
	sell-out	go-ahead	

1   Tomorrow I'm going to the dentist's for my six-monthly ....

2   I don't have to go to work tomorrow, so I'm going to have a ....

3   We can't begin this project until we get the .... from senior management.

4   The policeman reported a .... at the chemist's shop.

5   The World Cup Final .... is at 3 p.m.

6   There are no tickets left – the concert is a ....

7   If the leading actor falls ill, the .... will take his part.

8   Nobody met me at the airport because of a .... about flight times.

9   When he emigrated to Australia, Bill's friends gave him a wonderful .... that he would never forget.

10   Mrs Roberts gave her children a good .... when they spilt blackcurrent juice on the carpet.

5   Word-formation

Complete the sentences with the correct form of the word in capitals.

EXAMPLES: The prince spent his <u>boyhood</u> learning how to be king.   BOY
One positive aspect of army life is the <u>comradeship</u> between the troops. COMRADE

1   His .... was spent in the country.   CHILD

2   Their .... had lasted for over fifty years.   FRIEND

3   The family suffered considerable .... when they became refugees.   HARD

4   How has .... changed Jane?   MOTHER

5   The match was played in the spirit of great ....!   SPORTSMAN

6   All films released in Britain are subject to ....   CENSOR

7   She spent her .... in the East End of London.   GIRL

8   The furniture he makes shows superb ....   CRAFTSMAN

9   Is John ready for ....?   FATHER

10   It often sounds idealistic to talk of the .... of nations.   BROTHER

Exam Practice 2

1   (Exam Hints: Paper 1)

You are going to read an account of one man's day. For questions 1–8, choose the answer (A, B, C or D) which you think fits best according to the text.

My Kind of Day: **Mohammed Amin**

Somalia, Ethiopia, Namibia, Kenya, Britain – my day could start in any of these countries. And in the past year it has. As a television camera and photo-journalist – I am the Africa Bureau Chief for Reuters Television and I also run my own
5 company, Camerapix – I'm ready to fly out at a moment's notice. I keep three suitcases permanently packed.

I have an office in London, but I am based in Nairobi, Kenya, where I was born, though I tend to be away from home for nine months of the year. I co-ordinate Reuter's
10 television news coverage of the whole of Africa, but I prefer to 'shoot' rather than administrate – if a major story breaks I try to be there.

Some might think I keep the best jobs for myself, though dodging bullets and angry mobs is not everybody's
15 idea of 'best'. A rocket took off my left forearm and I got seven bullets in the right arm and shrapnel in my shoulder when an ammunition dump blew up in Addis Ababa, Ethiopia, while I was filming there in 1991. Now I have a computerised artificial arm – a lot of the components
20 come from space research at NASA – which is activated by my bicep and tricep muscles. I can open and close the hand and rotate the wrist but I only use it for camera work. I have always driven with one hand!

When I'm on location, whether it's for television news
25 or taking stills for one of the travel books I publish, the day inevitably follows the story. But the planning is vital. Ninety-five per cent of the work is logistics and your contacts are crucial. Knowing people opens every door. I am in the fortunate position of being able to get on the
30 phone personally to at least a dozen heads of state. And speaking fourteen languages helps.

I do have a daily routine when I'm home. I live with my 22-year-old son, Salim (he's just joined my company as a trainee) on the outskirts of Nairobi, though I don't
35 have much of a family life. I start my day at around two in the morning (I go to bed at 9 p.m.), working in my pyjamas from an office and editing studio behind the house. I drink tea – about twelve cups – until it's time to drive into the Reuters office at the Press Centre at 7 a.m.
40 The first thing to do here is sort out the overnight messages – which go into a computer system straight from London – and read the papers and bureau reports. Then I begin to arrange the day's coverage. There are always crews to get in and out of countries, rushes to view,
45 satellite links to be booked. Lunch is a waste of time and, anyway, I work better without food.

I get home about 7 p.m. and the cook will prepare an Indian or European meal. Then I listen to the BBC World Service news and go to bed – knackered! It's the same
50 routine at the weekend too, and I never have a holiday. Taking photographs for travel books in places such as the Maldives and the Seychelles seems holiday enough.

Hobbies? I collect stamps, especially African and Asian first-day covers. One day, when I am too old to
55 work, maybe I'll sit down and put them in an album. Or maybe I won't.

1   Mohammed keeps three suitcases packed because

   A   he doesn't like to pack in a hurry.
   B   he is not sure what he needs for each trip.
   C   he can't waste time when called to a job.
   D   he doesn't like being unprepared.

2   'shoot', in line 11 means

   A   move fast.
   B   take pictures.
   C   fire a gun.
   D   read quickly.

3 Mohammed was injured when

A he was attacked by a group of men.
B there was an explosion.
C someone wanted to shoot him.
D he was trying to keep out of the way of bullets.

4 'it', in line 22 means

A hand.
B wrist.
C arm.
D biceps.

5 Mohammed says his job would be impossible if he didn't have

A a wide circle of acquaintances.
B the best equipment.
C people telling him about new stories.
D a high reputation.

6 When Mohammed starts work in the morning,

A he is already in the office at the Press Centre.
B his mind is on the day's main story.
C he is still in his night clothes.
D he expects to go back to bed.

7 Regarding his eating habits, Mohammed

A enjoys different styles of cooking.
B thinks regular meals are important.
C cooks an evening meal.
D likes to work while he eats.

8 How does Mohammed view collecting stamps?

A as an essential part of his life
B as an investment for the future
C as a way of relaxing
D as a minor enjoyment

2 (Exam Hints: Paper 3, Part 2)

For questions 1–15, read the text below and think of the word which best fits each space. Use only **one** word in each space. There is an example at the beginning (0).

The achievement of Carolus Linnaeus

The names of animals and plants vary widely from country to country and often from region to region in the (0) ....*same*....... country. It is not unusual to travel to (1) .... part of your own country and find that the word for a common animal or flower (2) .... different from the one you are (3) .... to. This variety of terms (4) .... make life very difficult for scientists.

Fortunately, (5) .... is a set of international standard terms for describing all plants and living creatures. It was devised by Carolus Linnaeus, who was born in Sweden in 1707. By the time of (6) .... death in 1778, he had developed a system for classifying plants and animals which is (7) .... in use today. Using his system, any (8) .... of the millions of different plants and animals on Earth (9) .... be identified in such a way that a scientist will know exactly (10) .... it is.

It was Linnaeus (11) .... first divided the natural world into animal, vegetable and mineral. The first step in his system is (12) .... place something in one of these three 'kingdoms'. He then subdivided (13) .... kingdom into various categories. The words that are used in his system are all Latin, (14) .... the name by (15) .... he is known to the world. His Swedish name was Carl von Linné.

3 (Exam Hints: Paper 3, Part 3)

For questions 1–10, complete the second sentence so that it has a similar meaning to the first sentence using the word given. **Do not change the word given.** You must use between two and five words, including the word given.

EXAMPLE: I don't want to go out tonight.
   rather
   I 'd rather not go out tonight.

1 Both Tom and Laura are fond of chocolate.
 and
 Tom likes chocolate .... Laura.

2 Please inform me about the new regulations.
 some
 Please .... about the new regulations.

3 I haven't enough money to stay in this hotel.
 for
 This hotel is .... to stay in.

4 This car is the only one I considered buying.
 any
 I never considered .... this one.

5 Seeing the skill of the other competitors made me feel depressed.
 saw
 I felt depressed .... the other competitors were.

6 The committee has not decided who to invite.
 invitations
 No .... has been made by the committee.

7 Steven decided to try windsurfing.
 have
 'I think I'll ....,' said Steven.

8 The high jumper will attempt to break the world record any second now.
 about
 The high jumper .... to break the world record.

9 It's entirely your own fault.
 have
 You .... blame.

10 You must use black olives to make this dish.
 without
 You can't .... black olives.

4 (Exam Hints: Paper 3, Part 4)

Read the text below and look carefully at each line. Some of the lines are correct and some have a word which should not be there. Tick the correct lines and underline the wrong words in the incorrect lines.

EXAMPLES: 0 ✓
    00 <u>a</u>

When things go wrong

0 Last weekend, I had a fantastic adventure. Some friends of
00 mine at a college, Tom and Anna, invited me to Torquay for
1 a few days. It's near from the sea and a popular place for
2 a holiday. It's the town they come from and where their
3 parents still live in. They own a sailing boat and suggested
4 that all five of us go on sailing, since the weather was ideal.
5 I had never been in such a small boat before and I must
6 admit I felt myself rather anxious right from the start. As
7 soon as we were at sea, the temperature dropped and very
8 quickly the weather had got much worse. The wind was
9 very strong and it rained hardly. We became very cold
10 and then, to our terrible horror, a strong gust of wind blew
11 the sail away. This meant that we could not make the boat
12 go where to we wanted. We just drifted with the current.
13 There was no radio so we could not call for help. We were
14 in real danger. We could have been collided with another
15 boat or with rocks that might have done damaged our boat.
 Finally, just before dawn, the coastguard rescued us.

Listening

5 (Exam Hints: Paper 4, Part 2)

You will hear a woman talking about a visit to the dentist. For questions 1–10, complete the sentences which summarise what the speaker says. You will need to write a word or short phrase in each space.

When Rebecca last visited the dentist, it was
(1) ....

She had been (2) .... eating some (3) .... when she realised she had broken one of her (4) .... teeth.

The dentist said the tooth could not be
(5) ....

It had to be (6) .... immediately, to stop (7) ....

The whole experience lasted
(8) ....

During this time, Rebecca could not
(9) ....

She had a problem with her
(10) ....

6 (Exam Hints: Paper 4, Part 3)

You will hear five different men describing arrangements that went wrong. For questions 1–5, choose from the list A–F the reason why things went wrong. Use the letters only once. There is one extra letter which you do not need to use.

A He waited in a different place.

B He forgot something.

C He misheard what he was told.

D He lacked local knowledge.

E He couldn't find something out.

F He didn't write something down.

Speaker 1   ....
Speaker 2   ....
Speaker 3   ....
Speaker 4   ....
Speaker 5   ....

7 (Exam Hints: Paper 4, Part 4)

You will hear a conversation where a woman talks about her thirtieth birthday.
Answer questions 1–7, by deciding whether each statement is **true** or **false**. In the box, write **T** if the statement is true and **F** if it is false.

☐ 1 The woman was looking forward to her birthday celebrations.

☐ 2 She refused to get her friend a newspaper.

☐ 3 She got a shock when the door opened.

☐ 4 It was her flatmate who tricked her.

☐ 5 She thought everyone would get on well with one another.

☐ 6 A man she wanted to see had been invited.

☐ 7 She enjoyed the event.

unit 11 THINGS THAT GO WRONG

Lead-in **1** What has happened?
What sort of things can go wrong on
a typical day?
Think of five common examples.

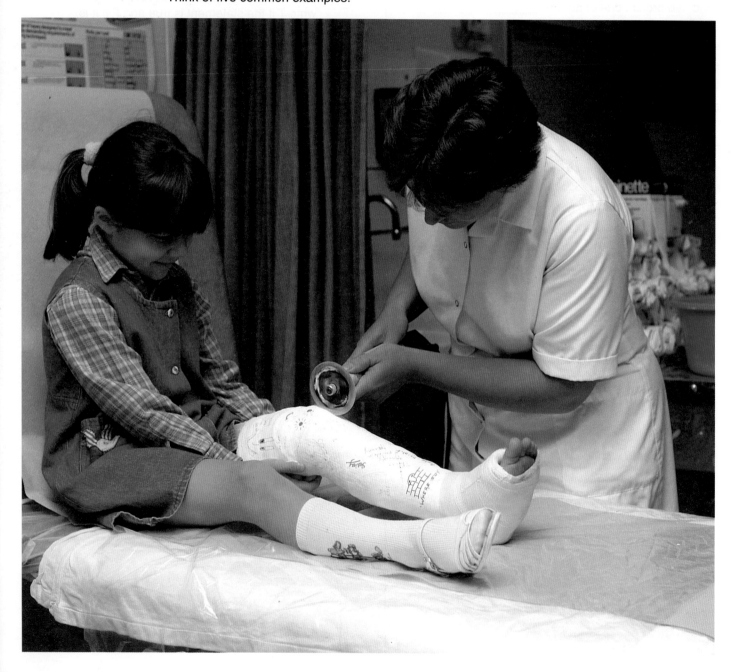

114

2 Choose the correct word or phrase for the gap in each sentence.

> disease   collapsed   trapped
> convalescing   precaution   symptoms
> wreckage   shock   plaster   survivors

1 The doctor asked Henry to describe his .... in order to diagnose what was wrong with him.

2 William was climbing the tree and lost his balance and that's why he's now got both his legs in ....

3 .... spread quickly in the unhealthy conditions of the prison camp.

4 All the .... of the crash were rushed by ambulance to the nearest hospital.

5 It's a good .... to have all the necessary vaccinations before you travel to tropical countries.

6 The plane exploded and the .... was strewn over an area of ten miles.

7 Anthony spent only three days being treated in hospital but he then spent another three weeks ....

8 There was an accident at the mine and over a hundred miners were .... underground for several hours.

9 A bridge over the river .... and three cars were left stranded.

10 Mary is still suffering from .... as a result of the accident, although she was not hurt physically.

3 Complete the text with the correct word or phrase.

> jaw   swollen   surgery   numb
> suffering   extraction   sore
> appointment   injection
> waiting room   toothache   check-ups
> decayed   take it out

One morning Jake woke up feeling terrible. His face was ....(1) and he had a throbbing pain in his lower ....(2). He thought he had never had such bad ....(3) in his life. He knew he would have to see the dentist as soon as possible. He rang up to make an ....(4) and luckily the dentist was able to fit him in at 9.30. Jake got to the ....(5) and sat down anxiously in the ....(6) to wait his turn. By now his face was extremely ....(7) and the pain had got much worse.

'How long have you had the pain?' asked the dentist. She looked inside Jake's mouth and told him that one of his bottom teeth was badly ....(8) and that the best thing would be to ....(9) immediately. She also wondered why Jake hadn't bothered to go for regular ....(10). He was ....(11) too much to be able to think of a suitable reply, and was just grateful when the dentist gave him an ....(12) to ease the pain of the ....(13). The tooth came out quite easily, and soon Jake was on his way to work. His face was still ....(14) as a result of the anaesthetic, but at least the dreadful pain, and a bad tooth, had gone.

Reading

A Describe an accident that you've seen.
Tell your partner about an accident or something unpleasant that has happened to you.

Unfortunate Incidents

1

On a cold dark night in December, John Campbell went to a reunion dinner with some old friends from university. It was a very pleasant evening and large amounts of food and drink were consumed. Just
5 before midnight, feeling not quite as alert as he had done earlier in the evening, John left the restaurant and got into his car. As he reversed he crashed into a vehicle parked behind him. He began to panic but then realised that the street was totally deserted and
10 no-one had seen him, so he put the car into first gear and pressed the accelerator. At first the car did not move, but then there was a second crashing sound and John drove off. He went straight home, without any further mishaps, put the car in the garage and
15 went to bed. He was going to check the damage in the morning. How lucky he had been to get away with it! After twenty minutes, his peace was disturbed by someone knocking at his door. He went down, opened the door and saw two policeman standing there.
20 'Is everything all right, sir?' said one policeman.
'Yes, perfectly,' replied John.
'Have you been out this evening, sir?'
'No, not at all. I've been at home all evening.'
'Then, in that case, sir, can you explain how
25 this came to be found lying in the road outside a restaurant in Dean Street?' said the policeman, producing from behind his back the rear bumper of John's car, complete with number plate.

2

On a very windy day in November David Myers went to Hampstead Heath to try out his brand-new kite.
5 His six-year old daughter, Emily, went with him. David assembled the kite, attached the string and let the wind take it into the air. It quickly
10 gained height and looked most impressive. Emily pleaded with her father to let her hold the kite. He handed her the string but at
15 that very moment a sudden powerful gust of wind blew the kite even higher and Emily was lifted off her feet. David watched in horror as
20 his daughter went sailing through the air, still holding the string tightly. Fortunately, the string got caught in the branches of a
25 tree and Emily fell to the ground, unhurt but very upset. The kite was never seen again.

3

One day last summer I was travelling on the London Underground, on the Piccadilly Line. We stopped at Green Park and a few people got on. Among them were an elderly lady and an elderly
5 gentleman, presumably her husband. Actually, he didn't quite get on the train, because the automatic doors closed on him as he was getting on. I knew from experience that this isn't really a problem – you just push with your arms and the
10 doors bounce back. However, this couple appeared to be unfamiliar with the Underground and this man did the worst thing possible – he stepped back but somehow leaned forward. This meant that the doors closed on his neck so his
15 head was inside the train but the rest of his body was outside. He had a most peculiar expression on his face and he was waving his arms up and down. His wife, who had found a seat, didn't seem to be in the least disturbed. I realised that
20 there was a real danger that he might be dragged along the platform and seriously injured, so I leapt from my seat and with two other men pulled at the doors, which soon sprang back. Nobody else did anything, apart
25 from one person who said, 'Pull the communication cord!' but remained seated. The man took his seat next to his wife. They were both completely calm and didn't say a word.

B Explain the meaning of the words and phrases:

text 1
1   a reunion (*line 2*)
2   alert (*line 5*)
3   reversed (*line 7*)
4   began to panic (*line 8*)
5   totally deserted (*line 9*)
6   his peace was disturbed (*line 17*)

text 2
1   try out (*line 4*)
2   brand-new (*line 4*)
3   gained height (*line 10*)
4   impressive (*line 11*)

text 3
1   elderly (*line 4*)
2   presumably (*line 5*)
3   didn't quite get on (*line 6*)
4   bounce (*line 10*)
5   leaned forward (*line 13*)

6   disturbed (*line 19*)
7   dragged (*line 21*)
8   leapt (*line 22*)

C Which accident

1   was the most dangerous?

2   was the most worrying for a parent?

3   involved damage to someone else's property?

4   showed a lack of reaction by the people involved?

5   showed someone to be telling a lie?

6   involved natural forces?

7   happened on public transport?

8   could easily have been avoided?

9   involved thoughtless behaviour?

Grammar: *past perfect*

 A Most of the following sentences can be completed with a verb in the *past perfect*. Some must be completed with a different tense.
(Grammar Notes **11.1**)

EXAMPLE: The strong man threw down the iron bar.
He ___had bent___ it into a U-shape.

1 Mark's arm was in a sling. He .... it while playing polo.   (break)

2 Diana looked delighted. The manager .... her for the team.   (choose)

3 The little boy screamed. His nose ....
                                                                              (bleed)

4 Lisa looked longingly at the new Porsche in the showroom. It .... her a lot of money. (cost)

5 I was amazed when I saw my niece. She .... a lot taller.   (grow)

6 John .... at the school from 1990 to 1994 and then .... to Canada.   (work, emigrate)

7 Both Andrew and his horse were exhausted. He .... all night to warn us of the danger. (ride)

8 In the morning we looked at the damage. The hurricane .... all the fences down.   (blow)

9 Sarah dropped her racket in amazement. She .... the champion.   (beat)

B In this exercise, use the *past perfect continuous* or another *continuous* tense. Decide which is the correct tense for each sentence.

EXAMPLE: Tom finally stopped work and went indoors.
He ___had been digging___ since early morning.

1 When the accountant checked the books she found that the manager .... from the company for years.   (steal)

2 John looked over his shoulder and saw that the other runners .... him up fast. (catch)

3 Sally desperately needed a bath and a hot meal. She .... for three days without a break.   (travel)

4 Patrick finally went to see the dentist. He .... great pain for several days.   (suffer)

C Comment on these situations, as in the example. Use the *past perfect*. Begin each sentence with '*It was the first time that ...*'

EXAMPLE: As he waited for the signal to take off, he felt very nervous.
It was the first time he had flown without the instructor.

1 Her knees felt like jelly as she walked onto the stage.

2 She tried not to look down as she waited for the signal to jump.

3 The surgeon tried to keep his hands steady and was glad he was wearing a mask.

4 Whenever he saw Margaret, Simon felt too confused to speak.

5 Lucy began to wonder how she would spend the prize money.

D Complete the sentences with either a *past simple* verb or a *past perfect* verb.

EXAMPLES: The prison officer opened the door of the cell. It was empty.
The prisoner ___had escaped___ .

The prison officer opened the door of the cell.
The prisoner ___refused___ to leave.

1 There was no-one in front of her. Lynne knew she .... the race.   (win)

2 John .... underneath his car and then got in.   (look)

3 I .... a fox in my garden.
It .... from the hunters.
                                                           (find, escape)

4 As soon as Charles .... on stage, the audience cheered.   (appear)

5 I realised with horror that I .... the tickets at home.   (leave)

6 I knew, even without looking, that the money ....
                                                       (not steal)

Listening

Listen to Rebecca talking about an accident that happened when she was riding her motorbike. Look at the statements and say whether they are *true* or *false*.

1 When the accident happened, Rebecca was riding home from work.
2 There was a lorry in front of her.
3 She was riding a powerful motorbike.
4 She suddenly put the brakes on.
5 She hit another vehicle.
6 She was thrown into the air.
7 The road was wet.
8 She was wearing trousers.
9 Her left leg was injured.
10 People in a garage nearby called an ambulance.
11 It took a long time for the ambulance to arrive.
12 She spent more than a week in hospital.

English in Use

1 Complete the sentences with the correct word, *wound*, *injure*, *injury* or *damage* in the correct form. (Grammar Notes **11.2**.)

EXAMPLES: The victim suffered minor __injuries__ .
Doctors tried to save the soldier's life, but he died of his __wounds__ .
Caroline fell off her bicycle, but it was not __damaged__ .

1 More than two thousand men were .... in the battle.
2 The house suffered major structural .... as a result of the storm.
3 You must report a road accident to the police if someone is ....
4 The general has an old war .... in his leg which causes him difficulty in walking.
5 Martin suffered brain .... as a result of the accident.
6 The builder fell from scaffolding and was taken to hospital with multiple ....
7 The building was badly .... by fire.
8 The .... were transported by helicopter from the battle front.
9 The wings of the plane were .... in the attack.
10 Clean the .... with running water.

2 Complete the sentences with the correct word, *heal*, *cure* or *treat*. (Grammar Notes **11.3**.)

EXAMPLES: Frankie grazed her leg and it took a long time to __heal__ .
For many years the patient was __treated__ for the wrong illness.
The doctors told the young man that there was little chance of his being completely __cured__ .

1 There is no .... but we can .... this condition with drugs.
2 I've been taking lots of medicine, but nothing seems to .... my cough.
3 John cut his finger two weeks ago and it still hasn't ....
4 'I went into medicine in order to .... the sick,' said the doctor.
5 There is still no .... for the common cold.
6 'There are no facilities in this hospital to .... these kinds of injuries,' the doctor stated.
7 You could put cream on the sore, but it will .... of its own accord just as quickly.
8 The doctors could offer no .... , she could only .... the symptoms.
9 It took three years before I knew I was .... of the disease.
10 'Yes, the skin is .... nicely,' said the specialist.

3 Complete each sentence with the appropriate preposition.

1 Julia has suffered .... back problems for a number of years.
2 I've got a pain .... my foot.
3 John had to undergo an operation .... his left knee.
4 Years of lifting heavy objects had caused damage .... Terry's spine.
5 My father is recovering .... a heart attack.
6 The Prime Minister entered hospital .... a check-up.
7 What's wrong .... Frank? He doesn't look at all well.
8 Many people in this village died .... tuberculosis.

Reading

A Is sport always good for you?

What dangers do you face when you practise different forms of sport?

The lifelong penalty facing football-crazy youngsters

A few years ago, Stuart Pow was convinced he would be a professional footballer. 'When I was at school, I thought I had it made.' Now, at the age of 23, he no longer plays football. His knee is 'too much of a mess,' he says. Stuart's professional aspirations were well founded. After
5 being spotted in his early teens by talent scouts from his local club in Southampton, he started training with about fifty other young hopefuls. 'I was playing four or five times a week,' he recalls. 'In summer, I used to go to camps for a solid month's training.' Within a couple of years, he began to have trouble with his right knee. His
10 doctor told him that the bones had gradually worn away, because he had played too much sport before they had fully hardened. Now, although he plays some squash, tennis and badminton, football is out. 'I never got over that,' he says, 'and I know I never will. It was my first love and giving it up took a big chunk out of my life.'
15 The wrecking of Stuart Pow's career is not an isolated case. The Football Association is becoming increasingly concerned that promising young footballers, aged between ten and sixteen, are injuring themselves as a result of playing too much. Charles Hughes, the association's director of coaching and education, estimates that at least
20 one young star player a year is lost to the game nationally because of overuse injuries or stress fractures. 'That means you could be losing a whole international team over a period of ten years,' he says.
The Football Association is working on a strategy for persuading clubs to limit the number of games played by their most promising
25 youngsters. Many of them play 140 or 150 games a season, Mr Hughes says, which makes it impossible for them to train properly. The pressure on such players is greatest towards the end of the football season, when the evenings are lighter and many competitions are coming to a head, he explains. Mr Hughes's association has
30 already held meetings for groups of doctors around the country, to alert them to the early symptoms of overuse injuries. The commonest symptom of this type of injury is pain. Mild stress fractures of the spine cause varying degrees of backache, and surgery may be needed to treat the most severe cases. Too much exercise while a child is
35 growing may also irritate the growth points in the long bones, causing what parents and teachers often dismiss as 'growing pains.'
Children who play other sports, such as tennis and gymnastics, are also at risk. Dr Tim Sonnex, a member of the FA's medical committee, has seen children who have been encouraged to start
40 weight training as young as eight. 'But no child should be doing weight training below the age of eighteen.' Other medical experts echo Dr Sonnex's warnings. Vivian Grisogono, a physiotherapist, explains that playing football but no other sport causes an imbalance in the way the body develops. The legs are well
45 developed, but when the child kicks the ball, the upper part of the body is too weak to act as a counterbalance, putting tremendous strain on the back. Boys should not do too much training during a growth spurt, because at this time, the difference in the lengths of a child's legs may be as much as three or four centimetres. Rapid
50 growth also causes an imbalance between the strength and flexibility of bones, making them more vulnerable.
'The better the players, the more likely they are to have these injuries,' says Dr Sonnex. They tend to be pushed more, sometimes even by their parents.

B Choose the most appropriate answer, according to the text.

1 What made Stuart Pow think he could be a professional footballer?

  A He was strong.
  B Other people told him he was good.
  C His teachers encouraged him.
  D He got summer training.

2 What is his view of football now?

  A He regrets devoting his time to it.
  B He envies other players.
  C He wishes his training had been different.
  D He wishes he could still play.

3 What does Charles Hughes want to do?

  A to encourage more young players to take up the sport.
  B to provide special training for selected young players.
  C to make those involved aware of the dangers to the young.
  D to improve the training of sports doctors.

4 According to the text, what is the usual reaction when children suffer pain?

  A to visit a doctor
  B to prescribe a different type of exercise
  C to pay little attention
  D to get annoyed

5 When are teenagers most at risk from injury?

  A when the evenings are light
  B at the end of a long season
  C when sudden growth occurs
  D when no attention is given to the back

Reading

A How do you think you would cope if something bad happened to you? What qualities help people to survive terrible experiences?

1

Survivors

Earlier this year Rachel Wilbourn was ill. Very ill. While she was having a liver transplant her heart stopped beating for 20 minutes. But Rachel came back to life to tell her story.

5 'It all started one day when out of the blue I started to vomit. And I kept on being sick. I went to the doctor and he sent me for some blood tests at the local hospital. Then I was transferred to a hospital in London. I felt like I was putting on a lot of weight. I felt so bloated. It turned out I
10 was retaining loads of fluid. Shortly after arriving at the hospital I went into a coma. My liver had failed because I had something called Wilson's disease, which is an inability of the body to get rid of copper. My body was poisoning itself, and I had to have an emergency
15 transplant. Apparently, during the transplant operation, I started to bleed internally and my heart stopped for twenty minutes. The doctors finally managed to revive me, but my mum was told that I would be definitely brain-damaged because the oxygen supply to my brain
20 had been cut off. When I finally regained consciousness after nineteen days, I couldn't talk, my arms were weak and I could hardly move. I kept asking for my mum but nobody understood. I was so lonely and frustrated.'

'I was in hospital for two months in all. When I started
25 to recover the doctors and my mum told me what I'd been through. When my mum told me they thought I would have brain damage I just couldn't believe it. It's so scary to think about how I could have ended up. I would have been a burden to everyone. I can't really think about it
30 too much. Suffering has really made me see how many friends I have. And I have come to appreciate even the tiny things in life. I am covered with scars. They are really hideous but they don't really bother me. They're certainly not going to stop me from wearing my swimsuit
35 when I go on holiday. When I think that I died and came back to life it puts having a few scars into perspective.

The illness has given me a new view on life. It's made me not want to sit around and do nothing. I am definitely more determined now and I really want to live
40 life to the full. You don't realise just how precious life is until you come so close to losing it.'

2

Twenty-two-year-old Karen Morgan thought she had it made. She had a good job as a secretary, her own house and a good social life. Then she was made redundant and everything changed. 'I was working for a firm of
5 surveyors and the recession hit the building trade really badly. Out of a staff of 60 they made 40 people redundant. I was so devastated that I literally couldn't speak. I felt like I was utterly worthless, just cast aside.

'To begin with, I thought that I wouldn't have much
10 of a problem getting another job. Because I had a mortgage I needed a certain wage, and I went for interview after interview, but either the money wasn't good enough or the job wasn't right or they didn't like me. At one stage I got so depressed that I just broke
15 down and cried. Eventually I got myself a bit of temping work but I just wasn't bringing in enough money. I was living with a friend and she was worried that I wasn't going to pay the bills. We had to move out. It's a shame because my friend and I parted on bad terms. So as well
20 as a job and a house I lost one of my best friends.'

'This experience has made me appreciate how lucky I was, and how we shouldn't take anything for granted. I went from being comfortably off to a situation where, if I fancied going to the corner shop and buying some
25 crisps, I had to think if I really could afford them. It took me eight months to sort everything out – slowly paying off my debts and coming to terms with what had happened. I've got a good job now with lots of prospects. I can see a good future and I'm a stronger
30 person. If it ever happened again, I'd be more prepared and able to cope much better.'

B In text **1**, find ten medical expressions that Rachel uses. Say what each means.

In text **2**, find the negative words that Karen uses to describe her emotions.

Look at the following statements and divide them into two groups, the first group applying to Rachel and the second group to Karen.

1 She is not worried about what people think of her physical appearance.
2 She mentions her financial situation.
3 She felt extremely depressed.
4 She is looking forward to many different experiences.
5 She was worried about being fat.
6 She took her life for granted.
7 She didn't believe what the experts had said.
8 She spent a long time learning to accept her situation.
9 She expects things to be better quite soon in the future.
10 She has had bad experiences with friends.

Talking Points

Section 1

Look at the pictures
What is happening/has happened?

What needs to be done?
Who is going to do it?

Section 2

Look at the five situations opposite.
Work with a partner.
Take it in turns to play either Student A or Student B.

Student A: explain what has happened
Student B: give advice. Use the phrases in italics when you give advice.

I suggest you put on the spare tyre.
You should change the tyre.
Why don't you get someone to help you put on the spare tyre?
What about ringing the Automobile Association for help.
Have you thought of getting out the tool-kit?
It would be a good idea to keep the spare tyre pumped up.

Situations

1   It's your best friend's birthday, and you had forgotten all about it.

2   You borrowed a book from a teacher at school and it got wet. Now there are marks all over it.

3   You've been lying in the sun for too long and your skin is very sore.

4   You borrowed your friend's bicycle and it crashed into a wall, leaving the wheels buckled and bent.

5   You have been looking after the neighbours' cat while they were away, and now the cat has disappeared.

Listening

Narrow escapes

Listen to the two people, Katherine and David, talking about accidents connected with a fire. Indicate whether the statements below refer to the incident described by Katherine or to the one described by David, or to both, by ticking the appropriate box.

1   The accident occurred in their own home.
2   A child was involved in the accident.
3   A child was in danger.
4   The person was alone at the time.
5   When the accident happened, other people rushed to help.
6   The house was damaged.
7   The people in the house had an open fire.
8   A meal was being eaten at the time of the accident.
9   The accident could have been very serious.
10 A building was burnt down.

	Katherine	David
1		
2		
3		
4		
5		
6		
7		
8		
9		
10		

Writing

A letter to a company

You have recently come back from an activity holiday where you went to get some tennis training. You were very dissatisfied for the following reasons:

1   The coaching was in large groups, so you got no individual attention.
2   The courts were all grass, so you couldn't develop your technique on different surfaces.
3   You couldn't use the courts when you wanted to because there weren't enough for all the participants.
4   There wasn't enough to eat and the food was of poor quality.
5   The bedrooms were crowded (six people sharing) and not cleaned often enough.

Write a letter to Mr McGregor, the director of the activity centre, telling him what was wrong and asking for a refund.

Look at the hints provided in the letter below which also shows you the layout for this type of letter.

```
                                    21 Blenheim Crescent
                                    Oxford
                                    OX8 9QR

                                    21 August 19—

Mr J MacGregor
Director
Thames Activity Holidays
362 Hills Road
Wallingford
Oxfordshire
WA7 6PT

Dear Mr MacGregor

1 Letters to companies are written in a clear
  and formal style.

2 You will need an introductory paragraph.

3 In the second paragraph, you will need to
  provide all the relevant details, about
  when and where you stayed and what was
  wrong. Arrange the information logically,
  and stick to reporting the facts.

4 In your final paragraph, say what action you
  want to be taken.

5 End your letter in a firm and polite way.

Yours sincerely

Charlotte Thompson

Charlotte Thompson
```

Which paragraph do these sentences belong to?

1   I expect a refund of the cost of the holiday.

2   I am writing to inform you of my dissatisfaction about the tennis training holiday organised by your company that I have just returned from.

3   I look forward to hearing from you in the very near future.

4   There were a number of things that were not satisfactory. First, ... In addition, ... Finally, and worst of all, ...

English in Use

1 Phrasal Verbs

Complete the sentences with a phrasal verb based on *stand*.

EXAMPLE: Jilly is so tall she always <u>stands out</u> in a crowd.

1 What do the initials UNESCO ....?

2 Everyone in court .... when the judge entered.

3 The plane was on the runway, ... for take-off.

4 Jonathan was an exceptional child – he .... from his fellow pupils in everything he did.

5 Mrs Smith refused to .... Tim's rude behaviour.

6 Paul was brought up in a rough neighbourhood where people learned early how to .... themselves.

7 The President was forced to .... when public feeling against him became intense.

8 John's a bully – if you want to work with him you'll have learn how to .... to him.

9 People .... to let the procession pass.

10 What does that political party ....?

2 Word-formation

Complete the sentences with the correct form of the word in capitals.

EXAMPLES: The commentator provided a detailed <u>analysis</u> of the situation. ANALYSE

There were many business <u>failures</u> because of the economic situation. FAIL

Matthew made a full <u>recovery</u> after his illness.

1 All the .... to the shop were made this morning. DELIVER

2 There's a space at the bottom of the form where you should put your .... SIGN

3 The .... of the factory caused many people to lose their jobs. CLOSE

4 What's the .... date of this season ticket? EXPIRE

5 Most people do well in times of economic .... PROSPER

6 This drug may cause temporary .... PARALYSE

7 Under .... the accused admitted he was guilty. PRESS

8 The boy suffered severe head .... as a result of the attack. INJURE

9 The teacher puts a lot of .... on not making grammatical mistakes. EMPHASIZE

10 The government ordered the immediate .... of the illegal weapons. SEIZE

WEATHER AND CLIMATE

Lead-in **1** Describe what is happening in the photographs.
What kind of damage can be caused by the weather?
How does your lifestyle change according to the different seasons?

2 Choose the correct word or phrase for the gap in each sentence.

drought   mist   lightning   gale   fog
heatwave   climate   hail storm
breeze   avalanche

1 The .... had caused temperatures to rise to over 45 degrees centigrade day after day.

2 The .... had lasted six months and farmers had hardly any water for their animals and crops.

3 There had been a heavy fall of snow followed by a rise in temperature, so there was great danger of an ....

4 The .... was so dense that visibility on the motorway had been reduced to 50 metres.

5 It was a lovely sunny day with a gentle .... just rustling the leaves on the trees.

6 In spring many farmers fear a .... which can cause severe damage to their early crops.

7 The winds had increased in strength during the night and were now .... force.

8 There was a violent thunderstorm and the old apple tree was struck by ....

9 New Zealand has a temperate .... with warm summers and mild winters.

10 At dawn there was a light .... rising from the sea which evaporated as the sun rose.

3 Choose the correct word or phrase for the gap in each sentence.

erode   irrigate   sunstroke   famine
frostbite   evacuate   flooded   swept
drenched   cut off

1 Years of battering by heavy seas had caused that part of the coastline to ....

2 The climbers were stranded on the freezing mountain and were in danger of suffering from ....

3 The farmers had set up a system of using water from the river to .... their crops.

4 There is a severe .... in that part of the country and people are dying of starvation.

5 The river rose rapidly and burst its banks, causing many homes to be ....

6 The tanker was battered by high seas and two sailors were .... overboard.

7 The children got caught in the rain on their way home and arrived home ....

8 If you stay out too long in a hot sun, you'll suffer from ....

9 There had been a landslide and five villages in the mountains were .... for three days.

10 The coastguard advised people to .... the town because a hurricane was approaching the area.

Reading

 A At what time of year is the weather at its worst in your country?
What problems are caused by bad weather?

STORMS SWEEP BRITAIN: *16 die*

AT LEAST SIXTEEN PEOPLE were killed as severe gales swept across Britain yesterday. There was
5 widespread flooding and many buildings were damaged by high winds. Several rivers, swollen by heavy rainfall, burst their banks. The worst
10 affected place was Towyn in North Wales. Yesterday morning, mountainous seas smashed through the sea wall that protected the town from
15 flooding. Floods up to two metres deep swept through the town. Lifeboats and helicopters were used to evacuate 2,000 people before
20 the midnight high tide brought even worse flooding. Fifty people were taken to hospital suffering from shock and exposure. A school outside the
25 town is being used as temporary accommodation for the evacuees, who are being looked after by voluntary workers. A police spokesman
30 said, 'If we hadn't got them out in time, many people would have died.' Police, ambulance crews and firefighters toured the town in boats in order to
35 check that everybody had been accounted for. A confused old lady, who had earlier hidden from police, was found and taken to hospital. Evacuees
40 claimed that the sea wall had not been repaired since 1980. 'We've been complaining for

years,' said one of them, 'but
45 nothing was done. Now we've lost our homes.' Experts predict that the damage caused by the midnight tide will be 'severe and extensive.'
50 No lives have been lost in Towyn but in other parts of Britain sixteen people died as 150 kph winds swept across the country. Eight of the
55 victims were motorists whose cars overturned on exposed roads. One man was killed when a parked car was blown onto him. A bus driver died
60 when his vehicle was crushed by a falling tree. A lorry crashed into a house after being hit by a falling lamp-post. Several people were
65 killed when walls, chimneys and roof tiles were blown down on top of them. Many roads are blocked by fallen trees and abandoned vehicles. All ferry
70 services have been suspended and many flights delayed.
A lorry driver was crossing the Humber Bridge when his vehicle was struck by a sudden
75 gust of wind and blown off the side of the bridge. Only the bridge suspension cables prevented the lorry from toppling over the edge into the
80 water. The driver managed to scramble to safety through a window. In the Humber estuary, several ships have been blown aground.
85 Weather forecasters warned that although the high winds would die down during the night, they would return with renewed force tomorrow
90 morning. Drivers are advised not to travel unless their journeys are absolutely necessary.

B What do the following numbers in the text refer to?

1 sixteen

2 two

3 2,000

4 fifty

5 eight

6 150

C List the phrasal verbs in the text which are based on *sweep* and *blow*, and, in pairs, discuss what they mean.

D Choose the correct answer A, B, C, or D.

1 Why was the midnight tide a serious threat to the town of Towyn?

A There were gale force winds.
B The seawall had been broken.
C Several rivers had burst their banks.
D There wasn't time to evacuate everybody.

2 Why are some evacuees angry?

A They knew the sea wall needed repairing.
B They are suffering from shock.
C They are afraid of the police.
D They expected a better weather forecast.

3 Forecasters think that the weather will

A stay the same.
B get better and then stormy again.
C get much worse.
D get worse for a short time and then better.

Grammar: *conditionals*

 A Look at these examples and answer the questions. (Grammar Notes **12.1**)

If I had known about the danger, I would have warned you.
Did I know? Did I warn you?

If you hadn't told me, I wouldn't have known.
Did you tell me? Did I know?

If John hadn't seen the cyclist in time, there would have been an accident.
Did he see the cyclist in time? Was there an accident?

B Match the two halves of each sentence.

1 If the soldiers had known about the ambush,

2 If we had invested more money in research,

3 If the weather forecast had given a warning about the high winds,

4 If the workers had known more about safety procedures,

5 If the sea wall had been strengthened,

a we could have produced a better product.

b people could have taken precautions.

c they wouldn't have advanced into the valley.

d the town would not have been flooded.

e the accident would not have happened.

C Complete the sentences.

1 If we had realised the water was polluted,
....

2 If John had known how poor the train service was,
....

3 If Mary hadn't been vaccinated,
....

4 The police car wouldn't have followed Peter if
....

5 The sailors would not have survived if
....

D Read the following text and write sentences which begin with *if*.

EXAMPLE: *If Bernard had got up in time, he would have caught the 8.10 train.*

Write at least five more sentences like the example. Some sentences can be negative.

The tenth of August was the first day of Bernard's holiday. He set the alarm clock for 6 a.m. but he didn't hear it and got up late. He missed the 8.10 train to the airport and had to take the 8.40. When he arrived at the airport, just in time, he discovered that his suitcase weighed more than 20 kilograms, so he had to pay a charge for excess baggage. Because he was in a hurry, and getting flustered, he went to the wrong departure gate. He found the right one with only a minute to spare. On the plane the food was horrible and he felt sick. When the plane landed he looked so ill that people asked him if he needed a doctor. By the time he got to his hotel he felt better and went to the beach. He lay in the sun for an hour but he didn't use any suntan lotion, so he was badly sunburnt. The rest of the holiday wasn't much fun. One day he left his room unlocked and his watch was stolen. Then he missed the return flight and had to stay another day.

E Study the following situations and write an appropriate conditional sentence. (Note: you do not need the same type of conditional in every case.)

EXAMPLE: The pool was one metre deep. Jack didn't know that and dived in.
If Jack had known the pool was one metre deep, he wouldn't have dived in.

1 It cost us £5 to enter the museum today but yesterday it was free.

2 I can give you an earlier flight but only on Friday. Your ticket is for Tuesday. Do you want to change?

3 Our friends left a note for us but we didn't see it, so we didn't know where they had gone.

4 The only way to make our house warmer is to replace the central heating system, which we can't afford to do.

5 We didn't see the signpost so we didn't take the right turning.

Listening

Weather forecasts

You will hear *four* weather forecasts. Match each weather forecast with the pictures below. There are four pictures for each forecast.

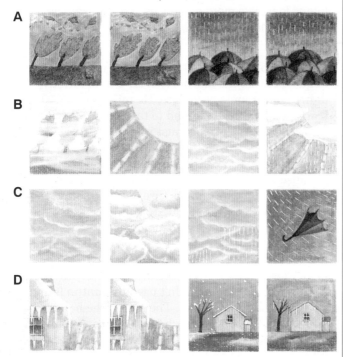

A

B

C

D

English in Use

Bath, bathe, sunbathe

1 Complete the sentences with these words. Use the correct form of the word *bath*, *bathe*, *sunbathe*. (Grammar Notes **12.2**)

1 I'd much rather have a .... than a shower.

2 I like sailing but the worst thing is that it is impossible to have a proper .... on a small boat.

3 On the first day of your holiday, don't .... for more than twenty minutes and use plenty of suntan lotion.

4 At this resort, you can lie on the beach, play football, water-ski, ... in the sea and enjoy many other activities.

5 Mrs Frost gave her children a .... and put them to bed.

6 The midwife taught the class how to .... a new-born baby.

7 It is inadvisable to .... between 12 noon and 2pm when the sun is at its strongest.

8 .... the wound with clean water.

9 Don't .... in the sea when the red flag is flying.

10 .... is not good for your skin.

2 Short forms

Complete the responses using short forms. (Grammar Notes **12.3**)

EXAMPLE: You don't know the answer.
<u>Yes, I do</u> .

1 John knows the answer.
Yes, he ....

2 Will Mary help us?
No, she ....

3 The students all arrived on time.
No, they ....

4 The soldiers have plenty of ammunition.
No, they ....

5 They've finished the painting.
Yes, they ....

6 The race started at 6 pm.
No, it ....

7 I should go and visit Aunt Lucy.
Yes, you ....

8 Ian can do the job by himself.
No, he ....

9 He'd filled the freezer before he left.
No, he ....

10 I don't think you would like it.
No, I ....

Reading

A At what time of year do you feel at your best?
If you travel to a country with a different climate, how do you feel?
Does climate have an important influence on personality?

Is winter a disease?

Few people in northern countries enjoy the long, dark nights and cold temperatures of winter. According to scientists, wintery conditions may be making some people ill. They suffer from Seasonal Affective Disorder (SAD) or
5 'the winter blues'. Sufferers become depressed as winter approaches, get even more depressed as the days become shorter but recover rapidly in spring. The symptoms can be very serious and may be mistaken for signs of mental illness. The further you live from the equator, the more
10 likely you are to be affected by SAD. It is believed that up to 20% of the population of northern countries suffers from SAD and that 5% are chronic cases.

Take the case of Janet Blake, a 30-year old public relations officer for a film distribution company. As the
15 temperature dropped and the nights became longer she found it more and more difficult to carry out her duties at work. Her job was very stressful and involved making speeches and appearing on television and radio. 'The pressure was just too much,' she said. 'Things became
20 unbearable. I felt really low. When I had to travel to my office in the dark and come home in the dark I could stand it no longer. I just couldn't cope anymore.' She started to sleep three to four hours longer than usual, felt drowsy, ate much more and spent hour after hour
25 slumped in an armchair in front of the T.V. She often burst into tears for no reason at all and had no interest in other people. 'I put on a lot of weight,' she said, 'and became very sluggish. I was in a state of utter despair.' In the end she was forced to give up her job.
30 At first, doctors tried to treat her with drugs, but without success. Fortunately, her case came to the attention of Dr Hamish MacRae, who has made a special study of SAD. His research had shown him that there was a simple and very effective cure – light. When SAD
35 sufferers are exposed to artificial light which simulates sunlight, they get better almost immediately. Dr MacRae had a special lightbox installed in Janet's home. She made a rapid recovery and was able to return to work. 'The problems seem to be caused by lack of light rather
40 than by low temperatures,' said Dr MacRae. 'It seems that some people feel the desire to hibernate in winter in the same way that many animals do. Ironically, SAD sufferers often become hyperactive in spring. They swing from one extreme to the other. In spring sunshine they
45 become very talkative and cannot sleep or sit still. The light box can help to keep their behaviour in balance.'

B Explain the meaning of these words and phrases in the text.

Paragraph 1
1 the winter blues
2 symptoms
3 chronic cases

Paragraph 2
4 things became unbearable
5 drowsy
6 slumped
7 sluggish
8 utter despair

Paragraph 3
9 hibernate
10 hyperactive

C

1 What is SAD?
2 How many people suffer from SAD?
3 What symptoms did Janet Blake have?
4 What finally convinced Janet Blake that she could not continue working?
5 Why was Janet fortunate to meet Dr MacRae?
6 What did Dr MacRae do?
7 According to Dr MacRae, what is the cause of SAD?
8 What problems do SAD sufferers have at other times of the year?

Reading

A What are the different ways of obtaining the water we need?
Why do we have to pay for water?
How is it paid for in your country?
In what ways is water wasted?
How could we be more economical in the use of water?

B Now read the article about water. Seven sentences have been removed from the article. Choose from the sentences A–H the one which fits each gap (1–7). There is one extra sentence that you do not need to use.

Water, water everywhere – *or is there?*

More than 70% of the Earth's surface is covered by water and a further 10% of the land is covered with ice. More than two-thirds of the human body is water and we cannot survive for more than four days without drinking water although we can survive without food for many weeks (the record for survival without food is 382 days). (1) .... Water is used in many manufacturing processes involving cooling and diluting, for transport and to extinguish fires. Water plays a part in many religious rituals. It also shapes the landscape by creating valleys and eroding coastlines. There is also a wide range of water sports that people enjoy such as swimming, diving, surfing, water polo, water skiing, canoeing and sailing.

Not everyone has access to a convenient and plentiful supply of fresh, clean water. It is estimated that two-thirds of households worldwide use a water source outside the home. In some parts of the world, water has to be carried by hand from a distant water source. (2) .... Water is heavy and a woman cannot carry more than about fifteen litres but one person needs at least five litres per day for drinking and cooking and a further twenty-five litres to keep clean. Consequently, women in some countries spend several hours a day in the backbreaking task of carrying water. (3) .... Even in advanced industrial countries, however, water is a cause for concern. Many people will not drink water from the tap but buy bottled water instead. They are concerned that tap water has not been adequately treated after leaving the reservoir and before being piped into their houses. (4) .... In agricultural areas, people are worried about the amount of chemical fertilisers that farmers spread on their fields. They believe that the rain washes these chemicals into the water supply. (5) ....

Water falls freely from the sky, as part of an endless cycle of evaporation, condensation and precipitation, but it has to be stored, treated and distributed and these processes cost money and have to be paid for. (6) .... In some parts of the world, countries are in dispute over the use of water from rivers and lakes that cross national boundaries. Some of these disputes could lead to war. The building of dams is particularly controversial because a large dam built to produce hydro-electric power may have effects outside the country where it has been built. Dams can have harmful social effects within a country because of the amount of agricultural land which is flooded and the number of people that have to move their homes.

(7) .... Floods lead to loss of life and environmental damage. Acid rain strips the leaves off trees and can destroy whole forests. Polluted water can kill fish and wildlife and cause fishermen to lose their livelihood. Perhaps worst of all is drought, when crops wither and die in arid fields, animals die of thirst, and people, unable to produce food, must move elsewhere or die. We are fortunate indeed if we can rely on a guaranteed, economical, unlimited supply of fresh, clean water.

A It is mostly women who have the job of carrying water.

B As well as being essential for our survival, water is also needed to wash our bodies and our clothes, for irrigating crops and for cooking.

C Compared with this, just turning on a tap in your house is sheer luxury, but a luxury we often take for granted.

D Water can be very destructive.

E Although it can cause damage, water is essential to life.

F Sometimes people are advised not to use water from wells because the water has been contaminated even at great depth.

G In many countries there are controversies about the private or public ownership of water and the amount of money that the consumer pays for it.

H They are worried that it is still polluted by chemicals that factories discharge into rivers.

Talking Points

Section 1

Work with a partner. Decide which sentence in list B comes after the sentence in list A.

List A

1 In the morning when he left his house there was a light drizzle but it soon began to pour with rain.

2 When she began the climb there was hardly a breath of wind. As the sun got hotter, a refreshing breeze helped to keep her cool.

3 A blanket of snow covered the fields, there were deep drifts in places and fresh snowflakes were falling.

4 Even inside his sleeping bag he was frozen stiff and his feet felt like blocks of ice.

5 The night sky was clear and bright and the stars twinkled. He could make out the Milky Way and the constellations of Orion and the Plough.

6 It was a mild day, slightly humid, with a few raindrops falling from a dull, overcast sky. The air seemed tense and heavy.

7 After six months of drought, the grass had turned brown, plants had withered in the heat, the ground was hard and cracked.

8 He stood on the rocks and listened to the sound of the waves crashing into the beach.

9 When the river burst its banks, the people in the small boat, struggling against the current, were in real danger.

List B

a He put his head outside the tent and felt the chill air on his face and saw that the grass was white with frost.

b By the time he reached his office he was drenched, soaked to the skin.

c There were plenty of meteors flashing through the sky but perhaps it was too early for the comet he really wanted to see.

d It was dusk and the tide was going out. Soon the surfers would give up and go home.

e After a couple of hours, however, there were strong gusts which almost blew her off her feet and soon gale force winds forced her to abandon her climb.

f He looked at the bleak, arid, barren fields that had once been a fertile farm.

g It wouldn't last long, however, a rise in temperature was forecast and soon it would all turn to slush before melting completely.

h Distant rumbles of thunder and flashes of lighting indicated that a storm was approaching.

i They were swept away and then became stranded in the branches of a tree.

Section 2

Climate change

Is it likely to get hotter or colder in the next fifty years?
What will happen if there is an increase or decrease in temperature all over the world?
What will the effects be in your own country?
Can ordinary people do anything to prevent changes in the climate?

Useful phrases:
global warming
greenhouse effect
damage to the ozone layer
increase in sea level
extremes of temperature
desertification

Section 3

'The way people think and behave is a result of the climate they grow up in.'

Discuss this in groups of three. Do you agree with the statement or not?

Listening

Freak weather

A Listen to this interview with Professor Marsh, a meteorologist who has a special interest in unusual weather conditions. Discuss the questions in pairs.

1 Why is Professor Marsh interested in unusual weather?

2 Which two strange phenomena are discussed by Professsor Marsh and the interviewer and what is the explanation for them?

3 Re-tell, briefly, the three stories about tornadoes that Professor Marsh tells.

4 Which story might not be true?

5 What strange phenomena cannot be explained by Professor Marsh?

6 What do some people believe is the explanation and what does Professor Marsh believe?

B Describe the most unusual weather that you have experienced. Have you heard or read any interesting stories about freak weather conditions?

Writing

Volcanoes

 Use the information below to write an article of about 150 words called 'Volcanoes'. You must use *only* the information given, but you need not use all the information. Write three paragraphs.

First paragraph: say what causes volcanic eruptions and explain what happens when eruptions take place.

Second paragraph: say which parts of the world have active volcanoes and mention some famous eruptions.

Third paragraph: refer to survivors' personal experiences of volcanic eruptions.

Famous Volcanic Eruptions		
1470 BC	THERA, GREECE	ISLAND DESTROYED (destroyed Minoan civilisation)
79 AD	VESUVIUS, ITALY	POMPEII DESTROYED (city preserved under the lava)
1669	ETNA, ITALY	20,000 DEAD
1883	KRAKATOA, INDONESIA	40,000 DEAD (created beautiful sunsets worldwide)
1902	MOUNT PELEE, MARTINIQUE	30,000 DEAD (only 2 survivors)
1985	NEVADA DEL RUIZ, COLUMBIA	25,000 DEAD

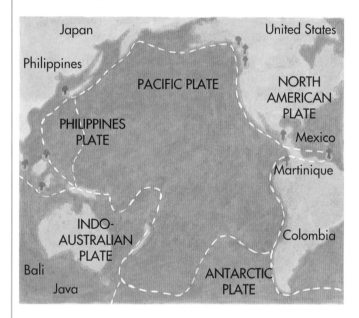

'The blinding fall of sand and stones, the intense blackness above and around us, broken only by flashes of lightning, and the explosive roars of Krakatoa, make our situation a truly awful one.'
The captain of a ship near Krakatoa.

'We closed the door and at that same moment came a terrible explosion that nearly burst our eardrums. The skylight was blown in and hot, moist ashes began to pour in on us; they came in boiling, splattering splashes like hot mud. In vain we tried to shield ourselves … When we could see each others' faces, they were all covered with black lava. The baby was dying and Rita, the elder girl was in great agony and every part of my body was hurting. A heap of hot mud had collected near us and as Rita put her hand out to raise herself up it was plunged up to the elbow in the scalding stuff.'
A maidservant on board a ship in Martinique harbour, 1902.

English in Use

1 What, which

Complete the sentences with *what* or *which*. (Grammar Notes **12.4**)

EXAMPLES: I don't know _____*what*_____ to do about it.
He bought a painting _____*which*_____ turned out to be worth a fortune.

1 He didn't tell anyone _____ had happened.

2 The workmen cut down the trees _____ were beginning to die.

3 Bernard identified the painting _____ had been stolen.

4 I didn't know _____ to wear for the garden party.

5 Madeleine showed me the cave _____ led to a secret world.

6 The chef rejected any mushrooms _____ were not fresh.

7 You can eat _____ you like.

8 I could not understand _____ he was trying to tell me.

9 The police recovered only two of the cars _____ had been stolen.

10 Tell me _____ Janet told you.

2 Phrasal Verbs

In many phrasal verbs the particle *off* indicates separation in distance or time. Complete the following sentences with a suitable verb.

EXAMPLE:
The football match has been _____*put off*_____ till next Saturday.
When will it take place? When should it have taken place?

Use the correct form of these words.

| get | cut | keep | see | run |
| break | blast | give | | |

1 Mr Jones didn't pay his bill so his telephone was _____ off.

2 We went to the airport to _____ our friends off.

3 The rocket _____ off into space late last night.

4 Take bus number 65 and _____ off at the railway station.

5 The gardener told the children to _____ off the grass.

6 Sarah has _____ off her engagement to George.

7 Can you _____ off twenty copies of this document?

8 These radiators don't _____ off much heat.

3 Word-formation

Complete the sentences with the correct form of the word in capitals.

EXAMPLES: The mayor made an interesting _____*suggestion*_____ about how the town should be developed. SUGGEST

The shop's policy was that all _____*breakages*_____ had to be paid for. BREAK

The student needed _____*encouragement*_____ to continue with his studies. ENCOURAGE

1 The weather was so bad that there had to be a _____ of the match. POSTPONE

2 There was a shocked _____ to news of the earthquake. REACT

3 Water _____ is a major problem in such a hot climate. STORE

4 There was an _____ in the condition of the accident victim. IMPROVE

5 Three ecologists stood for _____ to the town council. ELECT

6 The picture was too small for us to see all the details so we asked for an _____ to be made. ENLARGE

7 The _____ of the plane was scattered over the mountainside. WRECK

8 What are the current _____ about the effects of climate change? PREDICT

9 The coastline has worn away with the _____ of time. PASS

10 Our bodyguards provide _____ for people in danger. PROTECT

unit 13
HEROES AND HEROINES?

Lead-in **1** Look at the pictures. Who are they?

Are they heroes or villains? What makes you decide one way or another?

2 Choose the correct word for the gap in each sentence.

heroism   coward   success
criticism   star   failure   respect
defeat   legend   hero-worship

1 She had made just one film but suddenly she found she was a ....

2 Winning four Olympic medals made the skier a .... in her own lifetime.

3 The soldier acted so bravely in rescuing his colleague that he received an award for ....

4 There was a lot of .... of the politician for his dishonesty.

5 The footballer earned the .... of his captain by the way he fought to recover from injury.

6 The general had won many victories, and was shocked by his first ....

7 Although everyone admired Frances, she felt herself to be a ....

8 He won the tennis championship when he was only seventeen and found it difficult to cope with all the ....

9 She was so hungry for .... that everything else in her life came second to her sport.

10 Everyone called Henry a .... when he refused to fight.

3 Choose the correct word or phrase for each gap.

autograph   on show   achievements
privacy   well-known   in the public eye
dodge   interviews   celebrities
private life   publicity   commented
fans   intruders

*P*eople can become famous for many different reasons: through sporting .... (1), through acting – on stage, on TV or in films, through political activity or even through marrying someone already .... (2), such as a member of a royal family. But what is it like to be so .... (3) that you are recognised everywhere you go? What's it like to be in a restaurant and have people come up to you asking you for your .... (4)? How does it feel always being .... (5), with every move you make watched or .... (6) on by members of the public and the popular press? Is this lack of .... (7) a necessary price you have to pay? How does it feel if every time you leave the house you have to .... (8) reporters and .... (9), eager to get a picture of you or just touch you? Some .... (10) go to tremendous lengths to make sure that their .... (11) is kept that way. They protect their property with guard dogs and high wire fences to make sure no unwelcome .... (12) get in. When they give .... (13), they make it a rule not to discuss personal matters. For some the constant glare of .... (14) is too much and they never wish to come out from behind the wall they have built to protect themselves.

Reading

 A In your country, what famous events are there when people have been very brave? When people have done something considered brave, how are they treated?

Grace Darling

On 7 September, 1838, Grace Darling's life was changed forever by a single act of heroism. She was twenty-three years old, the seventh child of William Darling, a lighthouse keeper on Farne Island off the coast of
5 Northumberland. She had received little education and had had a very strict, religious upbringing. Her life consisted of the daily drudgery of cooking and cleaning. Then, on 7 September, 1838, the steamship *Forfarshire* was wrecked in a storm off Farne Island. Five
10 passengers managed to swim to rocks and hang on, but in the heavy seas they were in danger of being swept away by the huge waves. Grace Darling and her father got into an open boat and rowed out to the rocks, struggling against strong winds, driving rain and
15 dangerous currents. They reached the rocks and succeeded in rescuing all the survivors and taking them to safety.

News of Grace's exploit spread quickly and she soon became a celebrity. There were many stories about her
20 in newspapers and magazines, often written by journalists who had never met her. They made a lot of things up. Soon she was a household name. Portraits of her were painted by artists who had never seen her. She appeared on mugs, plates and other souvenirs,
25 always looking much prettier than she really was. Over £1700 was collected from people who admired her bravery. All this money was given to her and the Royal Humane Society gave her a gold medal. She received many offers of marriage from men she had never met,
30 but she turned them all down. She was invited to appear in a circus, but she refused. People wrote to her requesting locks of her hair and she also received many begging letters from people who thought that she was now rich (as indeed she was). She had become a legend
35 in her own lifetime. Grace, who was really a shy, plain, simple girl was very upset by the publicity and found it difficult to cope with. She lived at the beginning of the age of mass communication and was one of the first people to be 'famous for fifteen minutes'. Her father was
40 mystified by the hysterical public reaction. He regarded the rescue as a normal part of his job, and something he had done many times before. Cynics said that the publicity surrounding Grace was a way of distracting attention from the incompetence of the captain and
45 owners of the *Forfarshire*.

Grace did not enjoy being famous. Her health began to fail and four years after her heroic deed she died of tuberculosis. In the village where she was born there is a Grace Darling Museum where you can see the boat
50 she and her father rowed. It is 6.4m long and 1.8m wide.

B Use the context of the text to identify the meaning of the following words and phrases:

1 off the coast
  A on the beach
  B far out at sea
  C close to the coast

2 drudgery
  A pleasure
  B duty
  C boring work

3 wrecked
  A hit
  B destroyed
  C pushed

4 currents
  A waves
  B wind
  C movements of water

5 exploit
  A adventure
  B action
  C character

6 mystified
  A pleased
  B satisfied
  C surprised

7 incompetence
  A stupidity
  B lack of skill
  C worries

C Rewrite these statements so that they are correct according to the information in the text.

1 Grace's father was a sailor.
2 Her childhood was a time of enjoyment.
3 Her life before the accident was interesting.
4 Grace and her father rescued all the passengers from the *Forfarshire*.
5 The journalists who wrote about Grace interviewed her first.
6 The journalists told the truth about her.
7 People collected money for Grace because they felt sorry for her.
8 Grace was interested in several offers of marriage she received.
9 Grace enjoyed being famous.
10 Grace's father was pleased at the way people admired his daughter.

Grammar: *revision of past tenses*

A (Grammar Notes **13.1**) Look at the following sentences and answer these questions:

Which action happened first?
Were the actions finished or unfinished?
Was one action interrupted by another?

1 When I shouted to her, she walked away.
2 When I shouted to her, she was walking away.
3 When I shouted to her, she had walked away.
4 John died of food poisoning.
5 He was dying of food poisoning.
6 He was baking cakes when the children came home.
7 He made sandwiches when the children came home.
8 He had cooked dinner when the children came home.
9 The baby was crying when I picked him up.
10 The baby cried when I picked him up.

B Complete these sentences with the *past continuous* or *past simple* form of the verb. Some sentences need only one tense; others need two.

1 When the robber .... his gun, the police .... fire.   (draw, open)

2 The lifeguard .... into the pool because a man ....   (dive, drown)

3 The dog .... up the river bank and .... itself.   (climb, shake)

4 I .... a letter to Elizabeth when, to my surprise, she ....   (write, ring)

5 The plane .... at 10,000 metres when one engine .... fire.   (fly, catch)

6 The house .... when the firefighters ....   (burn, arrive)

C Is there a difference in meaning between these two sentences?

a John had hidden the money when the police arrived.
b John hid the money when the police arrived.

Which sentence means that John acted quickly when he realised the police were there?

Which sentence means that the hiding of the money took place before the arrival of the police?

In which sentence is John in more danger of being arrested?

Is there a difference in meaning between these two sentences?

c He finished before I arrived.
d He had finished before I arrived.

With the conjunctions, *before*, *after* and *until*, it is not always necessary for the first of two actions to be in the *past perfect*. There is no difference in meaning between the sentences. Would there be a difference if we changed *before* to *when*?

In this exercise, put the verbs in the *past simple* or *past perfect* as appropriate.

1 As he .... the runway, the pilot .... that he .... the undercarriage,
                (approach, realise, not lower)

2 Before Rebecca .... the train, she .... some glossy magazines.   (catch, buy)

3 By the time he .... , he .... over seventy fights.   (retire, win).

4 After he .... the deer, he .... it back to his car.   (shoot, drag)

5 When Lucy .... from the horse, she .... her arm.   (fall, break)

D Complete the following story using *past simple*, *past continuous* and *past perfect* verbs. The first three have been done as examples.

It **had been** a long walk from the station and my feet **were beginning** to ache but I **quickened** my pace when I (*1 see*) my *SAW* house ahead of me. I (*2 had*) a difficult three months away *HAD HAD* but I (*3 obtain*) the valuable information that my client (*4 OBTAINED* want). I (*5 look*) forward to a few days relaxation. As I *WANTED. WAS LOOKING* (*6 walk*) up the garden path towards the front door I (*7 had*) a *WALKED* strange feeling that someone (*8 watch*) me. I (*9 imagine*) things, I (*10 tell*) myself. Only a few trusted friends (*11 know*) of this address. I (*12 take out*) my keys, (*13 unlock*) all three locks and (*14 step*) inside. The house (*15 be*) empty during my long absence and (*16 seem*) cold and unwelcoming. To my surprise, the upstairs lights (*17 be*) on. Surely I (*18 not leave*) them on for three months! I (*19 be*) certain that I (*20 checked*) everything before leaving. I (*21 begin*) to wonder if someone (*22 break*) into the house but, if so, they (*23 take*) nothing from the downstairs room. Everything (*24 be*) just as I (*25 leave*) it. I (*26 check*) upstairs. I (*27 open*) the safe in my study in which, before leaving, I (*28 place*) the first part of my fee – £10,000 in cash. It (*29 be*) still there. Downstairs again, I (*30 examine*) the kitchen door. It (*31 be*) obvious that someone (*32 force*) it open. Someone (*33 enter*) my house but (*34 steal*) nothing. It (*35 be*) very strange. There (*36 be*) one room that I (*37 not check*). As soon as I (*38 open*) the door to the dining room I (*39 realise*) what (*40 happen*). Goya's 'Duke of Wellington', which, according to the newspapers, (*41 disappear*) from the National Gallery, (*42 lean*) against the fireplace. I (*43 hear*) the sound of a car braking and (*44 look*) out of the window. Four policemen (*45 get*) out of their car. Obviously, my enemies (*46 plan*) this to prevent me from continuing my enquiries.

Listening 📼

Women to admire

Listen to Claire and Mandy talking about women they admire. Claire speaks first.

Match the statements to the women they are talking about. Write **a** if the statement refers to the person Claire is referring to and **b** if it refers to the woman Mandy is talking about.

1 shows physical courage
2 possesses mental strength
3 enjoys her work
4 has worked to gain academic qualifications
5 speaks her mind
6 has spent time unemployed
7 ensures people are looked after
8 copes with situations when people disagree
9 has coped with the break up of a marriage

English in Use

1 Choose the correct word to fill the gap, and make any changes that are necessary. (Grammar Notes **13.3**)

EXAMPLE: Reading the governor's memoirs *reminded* Tom of details he had forgotten.

remember   remind   souvenir
memorise   reminder   memory

1 The book contains useful hints about ways of improving your ....

2 The spy had to .... all the information in the report before he burnt it.

3 Following the military victory, many firms produced .... to commemorate the great events.

4 These mountains .... me of the French Alps.

5 All members of the Tennyson Society were sent a .... that their annual subscriptions were due.

6 The author drew on happy .... of his childhood for a number of stories.

7 My mother .... meeting Ghandi when she was a child.

8 The judge .... the jury that they should not be affected by the accused's charming manner.

9 To publicise the film, there was a full-colour .... programme.

10 Do you .... what happened at the end of the film?

2 Complete each sentence with the correct form of the word in capitals. (Grammar Notes **13.2**.)

EXAMPLES: Some people found the film so *frightening* that they started to scream.   FRIGHTEN

Mary was so *frightened* by the film that she started to scream.   FRIGHTEN

1 The soldiers found the assault course quite ....   EXHAUST

2 The filmstar wanted to take a break after making three films in a year, but the offer was so .... that he couldn't refuse.   TEMPT

3 It's .... that such a nice girl should attract so much bad publicity.   SURPRISE

4 The safe breaker was .... at the difficulty he had getting the safe open.   FRUSTRATE

5 Being kidnapped was a .... ordeal for the young estate agent.   TERRIFY

6 The jury was .... by the evidence given by the spy.   FASCINATE

7 The general was talking about successful desert campaigns but he was so .... that three people fell asleep.   BORE

8 If anyone is .... in working on the dictionary of biography, would they please let us know?   INTEREST

9 The journey to Aunt Emily's cottage was very .... , especially in winter.   TIRE

10 Secretly, the politician was .... at the thought of having to face his critics.   SCARE

Reading

Tell the story of General Custer and explain the reasons behind the events.

Reading

A Before reading the article, discuss the following questions:
What's it like being famous?
What are the good and bad points?

B Now read the article where Boris Becker discusses his life. Seven sentences have been removed from the article. Choose from the sentences A–H the one which fits each gap (1–7). There is one extra sentence that you do not need to use.

LIVING WITH MY OWN LEGEND

Tennis star Boris Becker talks about his life

The brutal thing in my life is that I am famous twenty-four hours a day. I have no spare time and can never take a break. (1) .... Even after a tough tournament, when I need peace and quiet, I can never say: 'I am taking tomorrow off. Tomorrow I must relax.' I must give autographs. People are looking at me and trying to touch me. I am always under pressure. It's an enormous burden which creates enormous pressure. (2) .... I don't want to have to live in a castle like Michael Jackson, or like Ivan Lendl, who created his own empire with a few guard dogs. I want to be with normal people, go down to a bar, have a couple of beers and talk. (3) .... I have a great longing to be less well known one day. But it will probably never change. After big tournaments I cannot leave my apartment for two or three days. I am only free if I'm locked in my rooms, where no-one stares at me, no-one approaches me, no-one takes pictures, no-one says anything about me. (4) .... That's the toughest thing – that people can judge you and occasionally, convict you, although they don't even know you, people who tell me I'm happy or sad, who explain to me why I lost or won a match. They believe they know how I feel and think. And everyone is on familiar terms with you. (5) .... That's tough. Sure, one could say: 'I am well paid for this.' But should everything be ruled by money? (6) .... Only a few made it – only a few managed to say: 'No.' I try, and manage more often, to say 'No.' I've become stronger and freer. 'Would you like this contract?' 'No!' 'Why?' 'I've enough.' I have nothing against money but I know that money isn't everything. Sometimes I look at myself in the mirror and I am puzzled. I am surprised that I am this megastar. I, Boris Becker, from Leimen. And then I laugh at myself because I can't understand it. It is hard to understand that I am a legend at my age. (7) .... Old people, retired people, poor people. They often think that what I'm doing, and how, is great. Then it is beautiful to be a legend. Yet I long for the day when I will be unknown again.

A They call you by your first name and slap you on your back and, when you're in the middle of the meal in a restaurant, they ask you for your autograph.

B I think this is why so many stars move to solitary islands.

C So it is not amusing to be told how you should behave, how you should live your life.

D The price of fame was much too high for many people.

E But there is something positive, something beautiful in this, too – most of all when people like me who have nothing to do with tennis.

F Sure, there is often a certain distance with some people, which is hard to bridge, but with goodwill we make it.

G Except for the newspapers.

H My job goes on around the clock.

Talking Points

Section 1

Work with a partner and discuss the photographs and the questions.

What's happening in these pictures?

What makes people want to see/touch the people in the photos?

What makes them popular?

Section 2

Working in groups, find out who are the different people that members of the group admire.

QUESTIONNAIRE

1   Do you admire any particular public figure?   YES/NO

2   Which group does the person belong to?

Tick as appropriate:

pop singer
film star
sportsperson
musician
writer
other

3   Do you collect things connected with your idol?   YES/NO

If yes, what? Tick as appropriate:

photos
souvenirs
records
books
posters

4   Have you ever joined a fan club or a supporters club?   YES/NO

5   If yes, what benefits did this give you?

Listening

Oliver Cromwell

Listen to the discussion about Oliver Cromwell and answer the following questions.

1 What century did Cromwell live in?

2 What was the name of the King of England against whom Cromwell fought?

3 Did Cromwell become king himself?

4 When was the monarchy restored?

5 Whose rights did Cromwell fight for?

6 What countries did he keep united by his action?

7 Who did the Glorious Revolution of 1688 put on the throne of England?

8 What did Cromwell do in Ireland?

9 Of the three speakers, who speaks for Cromwell? Who speaks against him and who adopts a neutral position?

Writing

Biography

 A Part 1
Look at this brief biography

Marilyn Monroe was born in Los Angeles in 1926. Her real name was Norma Jean Baker. After an unhappy childhood, which was spent largely in foster homes, she became a model and started to get small parts in films. Realising her potential, the film studio she worked for launched a big publicity campaign, as a result of which she got better parts. Among her best films are 'Bus Stop' and 'Some Like it Hot'. Although she wished to be taken seriously as an actress and studied at Lee Strasberg's Actors' Studio in New York, she remained famous as a 'dumb blonde'. While at the height of her fame, she married the playwright, Arthur Miller in 1956, but this, like her two previous marriages, ended in divorce. She died in mysterious circumstances in 1961.

Time references:

In a biography, you need to make it clear what the order of events is, and instead of just writing a list, you can make a connection between events, by using words like:

Before starting her career in films, she worked as a photographic model.

After a childhood spent in foster homes, she …

You can also emphasise when things happened by using words like *when*, *while* and *during*.
While at the height of her fame, she …

Part 2
B Look at these notes about Martin Luther King and write his biography.

b 1929	in Atlanta, Georgia, USA, son of a Baptist pastor
	Studied theology at Morehouse College and Boston University
	Became a pastor in Montgomery, Alabama
1955	Ph.D at Boston University
1956	Organised boycott of buses in Montgomery
1960s	Worked against the segregation laws that operated against blacks in the southern states of USA
	Believed in non-violent resistance
	Famous speech: 'I have a dream that one day this nation will rise up and live out the true meaning of its creed: We hold these truths to be self-evident: that all men are created equal'
1963	Civil Rights march in Washington, D.C. in which 250,000 people took part
	Was successful in getting the legislation changed with the passing by the US Congress of the Civil Rights Act (1964) and Voting Act (1965)
1964	Awarded an honorary doctorate from Yale University, the Kennedy Peace Prize and the Nobel Peace Prize
From 1965	Turned his attention to social laws that operated against blacks in the north of USA
1968	Assassinated in Memphis

Part 3
C An international magazine for young people is running a competition with a prize of computer equipment for the school whose student writes the best biography of a person they admire. Your class teacher has encouraged all the members of your class to enter. Write your entry for the competition. Write between 120 and 180 words.

English in Use

1 Complete the gaps in the text with *one* word. Use the words below and seven others.

editorial   articles   quality   reviews
news   biased   circulation   mass

Newspapers play a very large part in determining how we form an opinion about people in the public eye. Although some people .... (1) the view that newspapers are objective, many others believe them to be very .... (2) in their reporting. This .... (3) of objectivity is seen in different parts of the paper – in the reporting of .... (4) stories, in feature .... (5), in cartoons and in the .... (6), where the editor of the paper puts forward his opinions.

Newspapers need to .... (7) money, and they do this in .... (8) ways, by trying to increase the .... (9) of copies that they sell (increasing their .... (10) figures) and by getting money from people and companies who pay to advertise in the paper.

In Britain the papers with a .... (11) market are the tabloids, which often run sensational stories. The .... (12) papers, which people read to .... (13) up-to-date with events at home and abroad, have much lower circulation figures, although they also provide .... (14) of the latest films and books. Most daily papers have a sports section .... (15) some readers find the most interesting section.

2 Phrasal Verbs

Complete the sentences with a phrasal verb based on *call*.

EXAMPLE: I'm afraid the manager is not here – he's been <u>called away</u> .

1 The police were .... to investigate the man's mysterious death.

2 Mrs Jones next door has plenty of people to .... if ever she needs help.

3 Tim's got a very demanding job, and he's often .... on business at very short notice.

4 The meeting had to be .... because of bad weather.

5 Don't hesitate to .... if you feel like some company.

6 I'll .... you at 7 o'clock and we'll go and see that film at the Odeon.

7 The doctor sometimes gets .... at night to attend to urgent cases.

8 The government .... aid from other countries to help with the disaster.

9 Roger is out at the moment but if you leave a message he will .... as soon as he can.

10 My father was .... to serve in the army just a month after war began.

3 Word-formation

Complete the sentences with the correct form of the word in capitals.

EXAMPLES: Anna told her brother not to be so <u>babyish</u> .   BABY

The children looked quite <u>wonderful</u> dressed up in their party clothes.   WONDER

1 The politician's .... good looks made him attractive to many voters.   BOY

2 This fly spray is .... to family pets.   HARM

3 A .... of people turned out to watch the match.   HAND

4 Such .... bad behaviour did little to make the princess popular with the public.   CHILD

5 The soldier was .... to carry out his orders exactly.   CARE

6 A .... athlete knows it's unwise to stop training hard.   SUCCESS

7 Although my mother is now in her fifties, she has a lot of .... mannerisms.   GIRL

8 It was .... of you to send flowers when I was in hospital.   THOUGHT

9 The tennis-player took a .... of water and spat it out.   MOUTH

10 The cook added a .... of sugar to the pudding.   TEASPOON

unit 14

VICTIMS AND VILLAINS

Lead-in **1** What can you see in these photos? What kinds of crime (major or minor) cause you problems in everyday life?

Match the criminal in List **1** with the description of the offence in List **2**.

List 1

1 a shoplifter
2 an arsonist
3 a burglar
4 a murderer
5 a pickpocket
6 a kidnapper
7 a smuggler
8 a mugger
9 a forger
10 a vandal

List 2

a sets fire to buildings
b attacks someone in a public place to get money
c kills
d takes things from people's bags and pockets
e steals from a shop
f seizes another person and takes them away
g destroys property
h tries to take things illegally into another country
i steals things from people's houses
j copies something to trick other people

 Choose the correct word for each gap.

> accused crime arrested found
> custody evidence court
> committed plead prison defence
> verdict charged witnesses acquit
> sentence convict fine bail

*I*f the police think that someone has ....(1) a crime, then that person is ....(2) and taken to a police station. Within forty-eight hours he or she must be ....(3) with an offence, or released. If a charge has been made, the accused is usually released on ....(4) until he or she stands trial at a later date. For very serious offences, such as murder, the ....(5) is remanded in ....(6), which means being kept in prison while awaiting trial. When someone appears in ....(7) before a judge and jury they have the right to be represented by a lawyer who speaks for the ....(8). When the trial begins, the accused has to ....(9), that is to say whether he or she is guilty or not guilty. The defence and the prosecution then call ....(10) to give evidence. After all the ....(11) has been heard, the jury retires to consider the ....(12). They can ....(13), which means they consider the accused innocent, or they can ....(14). If the accused has been ....(15) guilty, then the judge has to pass ....(16). He may impose a ....(17) or send the offender to ....(18). It depends on the nature of the ....(19).

Reading

A What clothes or shoes are very fashionable at the moment?

How can clothes indicate what sports' teams you support or people you admire?

Why do some clothes or shoes become extremely fashionable?

Dressing to kill leads to murder in Chicago

Being 'dressed to kill' is rapidly acquiring a macabre connotation in the streets of downtown Chicago, Detroit and Los Angeles. With disturbing frequency, young people, usually teenagers, are being murdered for the shirt or jacket on their
5 back or the shoes on their feet. The phenomenon has been called 'clothing-related violence', or 'killing to be cool' and the fatal fashion appears to be catching on. The most recent recorded incident occurred in Chicago and involved a 19-year-old man, Calvin Walsh. Mr Walsh was walking on the city's
10 West Side on Saturday wearing a brightly-coloured Cincinnati Bengals bomber jacket. Such jackets, and others featuring football team logos like those of the Washington Redskins and Chicago Bears, costing up to $200 (£130), are all the rage. And that's the problem. Mr Walsh's 'offence' was not that he was
15 wearing the wrong team colours. It was merely that the stranger who accosted him wanted his jacket. When Mr Walsh tried to make a run for it he was shot in the back and killed.

The trend was first spotted last autumn after the murder of a 24-year-old Chicago man by four youths who liked his jacket.
20 In November and December, Hawks jackets were the cause of two more killings. In Detroit last November, a school pupil was found dead and shoeless: his attacker had taken his $70 Nike sneakers. Police in Los Angeles and New York reported similar robberies. One mother whose son survived the theft of the $175
25 gym shoes he was wearing told a Chicago newspaper: 'These children are out here stealing from one another to be cool. It's a sad situation. Their parents can't afford to buy the stuff, so they do whatever they can to get it.' A Los Angeles policeman put it another way, 'The individual wants to hang on to the jacket
30 because he paid so much for it, so they just blow him away.' In some cases, the murders do appear to have been related to gang or team loyalties. Wearing the 'wrong' colour shoes, or even shoelaces, is enough to get you killed in some Los Angeles neighbourhoods. But the clothes-related violence phenomenon also reflects the cheapness of human life in some of America's inner city ghettos, the ready availability of guns to young people, and the poverty in which many of them live.

Ironically, perhaps, given the fashionable trend in the USA and Britain away from school uniform, the Detroit Board of Education has approved a schools dress code to be implemented this autumn in an attempt to control the problem of clothes-related violence.

B Find a word or phrase in the text that in context has a similar meaning to:

Paragraph 1
1 a frightening meaning
2 deadly
3 becoming popular
4 symbols
5 very fashionable
6 went up to him threateningly

Paragraph 2
7 noticed
8 expressed it differently
9 keep
10 shoot him
11 connected with

Paragraph 3
12 put into practice

C Work in pairs. Ask and answer the following questions.

1 What does the phrase 'dressed to kill' mean in this context? What does it normally mean?

2 What is the reason for the murders?

3 What happened to Mr Walsh?

4 When did murders of this kind begin?

5 What is meant by the 'wrong' colour shoes?

6 What reasons are given for these crimes?

7 What steps are being taken to control this problem?

Grammar: *revision of conditionals*

 A Match the two halves of the sentences. (Grammar Notes **5.1**, **12.2**, **14.1**)

1 If you give me your address,

2 If the garden were bigger,

3 If we had known about the bomb in time,

4 If the rescue workers had had better equipment,

5 If the experiment fails this time,

6 If we understood these coded messages,

7 If there is a further reduction in the price,

8 If his fees weren't so incredibly high,

9 If it hadn't been raining heavily,

a they could have saved more lives.

b I would ask him to represent me in court.

c we could arrest all the spies.

d the accident would probably not have happened.

e we could have evacuated the building.

f I'll send you the details.

g I could grow enough vegetables to feed us all year.

h we must abandon our research.

i we will make no profit.

B Re-write these sentences using *unless*. (Grammar Notes **14.2**)

EXAMPLE: If you haven't passed the test, we cannot consider your application.
Unless you have passed the test, we cannot consider your application.

1 If you are not a member, you cannot come in.

2 You will lose a day's pay if you don't produce a medical certificate.

3 There will be more accidents if traffic lights are not installed.

4 If we don't replace these old windows, we will freeze next winter.

5 If he isn't caught quickly, he will commit more crimes.

Complete these sentences. Begin with *unless*.

6 ....
you cannot get a job as an interpreter.

7 ....
you will not be allowed to enter that country.

8 ....
the shop will not accept your cheque.

9 ....
inflation will get out of control.

10 ....
that wall is likely to collapse.

C Three of these sentences are *incorrect*. The others are correct. Can you identify the incorrect sentences?

1 Even I had known, I wouldn't have told you, and I won't tell you now.

2 If I am ill on the day of the exam, could I possibly take it on another day?

3 If I forget to put the postcode on, does it make any difference?

4 If you haven't seen this film before, you don't know what you've missed.

5 If you would just come this way, I'll show you to the manager's office.

6 If we had a faster computer, we could have solved those problems easily.

7 If Martin is staying, I'm going.

8 If I would help you now, I know you wouldn't help me later.

9 If you are not sure about this, say so now.

10 Well, if you don't think John is being unreasonable about this, what do you think he is being?

11 If I would dig in that spot, would I find the treasure?

12 If you like Rachel, why didn't you ask her out?

13 If I could understand Swedish, I would translate the letter for you.

14 If I come back tomorrow, might there be some tickets left?

15 If the sun would shine, we would go for a picnic.

Listening

Being arrested

Listen to Rebecca describing an occasion on which she was arrested.
Complete the gaps in the text with *one* or *two* words.

Rebecca went out for a meal on her .... (1). She drank .... (2) of wine and had another drink later at a .... (3), which she left at about .... (4) a.m. When she was driving, she tried to turn .... (5) down a one-way street and was stopped by .... (6) police officers. They asked her to blow into a breathalyser and after .... (7) seconds a .... (8) light came on, so they arrested her. They waited for a .... (9) to arrive and then took her to the police station. At the station she had another test on a different machine which was .... (10) and more .... (11). The limit was .... (12) but she only scored .... (13) on the first test and .... (14) on the second, so the police had to let her go. The whole experience lasted about .... (15) minutes. Since then she has been careful not to drink more than .... (16) units of alcohol.

English in Use

 Rob, steal

Complete these sentences with the correct form of *rob* or *steal*. (Grammar Notes **14.3**)

EXAMPLES: Captain Blood __*stole*__ the crown jewels from the Tower of London in 1671. Since that time the Tower of London has never been __*robbed*__ .

1 Two banks have been .... in Cambridge this week.

2 He was found guilty of committing murder during a ....

3 Although the house was broken into, nothing was ....

4 Last week, Mrs Roberts .... from supermarkets on three occasions.

5 'I've been ....!' shouted Lady Brookes when she realised her necklace was missing.

6 Two .... were arrested by the police but the third escaped.

7 By the time he was fifteen, Tom was addicted to .... fast cars.

8 Don't leave your briefcase inside your car – it might get ....

9 Robin Hood .... the rich to pay the poor.

10 Marjorie was ashamed of .... money from her mother's purse.

 A Fault, blame

Re-write these sentences using the word *fault*. (Grammar Notes **14.4**)

EXAMPLES: Who is to blame for breaking the window?
Whose fault is it that the window is broken?

1 Richard was to blame for the accident.

2 They blamed the pilot for the crash.

3 The victim of this crime is partly to blame.

4 Don't blame me!

5 I will not accept any blame whatsoever.

B Re-write these sentences using the verb *to blame* in an appropriate form.

1 The accident was the other driver's fault.

2 People said that the heavy losses were the manager's fault.

3 The cyclist agreed that he was partly at fault.

4 It's not Peter's fault!

5 It's not your fault at all.

Reading

A How can criminals be persuaded to give up crime?
Why do young people begin to commit crimes?
What is the best way to deal with young people who commit crimes?

Lessons on a life of crime

It is Monday morning at the Cantell School in Southampton and a slight, attractive man of 45, wearing plain grey clothes, introduces himself to a group of 40 children. 'My name is John. How old are you … 13 or 14? Well, I've spent as many years as you've been alive in prison. At the moment, I am serving a seven-year sentence. This is my parole licence.' He waves a paper in front of them, then picks up three closely-typed pages and continues: 'This is my criminal record. Detention centre, Borstal, prison. That's a wasted life.' John Bower's visit is part of the children's personal development course, a chance to explore ideas about responsibility that they have already discussed with their teacher, John Jones. For Mr Bowers, it is a chance to redeem himself after 30 years of crime. On his release last February, he contacted New Bridge, a voluntary organisation that helps ex-prisoners find employment. He began giving talks about prison life to schools where the children might be at risk of getting into trouble. 'Those of us who are concerned with prisoners believe that the process of caring has to continue when they leave prison,' says Eric McGraw, the director of New Bridge. 'The main problem is that people are let out of prison with £20 in their pocket, no job and nowhere to go, and we expect them not to commit crimes again.'

At Cantell, a large secondary school, Mr Bowers writes 'prison' and 'prisoner' on the board and asks the children to suggest what the words mean. Hands go up and 'bars', 'bad news', 'lonely', 'isolation', 'terrible food', 'shame', and 'violence' are written down. 'Boredom' says one girl. 'That's exactly right,' says Mr Bowers. 'What do you think of me for wasting my life in a place like that? Honestly?' There is an awkward pause, then a boy at the back of the class whispers 'thick!' and everybody laughs. Later some of the questions reveal traces of anger, perhaps because the children have been victims of crime. 'Did you ever burgle a house at Christmas?' one girl demands. 'No,' Mr Bowers says. 'In some crazy moral way, I laid low at Christmas – as if that justified doing it at other times of the year'. Another child asks whether he had any regrets. 'You try and blot out what you are doing to people,' he explains. 'If I had robbed your house, it wouldn't have been anything personal. If I'd had any conscience, I wouldn't have lasted five minutes.'

Mr Bowers has written on the board all the words the children came up with. 'That's right,' he says. 'All these words apply to me.' This is the heart of his message. 'I'm here to say that all these words will apply to you too, if you embark on a life of crime, or waste your life through drugs, alcohol or, as I did, through imagining the world owes you a living.' He asks them to think about how their parents would feel if any of them were arrested for shoplifting or stealing a car radio. There is some uncomfortable shuffling as they volunteer 'ashamed' and 'upset'. He asks why they think people commit crime. Short of money, revenge on a society that does nothing for you, problems at home, no friends or the wrong sort of friends, they reply. But he accepts no excuses. 'Most prisoners are very selfish people,' he say. 'They'd rather rob than get a job. No friends, jealousy and idleness – this covers 99 per cent of the prison population.'

Mr Jones suggests that the children should tell Mr Bowers what they think of him now they've heard what he has to say. Replies come thick and fast: friendly, honest, willing, a good citizen, trustworthy, 'nearly a normal person'. In 40 minutes Mr Bowers has undergone a journey that is vital to his self-respect, from a criminal whom one boy said he wouldn't like to meet on a dark night, to being an ex-offender – 'nearly a normal person'. It is, after all, a course in personal development.

B Find a word or phrase in the text which in context is similar in meaning to:

Paragraph 1
1 time in prison
2 permission to leave prison
3 list of criminal convictions
4 regain his self-respect

Paragraph 2
5 stupid
6 slight indications
7 sense of right and wrong

Paragraph 3
8 begin
9 moving the feet

C Are the following statements *true* or *false*?

1 John Bowers has been a criminal for 14 years.

2 He has finished his prison sentence.

3 At first the children are hostile to Mr Bowers.

4 The children feel embarrassed.

5 Mr Bowers writes up all the words the children use to describe him.

6 Mr Bowers is more critical of criminals than the children are.

7 Mr Bowers makes a good impression on the children.

Reading

A Look at the map and read the text.

Two armed raiders killed in shoot-out with police

Police marksmen shot dead two armed robbers and wounded another yesterday, after a chase through North London. The three men had sprayed bullets and gunshot at the police officers, wounding one in the ankle, in their attempt to escape
5 after an unsuccessful raid on a post-office. It was the fourth occasion in two years that police have shot dead armed robbers. Commander John O'Connor said that his officers had acted 'correctly and courageously'. They had prevented any members of the public from getting hurt in the gun battle.
10 The incident has been justified by police as the inevitable response to armed robbery.

The incident began just before 9 am when the three men, who the police suspected of specialising in ramming security vehicles, pushed a steel girder out of the back of their van and,
15 reversing at high speed, used it as a battering ram to smash through the rear doors of the post office. Although the three, in balaclavas and motorcycle helmets, got into the post office, they failed to reach the area where valuables were kept. They had chosen the wrong doors. They abandoned their attempt at
20 robbery and drove off in a stolen car. Police who had been secretly observing them, gave chase but the robbers abandoned the car after driving into a side-street. Commander O'Connor said that the robbers then tried what he described as 'a classic ploy'. They ran down an alleyway so that the police car could
25 not follow them. The alley leads to a footbridge over a railway line and they had left a getaway car on the other side of the bridge. When the robbers got on to the bridge they opened fire. Commander O'Connor said, 'My officers shouted a warning 'Armed police! Drop your weapons and surrender!' but the
30 robbers continued firing and police officers returned fire.' He denied suggestions that officers were waiting for the men and 'staking out' the stolen getaway car. The robbers continued firing, spraying bullets everywhere. In all, about thirty shots were fired. Some bullets hit parked cars and spent cartridges
35 still littered the scene several hours later.

Mr Paul Duego, who lives nearby, said. "During the shooting, one old man was right in the middle of it. He turned back and said, 'What are they doing – are they shooting a film?' He was completely oblivious to what was really happening." Tony
40 Dewsnapp, aged 48, a married man, died at the scene. James Farrell, 52, also married, died in hospital. The third man, who has not been named, has shoulder and leg wounds but is not in a serious condition. The robbers were armed with a sawn-off shotgun, a Colt 45 revolver and a Luger pistol. Commander
45 O'Connor said that the police regretted incidents involving loss of life and extended sympathy to the dead men's families.

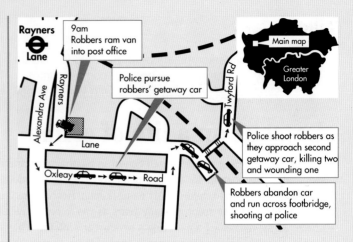

B Find a word or phrase in the text which in context is similar in meaning to:

Paragraph 1
1 men who shoot accurately
2 bravely
3 unavoidable reaction

Paragraph 2
4 crashing into
5 large metal bar
6 going backwards
7 gave up
8 narrow street
9 started shooting
10 watching and waiting

Paragraph 3
11 unaware
12 were sorry about
13 offered

C Work in pairs. Discuss the following questions. You will have to 'read between the lines' to produce your answers. Refer to the map.

1 How did the robbers prepare for the raid?

2 How did they feel when they got into the post office?

3 What did the robbers say to each other when they were inside the post office?

4 How did the robbers react when they first saw the police?

5 How much did the police know in advance?

6 Where were the armed police?

7 Describe the reactions of the old man.

D Write a description of the incident

1 from the point of view of one of the policemen who gave chase.

2 from the point of view of the wounded robber.

Talking Points

Section 1

Read the poem: working with a partner, how many strange points can you find?

One fine day in the middle of the night
Two dead men got up to fight
Back to back they faced each other
Drew their swords and shot each other.

Anon

Section 2

When people do wrong, how should they be punished?

Working in groups of three, look at the list and put these actions in order, with the one you consider to be most serious first, and the least serious last.

1 A man was driving a car and a child ran out into the road. Although he tried to stop, he hit the child, who was killed.

2 A seven-year old boy took his friend's bicycle and hid it where it could not be found.

3 A woman was beaten by her husband for many years, and then one day, she attacked him with a kitchen knife and killed him.

4 A teacher sold a group of students a copy of the examination paper in advance and was then discovered by the head of the school.

5 Two teenagers went into a shop after school and stole three bars of chocolate.

6 A woman made a serious mistake on the firm's computer, but blamed the error on her colleague, who was dismissed.

7 Two visitors to Britain brought a dog into the country from overseas, although they knew it was against the law.

What punishment is suitable in each situation?

Section 3

Describe the man in the photo.
How will his life be different?

Listening

Witnessing a crime

Listen to three people describing crimes they have seen or experienced. Tick the box if the statements apply to the incident described by that speaker.

	Speaker 1	Speaker 2	Speaker 3
1 happened in the evening			
2 committed by teenagers			
3 police were informed			
4 speaker was very upset			
5 damage was done			
6 more than one criminal			
7 criminals were not caught			
8 nothing was stolen			
9 happened quickly			
10 happened indoors			
11 speaker was near criminals			
12 criminals had a weapon			
13 speaker could recognise the criminal			

Writing

Story writing

 A The first sentence of a short story or novel must seize the attention of the readers and encourage them to read on. First sentences may:

a introduce a character
b describe the background or setting
c start the plot by describing action
d describe the start of a journey
e flashback to a time before the beginning of the story
f describe something mysterious and unexplained
g make a statement about life, with which you may agree or disagree

What kind of first sentences are 1–7? Do they make you want to read the rest of the story? Match the sentences with the descriptions a–g. You may choose more than one description for some sentences.

> 1 It was a bright cold day in April and the clocks were striking thirteen.
>
> 2 Many years later, as he faced the firing squad, Colonel Aureliano Buendia was to remember that distant afternoon when his father took him to discover ice.
>
> 3 All happy families resemble one another, but each unhappy family is unhappy in its own way.
>
> 4 I will begin the story of my adventures with a certain morning early in the month of June, the year of grace 1751, when I took the key for the last time out of the door of my father's house.
>
> 5 This is the saddest story I have ever heard.
>
> 6 It is a truth universally acknowledged, that a single man in possession of a good fortune must be in want of a wife.
>
> 7 The cell door slammed behind Rubashov.
>
> 8 Someone must have been telling lies about Joseph K., for without having done anything wrong he was arrested one morning.

B Choose one of these first sentences. Continue and finish the story in your own way. Write about 150 words.

English in Use

1 Phrasal Verbs

Some phrasal verbs consist of *three* words. Complete the sentences using the phrasal verbs below. Use the correct form of the verb.

to get away with	to get rid of
to make off with	to catch up with
to break out of	to come forward with
to face up to	to keep up with
to come up with	to make up for

1 Bill decided to study for a university degree while in prison in order to .... the opportunities he had wasted in his life.

2 The convicted burglars had to meet the victims of their crimes and .... the distress they had caused.

3 Charles committed the robbery because he thought he could .... it but he was arrested at the airport.

4 Several witnesses have .... new evidence.

5 The policeman ran after the thief and soon .... him.

6 Andrew spent a lot of money in order to .... the latest fashions.

7 The robbers .... the stolen car by dumping it in a lake.

8 Scientists have .... a new and effective way of identifying DNA in blood samples.

9 The thief smashed the window of the shop and .... some diamond rings.

10 Three prisoners .... their prison cell last night.

2 In prison, in the prison

Complete the sentences with the phrases below. (Grammar Notes **14.5**)

EXAMPLE: Mr Smith goes ..*to church*.. every Sunday. Deliver these supplies *to the church* in the square.

in prison	in a prison	from prison
to prison	in court	in the court
from hospital	to hospital	to the hospital
in hospital		

1 Three days after his operation, Mr Jones was discharged ....

2 After finishing work, Peter drove .... to visit his sick mother.

3 Paul was released .... after serving ten years.

4 Mrs Richards was admitted .... hospital with suspected appendicitis.

5 She has been .... for three weeks and is not well enough to leave.

6 The arrested man will appear .... on Tuesday charged with murder.

7 Michael's company has to install a new ventilation system ....

8 For six years John worked as a cook ....

9 This prisoner is expected to remain .... until he dies.

10 He has been sent .... for six years.

3 Word-formation

Complete the sentences with the correct form of the word in capitals.

EXAMPLES: The thief escaped into the ..*darkness*.. of the night.   DARK

The prisoner said he was innocent but the ..*reality*.. was that he was guilty.   REAL

1 The police inspector insisted on .... at meetings.   PUNCTUAL

2 My grandmother suffered from .... from the age of fifty.   DEAF

3 The accused was not aware of the .... of the charge.   SERIOUS

4 It was just his own .... that made John act that way.   STUPID

5 The prison warder showed a lot of .... to all the inmates.   KIND

6 There was so much .... among the hospital staff that there were not enough people to look after the patients.   ILL

7 The police assured the man that their enquiries were merely a ....   FORMAL

8 The new police chief was not at all concerned about his .... , he just wanted to get the job done.   POPULAR

unit 15
LIES, TRICKS AND DECEIT

Lead-in | **1** | What is happening in these pictures? What tricks and deception are involved?
What other examples can you think of people using tricks?

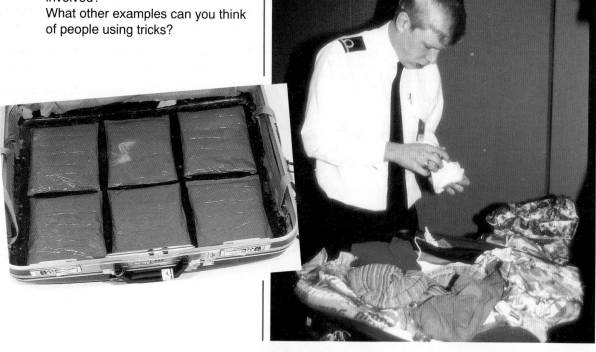

2 Choose the correct word to fit the gap in each sentence.

disguised	tricked	cheats	betraying
posed	suspected	forged	misled
	impersonating	deceive	

1 The thief .... as an electrician in order to be allowed into the house.

2 The soldier got across the border .... as a woman.

3 In order to get some money the young man .... his father's signature on the cheque.

4 No-one believed that their neighbour was a spy – she had managed to .... everybody.

5 The person .... of the theft was the woman who cleaned the office.

6 People who reveal secrets are .... the trust placed in them.

7 I never play cards with Rachel because she always ....

8 The businessman was .... into signing the cheque.

9 The woman was found guilty of .... a police officer.

10 The politician revealed that he had been .... by reports in the newspaper.

3 Choose the correct word to fit the gap in each sentence.

fake	espionage	deception	
swindler	artificial	fraud	lie
	counterfeit	hoax	false

1 John was accused of passing .... money.

2 The museum thought the painting was a genuine Constable, but it turned out to be a ....

3 The actress was wearing .... eyelashes.

4 I liked the way the restaurant looked, apart from the fact that there were .... flowers on the tables.

5 After a bomb was discovered at the station, the police received a number of .... phonecalls.

6 The man's a .... ; he got money from those people by telling them deliberate lies.

7 The only way the accountant could see of making some money was through ....

8 The company warned its staff against industrial .... by rival companies.

9 The accused was found guilty of obtaining money through ....

10 The judge said the young conman had been living a ....

Reading

 A Have you ever had anything stolen? How did you feel?

MOMENT OF TRUTH

Jennifer describes how she learned to stop stealing.

The first time I took something which didn't belong to me, I was thirteen. That tortoiseshell hairslide became my most treasured possession, even after the box where I hid it had filled up
5 with pens and purses 'mislaid' by the other girls at school. I don't think I was ever suspected – not even later, when an expensive watch disappeared from the shop where I worked. Then I married, and my husband believed I was a marvellous
10 housekeeper when luxuries appeared which we couldn't possibly afford.

After my baby was born, our doctor asked me to help look after his mother, who was in her seventies and almost blind. She had a lovely old
15 house, full of nice furniture and antiques. We got on really well and I was very happy working for her. I'd read to her and she'd tell me I should have studied, gone to college.

There were three things in that house I really
20 liked: a small silver box, one of her rings and a framed mirror. I stole them, one by one. I thought that as the old lady was blind she would not realise they were missing. Just before she died, she changed her will and left me the silver box, the
25 ring and the mirror 'to remember her by'.

I have never stolen since. I went to college as a mature student and now work with the elderly.

B Explain the meaning of these words and phrases:

1 my most treasured possession (*line 3*)

2 mislaid (*line 5*)

3 suspected (*line 6*)

4 luxuries (*line 10*)

5 antiques (*line 15*)

6 I'd read to her (*line 17*)

7 missing (*line 23*)

8 a mature student (*line 27*)

C Now answer these questions.

1 Name the things Jennifer stole.

2 Why did Jennifer like working for the old lady?

3 What made her think the old lady would not be suspicious if things disappeared?

4 What happened when the old lady died?

5 Do you think that the old lady realised that her things had been stolen?

6 How did Jennifer feel?

7 How did her life change?

Grammar: *indirect speech (1)*

 A You may like to refer to Grammar Notes **15.1** first. Now look at these sentences.

'What time will you get here tomorrow, John?' asked Peter.

Peter asked John what time he would get there the following day.

How many changes have been made in the second sentence?

Look carefully at: *verb form*
word order
pronouns
time words
place words
punctuation

B Now change these sentences into *indirect speech*.

1 'When will you give me the tickets, Sally,' asked Sarah.
Sarah asked Sally when ....

2 'What will you say at the meeting tomorrow?' Michael asked me.
Michael asked me what ....

3 'Where will you put your new bookcase, David?' asked Victoria.
Victoria asked David where ....

4 'Will you be staying in this village until tomorrow, Jane?' said William.
William asked Jane if ....

5 'Will you come by yourself or bring your family, John?' asked Robert.
Robert asked John if ....

6 'Will you help me move these filing cabinets, Arnold?' said Lucy.
Lucy asked Arnold if ....

Remember that in real life situations the words referring to time and place only change if the time and place have really changed. Remember also that if people report what someone else has said immediately after they have said it, after making a telephone call, for example, they usually repeat the exact words that were used. Exercises on indirect speech normally assume that some time has passed since the words were actually spoken.

C List the changes that have been made in these sentences.

1 'What is the answer, Ian?' asked Paul.
Paul asked Ian what the answer was.

2 'Do you know Ann's address, Jack?' asked Melissa.
Melissa asked Jack if he knew Ann's address.

3 'Did you bring the map and compass, Patricia?' asked Katherine.
Katherine asked Patricia if she had brought the map and compass.

4 'How much money have you won, Brian?' asked Janet.
Janet asked Brian how much money he had won.

D Change these sentences into *indirect speech*.

1 'What can I do to improve things,?' Maria asked me.

2 'Where is the emergency exit?' I asked the stewardess.

3 'Why did you see a lawyer, Mary?' I asked.

4 'Where have you put the passports?' Tony asked me.

5 'What do you want to do tomorrow, Lisa?' asked John.

6 'Do you like spicy food, Bernard?' asked Julia.

7 'Did you enjoy the performance?' Mrs Osborne asked me.

8 'Are you coming to my party next week, Charles?' asked Louise.

9 'Can you wait two more days?' the shop assistant asked me.

10 'Does your brother always visit you on Saturdays, Lucy?' asked Jenny.

Listening

The great tortoise mystery

 A Are these statements *true* or *false*?

1 The story is about a friend of the speaker.

2 Peter was the only student in the house.

3 The landlady lived in the same house as Peter.

4 The tortoise was given as a birthday present.

5 The landlady was interviewed on television.

6 The landlady gave the tortoise too much food.

B Work in pairs.
Re-tell the story.
Do you know any similar stories?
Is it right to play practical jokes on people?

English in Use

1 Prepositions

Complete the sentences with the correct preposition.

1 When Mary's father was sent to prison her relatives tried to keep the truth .... her.

2 Philip lied .... his age.

3 Anthony told such convincing stories that everyone was completely taken .... by them.

4 It's best to be honest .... your past.

5 'My boyfriend was with me all the evening, and I'll swear .... it in court,' the young woman told the police.

6 We know this man was responsible .... the disappearance of the money, but he refuses to confess .... it.

7 The schoolboy was tricked .... helping the gang.

8 What you are saying is far .... the truth of the matter.

9 Alexander lied .... his whole family about where he had spent the last three months.

10 The heiress was cheated .... of her inheritance.

2 For questions 1–15, read the text below and look carefully at each line. Some of the lines are correct, and some have a word which should not be there. Tick the correct lines and underline the wrong words in the incorrect lines.

EXAMPLES: 0 ✓
00 <u>to</u>

A distressing incident

0 Thank you for your letter in which you tell

00 to me all the good news about your family.

1 Nothing much has changed since you were last

2 visited us. However, my grandmother is rather

3 upset right now because of a deep distressing

4 incident that it happened to her while she was

5 being shopping. She went into a shop to buy

6 two birthday cards for her grandchildren. She

7 knew they wouldn't cost her much so did she

8 checked her purse before she entered into the

9 shop to make sure she had enough change.

10 While she looking at the cards, my grandmother

11 noticed by a woman of about her own age

12 standing near her. When she went to pay for she

13 realised her purse was no longer than inside her

14 bag! The woman must have been stolen it! You

15 don't expect elderly ladies to be the thieves, do you?

Reading

What do confidence tricksters do?
What techniques do they use?

Work with a partner. Student A reads text **a**, and Student B reads text **b**.

As you read your own text, write down the answers to the questions. When you and your partner have finished, compare your answers. Then read your partner's text and compare it with your own.

1 How old is Mark now?
2 How old was he when he committed the crimes?
3 What did he pretend to be?
4 How much did he say he earned?
5 How much was the mortgage for? And what was the cost of the house?
6 How did he get money to spend?
7 What did he spend the money on?
8 What did his father do when he realised what Mark was doing?
9 What did his lawyer say about him?
10 What did the judge say about him?
11 What was his sentence?

Text **a**

Four years' jail and a ruined life for conman, 18

'I took them for a million,' he boasts.

Teenage conman Mark Acklom, who duped a building society into giving him a £500,000 mortgage, began a four-year jail sentence last night with his make-believe world in ruins. He was 16 when he swindled £1 million to live a champagne lifestyle.

Now 18 and virtually penniless, he stood stony-faced in court as Judge Brian Pryor branded him 'utterly selfish and completely ruthless.'

The fresh-faced public schoolboy glanced towards his family as he was led from the dock. 'Everything was so easy. I took about a million, I suppose. They've got to be mugs, all of them. It's their stupid fault,' he told reporters.

The judge dismissed defence claims that Acklom was suffering from mental illness. He said: 'You show all the typical symptoms of a conman, telling sophisticated lies to your victims, cleverly adapted to suit their circumstances'.

While still a sixth-former at Eastbourne College, Sussex, smooth-talking Acklom posed as an international investments advisor earning £200,000 a year to trick a building society. It gave him a £466,000 loan for a luxury house in South London. The plausible youngster also hired private jets and drove Ferraris and Porsches. With attractive girls on his arm he flashed a gold credit card stolen from his father round top London nightspots. He went on a £1700 shopping trip to Harrods. In all, his credit card spree led to £11,000 in bills from shops, nightclubs, hotels restaurants and garages.

During his three months of swindling he also got a former teacher and his girlfriend to invest £13,000 in a bogus share deal. This crime, said Judge Pryor, was 'the worst of all. You told lie after lie in order to get their money so that you could squander it on self-indulgent pleasure or gratify your gambler's desire to speculate with it.'

Acklom admitted nine thefts, deceptions and forgeries and asked for 119 others to be considered. He will serve his sentence at a young offenders' institution. His parents, John and Diane, had to move out of their plush home in Kent, to help pay their son's debts. But they left the court vowing to appeal against the sentence. Fighting back tears, Mrs Acklom said: 'It's disgusting, unwarranted.'

Text **b**

Teenage conman gets four years

A teenager who posed as a City stockbroker in a £466,000 mortgage fraud was yesterday sentenced to a total of four years in a young offenders' institution. Judge Brian Pryor, QC, described Mark Acklom, aged 16 at the time of the offences, as 'utterly selfish and completely ruthless'. Mr Acklom, who was educated at Eastbourne College, an East Sussex public school, spent £11,000 after stealing his father's credit card, swindled Ian Markland, a former teacher, out of £13,000 and ran up a £34,000 bill with a private jet company. Charles Conway, defending, said he was out of touch with reality. But the judge told Mr Acklom: 'I do not accept for one moment that you were a character believing in a fantasy world.'

Mr Acklom, who last month admitted charges of theft and deception, convinced a building society, at the age of 16, that he was a 25-year-old stockbroker earning £214,000 a year. They gave him a £466,000 mortgage for a £516,000 home in Dulwich, south London.

Mr Acklom, now 18, was given concurrent sentences, including four years for swindling the teacher, three years for obtaining the mortgage, and two years for deceiving the air firm. The judge said the sentence was 'to reflect what I regard as the overall wickedness of your crimes.' He said Mr Acklom did not suffer from mental illness, but showed 'all the typical symptoms of a conman, telling sophisticated lies to your victims.' Earlier, Mr Conway said Mr Acklom, who had boasted he was the youngest stockbroker in the City, was in need of urgent psychiatric treatment. While others saw him as a conceited, self-centred conman, he was an inadequate boy living without any sense of reality. He stole the credit card for wining and dining girlfriends, and to live an extravagant lifestyle beyond his means. He could not have hoped to get away with it.

One girlfriend stayed with him in the £600 a night presidential suite at Brighton's Grand Hotel. He took another abroad in chartered jets. Mr Conway said Mr. Acklom's father, an insurance consultant, wrote to solicitors and accountants informing them of the youngster's real age, but 'to some limited extent, these people shut their eyes.' After the hearing, Mr Acklom's mother, Diana, said: 'We're going to appeal against this sentence.'

159

Reading

A What cases do you know of people pretending to be someone else?
Why should people want to pretend to be other people?

The Tichborne case

In 1854 a young English aristocrat, Sir Roger Tichborne, fell in love with his cousin Katherine, and proposed to her. Both families were strongly opposed to the marriage, and Sir Roger, heartbroken, left England to travel around the world and try and
5 forget. His ship sank off the coast of America and he drowned. His body was never recovered but after three years he was officially declared dead and the family fortune passed to his nephew, Henry. Sir Roger's mother, however, refused to believe that he was dead and advertised all over the world for news of
10 her long-lost son. In 1866, one of these advertisements came to the attention of Thomas Castro, a butcher in Wagga Wagga, Australia. He wrote to Lady Tichborne claiming to be Sir Roger and apologising for not having written to her for twelve years. He said that he would like to come home but had no money. Lady
15 Tichborne was overjoyed that her 'son' had been found. She wrote back suggesting that he should call on a former family servant, named Bogle, who was living in Sydney. Castro discovered as much as he could about the Tichborne family and visited Bogle, an elderly and rather short-sighted gentleman. Despite the fact
20 that Castro was ten centimetres shorter and ten kilograms heavier than Sir Roger, Bogle confirmed that he was genuine. Castro explained that the hardships of life in Australia had changed his appearance. On receiving a letter from Bogle, Lady Tichborne sent enough money to pay the fare back to England.
25   When she met Castro, Lady Tichborne was convinced that he was her son and arranged for him to receive £1000 a year, a very large sum of money in those days. If Castro had not been greedy that might have been the end of the matter, but he insisted that he was the rightful heir to the title and to the
30 entire family fortune, which was extremely large. Apart from Lady Tichborne and the family solicitor, members of the family and friends were not convinced and started to look for evidence to disprove his claims. The real Sir Roger had been brought up in France and spoke French fluently but when Thomas Castro
35 was addressed in French, he could not reply. He said that he had forgotten how to speak French because there had been no opportunity to use that language in Australia. Eventually, in 1871, the matter went to court and although his two principal allies had died by that time, Castro pressed ahead with the case.
40 Henry Tichborne's lawyers soon discovered that not only was Thomas Castro not Sir Roger Tichborne, he wasn't Thomas Castro either. In fact, he was Arthur Orton, who had been born in Wapping in London and had spent most of his life in Chile. He was also wanted by the Australian police for horse-stealing.
45 Nevertheless, the Claimant, as he was now known, since no-one was quite sure what to call him, managed to produce a hundred witnesses who swore on oath that he was who he claimed to be.
    After a hearing of 102 days, the court found that he was not Sir Roger Tichborne. Castro, alias Orton, was then arrested and
50 charged with perjury, that is, with telling lies in court. After a second trial lasting 188 days, he was found guilty and sentenced to fourteen years in prison. He still maintained that he was Sir Roger, but when he was released from prison in 1884, he finally admitted that he was an imposter. He died on 1 April 1898.

B Now answer these questions:

1 Why did Sir Roger Tichborne leave England?
   A He had always wanted to see other parts of the world.
   B His mother told him to leave the family home
   C His fiancée refused to marry him.
   D He wanted to escape from a difficult situation.

2 When Sir Roger was officially declared dead, what did his mother do?
   A She accepted the fact.
   B She went in search of her son.
   C She used the press to help look for him.
   D She gave away the family fortune.

3 How did the claimant account for the fact that he was physically different from Sir Roger?
   A He said the climate in Australia had affected him.
   B He explained that he had had little to eat.
   C He declared that he had had a very tough life.
   D He said an accident had damaged his back.

4 When Lady Tichborne gave Castro £1000 a year, how did he react?
   A He asked her for more money.
   B He was pleased with what he had received.
   C He wanted the family fortune.
   D He immediately went to court.

5 When the case came to court, what affected Castro's chances of success?
   A He was being greedy.
   B Lady Tichborne's solicitor opposed him.
   C People important to his case were not available.
   D He was unable to answer questions in French.

Talking Points

Section 1

Look at the advertisements.
Describe what's for sale.
Would you be tempted by any of these offers? Why/why not?

TRAVELLING SET OF ENCYCLOPEDIAS

£25.99

4947

This easy to carry portable set of encyclopedias means you never have to get caught short on holiday again. **A BOON TO THE MODERN TRAVELLER. PRINT NAME AND ADDRESS CLEARLY ON ORDER.**

SOLAR POWERED

£8.99
inc vat

NITE LIGHT

SAVE a fortune on electricity with the original patented solar powered nite light, use at any time – as long as the sun is shining. **WORKS FROM DIRECT SUNLIGHT.** £8.99 (inc vat) + 75p p+p 10 DAY TRIAL MUST SATISFY OR MONEY WILL BE REFUNDED. STATE COLOUR PREFERENCE.

Section 2

Moral dilemmas:

How would you react if

1   you found a £50 note on the pavement?

2   you didn't have enough money to pay the fare on the train?

3   you wanted to see a film but didn't have enough money for the ticket?

4   you were in a supermarket and needed food but had no money?

5   you had the chance to see exam papers in advance?

6   in an exam, you were sitting next to the best student in the class and could see that person's answers?

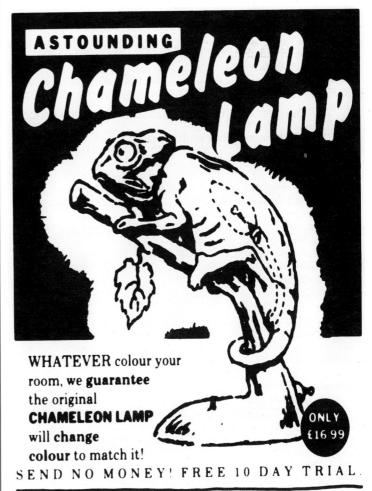

ASTOUNDING Chameleon Lamp

WHATEVER colour your room, we **guarantee** the original **CHAMELEON LAMP** will **change colour** to match it!

ONLY £16.99

S E N D   N O   M O N E Y !   F R E E   1 0   D A Y   T R I A L .

Listening

Deceiving people

Listen to Mandy and James talking about incidents when they deceived people.

Look at the statements and say if they are *true* or *false*.

1 Mandy's incident happened when she was a student.

2 This was the first time she had cheated on the tube.

3 The ticket collector at Charing Cross asked to see her ticket.

4 She said she had travelled from the nearest station.

5 She kept telling the same story.

6 In the end she decided not to appear in court.

7 The court found her guilty.

8 She had to pay a sum of money.

9 James's story happened when he was about to leave school.

10 He arranged everything by himself.

11 The reunion was for all James's friends.

12 Mr Gateshall was about to end his career as a teacher.

13 There was a big show.

14 The people invited were associated with the school.

15 James was rather embarrassed.

Writing

A letter giving advice to a friend

Here is part of a letter you have just received from your close friend, Elizabeth.

> Well, you know that Tony and I have been seeing each other for five months – and it's been just wonderful. We were making lots of plans and I thought everything was going so well. Anyway, last week a girl at college told me she had seen Tony at a disco with someone else. At first I didn't believe her, and then I talked to Tony, and he said, yes, it was quite right, he took this girl, Mariella, her name is, to the disco. But he says he still wants to go on seeing me.
>
> I just don't know what to do. I mean, I'm really angry, and part of me wants to tell him to go. But I love him. And in a way, can't he have some freedom to see other people? I mean, I meet people at college all the time, though I don't go out with them. I'm confused. What do you think about this? And what should I do?

Write to your friend.
Use some of these ways of expressing an opinion:

I believe ....
  think ....
  consider ....

It's my view/my opinion that ....
In my opinion, ...
I agree with the idea that ....

I don't believe that ....
I can't/don't agree that ....
I disagree with the idea that ....

I advise you to ....
If I were you I would ....
I suggest that you should ....

English in Use

1 Complete each gap in the text with *one* suitable word.

Matthew Patterson found the perfect way to travel to the faraway places you see advertised in the travel brochures. He managed _____(1) make the crews of Pacific Airways believe that he really was _____(2) airline steward.

Over a period of three years, he travelled _____(3) the world making frequent visits to New York, Sydney, Hawaii and Tokyo. _____(4) did he do it? Twelve years _____(5) he started his trips, Matthew _____(6) as a steward with Pacific Airways. When the training was over, he decided _____(7) to take the job. But he kept his uniform, and _____(8) it on when he decided, three years _____(9), that he wanted to see more of the world.

Because of the smart uniform, he was able to walk _____(10) security guards and to _____(11) members of the flight crew that he had _____(12) transferred to their flight at the last moment. But Matthew had one problem. He was so good _____(13) his job and so successful at _____(14) with the passengers on Pacific Airways planes that reports started to reach the airline about _____(15) a good steward he was. When the airline _____(16) for his file, they couldn't find it, because of course Matthew didn't have _____(17). Eventually the police were called in and Matthew had to _____(18) what he had been doing. Now _____(19) of seeing the world on his free trips he _____(20) a few years in a prison cell.

2 Phrasal Verbs

Complete the sentences with a phrasal verb based on *cut*.

EXAMPLE: John ___cut off___ the legs of his jeans to make a pair of shorts.

1 The cook _____ the meat into small pieces.

2 Those people who want to lose weight should _____ sweets and chocolates from their diet.

3 The forest was _____ in order to make way for the motorway.

4 We were _____ in the middle of our phone conversation.

5 Several villages were _____ by the unexpected heavy snowfall.

6 When he wrote his will, the tycoon decided to _____ his eldest son.

7 They _____ their food expenses in an effort to save money.

8 It's annoying when you're driving and a motorist _____ directly in front of you.

3 Word-formation

Complete the sentences with the correct form of the word in capitals.

EXAMPLE: There is a wonderful ___simplicity___ about the way Jerry tries to trick people. SIMPLE

Tom suffers from ___jealousy___ whenever he sees his wife dancing with another man. JEALOUS

The company advertised a ___vacancy___ in the accounts department. VACANT

1 The journalist thought there was nothing wrong with invading people's _____. PRIVATE

2 There can be no _____ that this man is the spy. CERTAIN

3 Mark felt considerable _____ when circumstances forced him to tell a lie, ANXIOUS

4 The investigators completed the job with great _____. EFFICIENT

5 The general was unsure of the _____ of the reports. ACCURATE

6 We have to act fast – it's a matter of _____. NECESSARY

7 The conman spoke a number of languages with great _____. FLUENT

8 There was little _____ in the schoolgirl's life. VARIOUS

9 _____ led him to investigate the circumstances of the accident. CURIOUS

10 Stephen's wife and children were killed in a accident and he never got over the _____. TRAGIC

Exam Practice 3

1 (Exam Hints: Paper 1)

You are going to read a newspaper article about a man who made a parachute jump. Seven sentences have been removed from the article. Choose from the sentences A–I the one which fits each space (1–7). There is one extra sentence which you do not need to use. There is an example at the beginning (0).

The Man Who Fell To Earth

Simon Walsh's first parachute jump was an experience he'll never forget.

When actor Patrick Swayze insisted on doing his own jumps for the skydiving sequence in the film Point Break they put him on the AFF course. (0) __C__ Normally, novice parachutists start jumping from 2,000 feet (670 metres) under chutes that open automatically while they practise pulling a dummy ripcord. This can take 25 jumps or more. On an AFF course, lesson one sees you out of the plane at between 8,000 and 12,000 feet (2,500 and 4,000 metres) with two instructors hanging onto you as you perform a series of pre-arranged exercises while freefalling down to 5,000 feet (1,700 metres), when you pull your ripcord.

It normally takes a bit of saving up to do an AFF. (1) _____ Which is how I came to be perched 11,000 feet (3,700 metres) over Headcorn one afternoon, believing that a man cannot, repeat, cannot fly.

(2) _____ Chief instructor Jane Buckle has done more than 3,000 jumps plus further rigorous training to qualify as an AFF instructor. I also have the benefit of a very thorough day's ground training. Jane and her colleague, Chris Lynch, told me they would be holding on to me to ensure I stayed in that all-important 'stable position': spine arched, arms and legs spread like a frog in mid-leap.

Sitting with my back pressed up against the pilot's seat, I sense the air turning noticeably colder as we pass through 7,000 feet (2,500 metres). Eleven thousand feet (3,700 metres) and the engine noise lowers as we throttle back to 70 miles (110 km) per hour. I'm next. (3) _____ 'Yo!' I shout.

Fresh air, open space, the engines' deafening roar. There's a lot of gravity down there. Behind me, Jane grips a purpose-made tuck in my jumpsuit while Chris, to the left of me, does likewise. I fling myself into space. The steady blast of rushing wind fills my ears, and then, a pleasant surprise. (4) _____ Instead, well, have you ever seen a scrap of paper hovering over a ventilator shaft?

Time to do the 'circle of awareness': look at the ground. (5) _____ Now I look at the altimeter. There it is on my chest strap: 10,500 feet (3,500 metres). I turn to Chris on my left, and shout the altitude. He gives the thumb-up signal for OK. I turn to Jane and repeat the altitude. 'OK', she says.

Five thousand feet. Time to 'live pull'. (6) _____ It is what we skydivers call a parachute that has opened out.

Silence. Far below me and all around is a great green floor, blotched with trees and speckled with tiny shapes. I'm king of the sky, and it's beautiful. I actually sense myself losing height. There's the airfield. I can see it all quite easily now…ground rush! Feet and legs together, and 'whummmp' – a three-point landing on two feet and posterior.

I'm here! I'm alive! (7) _____ Apparently so. I want to kiss the chief instructor; so I do, while the chief instructor would rather I gathered together and picked up my chute, so I do that as well.

Off into the sunset I walk creasing my features with that particularly space-cadet smile that only first-time jumpers ever wear. And I keep telling myself: 'That wasn't just a film, that wasn't just a film…'

A Chris turns, braces himself in the doorframe and shouts: 'Ready to sky dive?'

B Look, reach, pull, and something immensely powerful grips me under the armpits and hoists me back up the way I've come.

C AFF stands for Accelerated Freefall.

D I am in safe hands, though.

E I swing left, along a bit, and left again, and start to look out for the 'drop zone'.

F I had been bracing myself for the awful plunging sensation I was sure would come.

G So when a couple of instructors asked if I would like to try a level one jump with them, it seemed like an offer I couldn't refuse.

H Did I just do what I think I did?

I It's just lying there, not rushing towards us.

Listening

5 (Exam Hints; Paper 4, Part 1)

You will hear people talking in eight different situations. For questions 1–8, choose the best answer, A, B or C. You will hear each piece twice.

1 You are listening to a radio programme. What is the speaker describing?

   A a helicopter
   B a rocket
   C a submarine

2 You overhear this conversation in a shop. Why is the card needed?

   A to pay for the goods
   B to check identity
   C to operate a machine

3 A friend describes something he has sold. What is he describing?

   A a painting
   B furniture
   C a clock

4 A friend tells you about a competition he entered. How does he feel?

   A pleased
   B angry
   C disappointed

5 You overhear part of a conversation between two people. Who is speaking?

   A a parent
   B a shop assistant
   C a teacher

6 A friend is telling you about a sport he plays. What exactly happened?

   A They were defeated in the last minute.
   B They played much better than last time.
   C The match did not take place.

7 You hear someone talking to a group of people. Why does he interrupt?

   A to apologise
   B to inform
   C to praise

8 You hear two people talking about a meeting. What is the man doing?

   A refusing
   B arranging another time
   C agreeing reluctantly

6 (Exam Hints: Paper 4, Part 2)

You will hear Katherine talking about a special place in Devon, in the West of England. For questions 1–10, complete the sentences which summarise what the speaker says. You will need to write a word or a short phrase in each space.

Katherine was taken to Clovelly by her (1) ....

The village was located (2) ....

By the sea, there was a place for (3) ....

Years later, Katherine went there with a (4) ....

The first thing they saw was a (5) ....

You had to go through a building with shops in and then you had to (6) .... to visit the village.

People were allowed in in groups of (7) ....

Katherine thought the village was now organised for (8) .... and not for (9) ....

She was very (10) ....

unit 16
A THING OF BEAUTY IS A JOY FOREVER

Lead-in **1** Are these things beautiful? What makes them beautiful?
What things that you have seen do you consider to be beautiful?

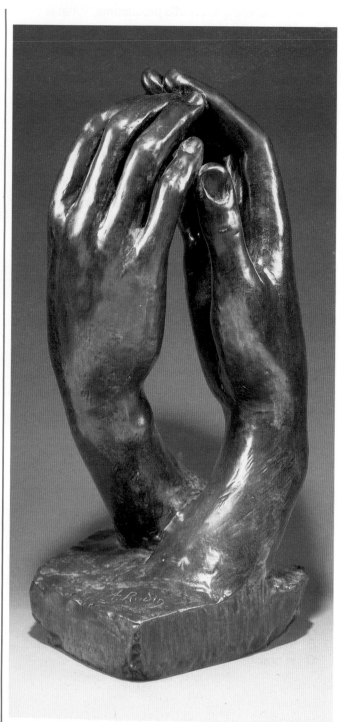

2 Choose the correct word to fill the gap in each sentence.

> carved   original   architect   creative
> potter   artists   reputation
> masterpiece   designs   restored

1   The artist is so .... that it's difficult to imagine what he will think of producing next.

2   The men who make money from the sale of paintings are not the .... themselves but the dealers.

3   Until I visited Peter's house I had never seen an .... Picasso in a private house.

4   Constable produced many good paintings but this is considered to be his ....

5   The sculptor .... the stone until his vision of a young man emerged.

6   Many .... were submitted for the new building, and the committee chose the one that was the least expensive to build.

7   The artist was not well-known in his lifetime but his .... has grown rapidly since his death.

8   The .... became famous after he won the competition for a plan for the new concert hall.

9   The painting was badly damaged in a flood and has not yet been ....

10   The .... worked the clay on a wheel and then fired it in a kiln.

 3 Choose the correct word to fill the gap in each sentence.

> gallery   reproductions   display
> exhibition   cases   preserve   guide
> entry fee   curator   alarm

1   The museum publishes a useful .... which will help you find your way round.

2   The .... of the museum was anxious to maintain the building in the best possible condition.

3   The critics recommended everyone to visit the current .... at the gallery.

4   All the museum's exhibits were kept in glass ....

5   This museums owns so many objects that they only have a small amount of the collection on .... at any one time.

6   This is a small museum with only one main ....

7   All visitors to the museum are required to pay the ....

8   We have two main aims in this museum – to .... the objects in our care and to educate the public who come to see them.

9   Mary's little boy touched the painting and set off the ....

10   The shop does a good trade in .... of the museum's most popular paintings.

Reading

Can you think of one work of art
(for example, a painting or sculpture) that you
admire very much?
Why do you like it?
What kind of exhibitions do you like to visit?

Three people describe objects they have seen which
they found particularly beautiful.
Read the three descriptions and decide if the following
statements apply to description **1**, **2** or **3**, or to more
than one description.

a   depicted real people

b   belonged to the state

c   intended to be handled

d   disliked by some people

e   about 400 years old

f   mainly made of metal

g   almost abstract

h   depicted natural objects

i   used in a ceremony

j   produced over a period of more than 2,000 years

k   made by one person

l   influenced by one person's taste

m   part of a larger exhibition

Works of art

1

A few years ago I went to an exhibition of art treasures that
had been lent by the government of Nigeria. The exhibition was
travelling to several different museums in different countries.
The objects on display spanned a period of more than two
5 thousand years, from the fifth century B.C. to the late
nineteenth century. They were all small sculptures, mainly in
bronze and other metals, but also in terracotta and ivory. The
most striking objects were bronze heads from Benin. These were
life-size and represented the heads of kings. Apparently, they
10 were used in ceremonies after the king's death. They had been
made by a guild of specialist craftsmen whose sole activity was
to produce artistic objects for the king. I was struck by how
lifelike they were and by the delicate modelling of the features.
The heads have a serene, dignified, rather detached expression,
15 embodying the majesty of the king. The bronze heads were all
cast by pouring molten metal into moulds of clay and beeswax,
and a very high degree of technical skill went into their
production. A few heads are pure copper which is a particularly
difficult metal to cast.

2

For me the most interesting part of the exhibition
was the section devoted to Japanese ceramics of the
late sixteenth and early seventeenth centuries. The
pottery on display was used in the tea ceremony at that
5 period. What impressed me very much was that the
objects were, quite deliberately, asymmetrical, almost
misshapen. As well as the irregular shape, they had a
rough, natural, texture in earthy colours which gave
them a rustic appearance. Most of them had not been
10 made on a potter's wheel. There was clearly no desire
to have an exact, regular shape. This preference for the
natural and unobtrusive reflected the taste of the great
tea-master Sen Rikyu (1552–1591). The tea-bowls,
water vessels and vases were simple, informal,
15 harmonious and intensely beautiful. They could not be
touched, of course, but I felt that their sensuous beauty
could only really be appreciated by handling them.

3

Yesterday I went to an exhibition of paintings by the
French Impressionist painter, Claude Monet. Because
he is a very popular painter some critics dismiss his
work as 'chocolate box' art, meaning that it is very
5 pretty but not very serious. This exhibition certainly
refuted that view. On display were several paintings of
the same scene with slight but significant changes.
There were a variety of themes, such as haystacks in
different light and weather conditions and the bridge
10 over the pond in his garden, but best of all, in my
opinion, were his paintings of the tall and slender
poplar trees that grew by the River Epte, close to his
home. He painted these trees at different times of the
year and there is a fascinating contrast between the
15 shapes of the tree-trunks and the curve of the river. In
these paintings, Monet is clearly a forerunner of the
abstract movement that dominated early twentieth
century art.

Grammar: *indirect speech (2)*

 A Change these sentences from direct to indirect speech. (Grammar Notes **16.1**)

EXAMPLE: 'I take my sons swimming every Sunday,' said Peter.

Peter said that he took his sons swimming every Sunday.

1 'My daughter is getting married next month,' said Mrs Morse.

2 'I go to the cinema every week,' said Barry.

3 'We didn't enjoy our holiday at all,' complained Mr and Mrs Leech.

4 'I'll make sure that the goods arrive on time,' Mr Barnes told me.

5 'I can't order any more goods until I've sold what I have in stock,' said the shopkeeper.

B Change these sentences from indirect speech to direct speech.

EXAMPLES:
The doctor asked me if I was feeling better.
'Are you feeling better?' the doctor asked me.

Michael said that he couldn't come unless we met him at the station.
'I can't come unless you meet me at the station,' said Michael.

1 Sarah claimed that she had seen a ghost the previous night.

2 Peter said that he was going to stand for election to Parliament.

3 Mr Blake said that he always took a packed lunch with him to work.

4 Bernard said that he would order the food for the party.

5 Lisa said that she had been waiting for me for half an hour.

6 Jack asked me if I knew what had happened to his cassette-player.

7 Mary asked me where the college was on the map.

8 Oliver asked Jenny why she hadn't taken part in the race the previous day.

9 Lucy asked Paul how he managed to remember so many telephone numbers.

10 George asked the receptionist what the manager's name was.

C Sometimes we can express the meaning of what someone said without following the tense-changes of indirect speech by using a different verb where given.

EXAMPLE:
'Really? I can't believe it!' said Tom.
Tom expressed his disbelief.
(Instead of: *Tom said that he really couldn't believe it.*)

'I'm sorry I lost your book, Amanda,' said Penny.
Penny apologised to Amanda for losing her book.
(Instead of: *Penny said to Amanda that she was sorry that she had lost her book.*)

Change these sentences using the introductory verb and make any other changes necessary.

1 'You stole the camera, John!' said Tim.
Tim accused ....

2 'Why don't we visit the exhibition?' asked Charles.
Charles suggested ....

3 'It was me that set fire to the house,' said Martin.
Martin admitted ....

4 'I did not meet Professor Wilson in Zurich,' said the Inspector.
The Inspector denied ....

5 'I'm sorry I'm late,' said Norman.
Norman apologised ....

6 'Don't skate on the ice, Barbara,' said John.
John told ....

7 'Wait for ten minutes, everyone,' said Bill.
Bill told ....

8 'I will do everything possible to help you,' Tom told us.
Tom promised ....

9 'I will not make a statement to the police,' said Angela.
Angela refused ....

10 'Well … er … um. … I … er … ,' said Christopher.
Christopher ....

Listening

Visiting museums

A Listen to four people talking about museums. Look at the list below. Tick the box if the speakers mention a museum devoted to something on the list.

1 film and television	
2 the Victorian period (1838–1901)	
3 music	
4 live theatre	
5 science	
6 Japanese art	
7 natural history	

B The speakers mention good points and bad points. Tick the boxes below if the speakers mention these points.

Good points

1 a chance to do things as well as look	
2 good cafés and restaurants	
3 staff who answer questions	
4 unusual presents for sale in shop	
5 things that appeal to children	

Bad points

1 many museums are badly organised	
2 objects in glass cases	
3 very crowded	
4 poor access for disabled people	
5 long distances to walk	
6 closed on Sundays	
7 having to pay for admission	
8 things in museums are dead	

English in Use

1 So, such (a)

Finish each of the following sentences in such a way that it means exactly the same as the sentence printed before it. (Grammar Notes **16.2**)

EXAMPLE:
It was _____such a_____ high admission fee that I decided not to visit the museum.
The admission fee was _____so high_____ that I decided not to visit the museum.

1 It was such an expensive vase the museum couldn't afford to buy it.
The vase ....

2 Patrick knows such a lot about Renaissance art that I daren't disagree with him.
Patrick knows so ....

3 They are such old books that they are beginning to fall to pieces.
The books ....

4 The artist became so famous that it was difficult for him to find time to paint.
He was such ....

5 The sculpture was so heavy that a crane was needed to move it.
It was ....

6 The exhibition was so popular that people had to queue for three hours to get in.
It was ....

7 It was so far to walk to the museum that I decided to take a taxi.
It was such ....

8 Anthony has read so many books on art that he can answer all your questions.
Anthony has read such ....

 2 Note the difference between these sentences.

The furniture was *so* heavy that I couldn't move it.
It was *such* heavy furniture that I couldn't move it.

1 Security in the museum was so poor that several paintings were stolen.
There was ....

2 The painting was so severely damaged it could not be repaired.
There was ....

3 The furniture was so old that nobody was allowed to sit on it.
It was ....

4 The expert's advice was so good that the museum always bought the right things at the right time.
The expert gave ....

5 The people at the club are so friendly that I always look forward to going there.
They are ....

Reading

A When did you last go to a museum?
How could museums improve their services?

B Allow yourself *three* minutes to read through the following text and make a list of:

1 *four* ways in which museums try to attract children.

2 *three* advantages of belonging to a museum society.

3 *two* museums which are mentioned by name.

C Think of a title for this text.

In recent years, there have been many changes in the way museums present their exhibits to the public. The days of large, dusty rooms full of glass cases with 'DO NOT TOUCH' signs on them are long gone, together with free admission. Until recently, most museums in Britain did not charge admission fees. They received a grant from the government which covered the cost of running the museum. These grants have been abolished or reduced. Consequently, many museums now charge for admission and need to attract large numbers of visitors in order to generate the income to maintain the building, pay the staff, finance research and restoration services and buy new exhibits. In order to persuade people that it is worth paying for a quite expensive admission ticket, museums have tried to make their exhibitions brighter and more appealing. Many museums, especially those devoted to science and technology, now have 'interactive exhibits' which means that you can, in fact, touch the exhibits. For example, you can learn how a television camera works by actually using one, or operate the controls of an aeroplane and watch the wings and tail move. Such exhibits appeal strongly to children and most museums, in order to encourage children to visit, have special 'museum trail' worksheets which direct them to particular exhibits and have questions for the children to answer. These worksheets are very popular with school parties. One of the biggest changes to take place in recent years is that large numbers of teachers are now employed by museums. Their task is to prepare material that makes the museum interesting to children and young people and to advise the curator on how to create strong links with schools and colleges.

Museums have also introduced new features which appeal to adults. For example, you can join, for an annual fee, a society linked to your favourite museum which will enable you to visit the museum without paying or to visit at times when it is normally closed, so that you can then admire the exhibits when the crowds have gone. These societies usually publish regular newsletters and organise social events at the museum where you can meet like-minded people. Indeed, because of their need to increase their income, many museums can be hired for social events – a room full of dinosaur skeletons, old locomotives or mummies makes an interesting venue for a party. Many museums now have impressive cafés and restaurants as well as large gift shops selling books, reproductions and models. These are often more crowded than the museum itself. Museums also seek commercial sponsorship as another way of increasing their income. In return for publicity and advertising, large companies will, for example, cover the cost of a special exhibition.

Some museums create a realistic environment into which the visitor can enter. An example of this kind of museum is Jamestown in New England where a seventeenth century village has been re-created. There are actors in seventeenth century dress performing seventeenth century tasks. If you speak to them as you wander around, they will reply using seventeenth century English accents and vocabulary. At Blists Hill Open Air Museum in England an entire street from the early nineteenth century has been re-created and the visitor can enter commercial and industrial premises from the time of the Industrial Revolution and observe working machinery and old methods of production.

Reading

A What problems are involved in copying works of art?
When is a copy a forgery?

Just as good as the original?

In 1979, the painter Tom Keating was arrested and charged with forgery. He was accused of faking and selling a painting by Samuel Palmer, an early nineteenth-century British artist. Everyone in the art world was
5 shocked when Keating admitted faking more than 2,000 paintings by various artists over a period of twenty years. He couldn't remember the exact number. Nor could he remember who he had sold them to, which meant that many of his fakes could not be traced. As a young man,
10 Keating had been employed by art dealers to make copies of paintings by well-known artists whose original paintings sold for high prices. He was paid very little for this work and assumed that his paintings were being sold for what they were – copies. He then discovered by chance
15 that the dealers who employed him were selling his copies as originals for hundreds of times the price that they paid him. This experience made him very cynical and he decided to take his revenge. He set about producing large numbers of fakes by over a hundred artists, convinced
20 that most art dealers and art critics could not tell the difference between the genuine and the fake.

Keating had a rather casual attitude to his paintings. He often gave them away or sold them cheaply. Many unsuspecting people thought they had picked up a
25 bargain from him. In fact, he had not made himself rich but he took great delight in fooling so-called experts. Before starting to paint, he would write the word 'FAKE' or 'KEATING' or sometimes a rude word on the canvas. The word would be covered by paint but would show up
30 if anyone took the trouble to X-ray the paintings. This has enabled some famous museums to discreetly remove Keatings from their walls. Although he faked paintings by many artists, Keating specialised in the works of Samuel Palmer. Unfortunately, Palmer's genuine output
35 was quite small, much less than Keating's in fact, and soon the number of 'previously unknown' or 'just discovered' Palmers coming on to the market began to arouse suspicion. He admitted in court that he was rather ashamed of the particular painting he had been
40 charged with faking. It wasn't up to his usual standard. He admitted everything and took great delight in exposing the greed of the dealers who had once exploited him and cheated their customers. He did not go to prison because the charges against him were dropped on
45 account of his poor health. After the trial, which had received a lot of publicity, he became very well-known and appeared on television. He actually painted a Samuel Palmer in about half an hour in the television studio, with the whole process being filmed. Later he
50 had his own television series in which he taught his painting techniques. There is no doubt that Keating had remarkable natural talent and at the end of his life he received many orders for his own work. Nowadays even his fakes sell for quite high prices.

B Find a word or phrase in the text which, in context, is similar in meaning to:

Paragraph 1
1 precise
2 found
3 started
4 certain

Paragraph 2
5 not very serious
6 very much enjoyed
7 acquired a painting at a low price
8 without any publicity
9 production
10 revealing
11 tricked
12 because of

C The following sentences contain incorrect information. Re-write them correctly, according to the information in the text.

1 Keating faked nearly 2,000 paintings.

2 All his fake paintings have now been identified.

3 As a young man, Keating knowingly produced fake paintings for dishonest dealers.

4 Although he despised art dealers, Keating had a high opinion of art critics.

5 His main reason for faking paintings was to make money.

6 Keating was ashamed of what he had done.

7 He seems to have had no sense of humour.

8 He was found guilty in court.

9 It took him a very long time to fake a Samuel Palmer.

10 He never produced paintings in his own style.

Talking Points

Section 1

Work in pairs.
What is the person doing?
What is involved in restoring a painting?
What problems are involved in looking after beautiful objects from the past?

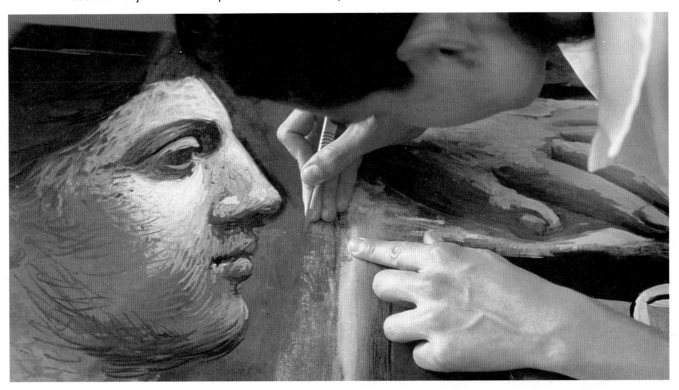

Section 2

Discuss these questions in groups of three.

If you had £10 million pounds to spend, what would you spend it on? Would you do any of the following? Why? Why not?

Would you buy a painting? A racehorse? A piece of memorabilia?

Would you give your money away?

Would you spend it on other people?

Would you set up an organisation to provide:

care for the homeless?

educational opportunities for the deprived?

counselling services for those in need?

Listening

Restoring works of art

A Listen to the talk and answer these questions.

1 Name four things that cause works of art to deteriorate.

2 What three examples of vandalism are given?

3 In what two ways did owners of oil paintings damage them without realising it?

4 Why are people often surprised by newly-restored paintings?

5 If sculpture has been badly-eroded, what important decision do restorers have to make?

B What paintings, buildings or archeological sites have you seen which have been restored? Did you like the way they had been restored?

Writing

A report

In the early nineteenth century Sir Henry Morton made his fortune by importing tea and coffee. He used his money to build up a magnificent private art collection. Just before he died, in 1842, he put all his paintings and sculptures in a small museum which was open to the public. In his last will and testament he left money for the maintenance of the museum. According to the terms of the will, nothing in the museum must ever be sold and entrance to the museum must be free.

The management committee of the museum now face a number of serious problems and cannot agree on what should be done. The museum's income, from investments made with the money Sir Henry left, is only £100,000 a year and much more money is needed for important projects. Read the information below and decide on the best action to take. Write a report to the management committee, advising them what action to take. Give reasons for your advice. Write about 150 words.

MEMO

The following projects must be started as soon as funds are available.

	Cost
New roof	£500,000
New heating and ventilation system	£500,000
Computerised security system	£300,000

These are matters of extreme urgency. Several paintings have been damaged by water and all of them are being badly affected by inadequate temperature control. We are fortunate that, so far, there have

> We should sell Hartog's 'The Tulips'. It was acquired after Sir Henry's death and is not covered by the terms of his will. It would sell for at least £12,000,000 - far more than we need.

> We cannot sell the Hartog - it is the painting everyone comes to see. If we sell it, people will stop coming.

> Why don't we charge £2 for admission? Since we have 100,000 visitors per year, we could raise £200,000. Our lawyers will find a way round the terms of the will.

> There are some minor works of art, purchased after Sir Henry's death, which we could sell for about £50,000 - but we mustn't sell the Hartog.

> We should launch a 'Save the Museum Appeal' and ask people to make donations to the museum - I'm sure people would be generous. We could ask large companies and banks to sponsor the museum.

> Sell the Hartog - it will solve all our problems.

English in Use

 I wish, if only

A Comment on these sentences using *I wish …* or *if only*. (Grammar Notes **16.3**)

1 I bought the painting for £5,000 but it turned out to be a fake.

2 The exhibition was open from January to June but I didn't go.

3 I didn't buy an advance ticket so I had to queue.

4 I forgot to take a map so I couldn't find the museum.

5 I once owned a Picasso but unfortunately I sold it.

B Write similar sentences starting with the words given.

EXAMPLE:
I don't know when the museum opens.
I wish I knew or *I wish I did.*

1 Sally can't tell the difference between a Rembrandt and a Rubens. She wishes ....

2 I haven't got the catalogue. I wish ....

3 I'm working all day Sunday. I wish ....

4 Tom lives in the centre of town. He wishes ....

5 I can't reach the shelf. I wish ....

C *I wish* and *if only* + *would* is often used to complain about things. Comment on these sentences using this pattern.

EXAMPLE:
My brother won't help me.
I wish he would.

1 Martin won't tell me the answer to the question.

2 Neil came to stay for the weekend but he's been in my flat for six weeks.

3 It's been raining all day and I want to play tennis.

4 My neighbours have been playing loud music all day.

5 Michael hasn't rung me all weekend.

2 Phrasal Verbs

Many phrasal verbs which include the word *back* have meanings which include the idea of *return*. Complete the sentences with a suitable word in the correct form.

fight	win	date	pay	read
send	answer	take		

1 Manchester United lost the final last year but this year they hope to .... back the cup.

2 I lent Tom £10 last week and he .... me back yesterday.

3 The book had been damaged in the post so I .... it back.

4 Looking at the old photos .... Frank back to his childhood days.

5 His criminal offences .... back to 1950.

6 Mrs Thomas was annoyed when her five-year old son .... her back.

7 Can you .... back what I dictated to you?

8 When he was attacked by two muggers, Frank .... back.

3 Word-formation

Complete the sentences with the correct form of the word in capitals.

EXAMPLES: The introduction to the catalogue gives details of how the exhibition was put together.   INTRODUCE

Admission to the museum costs £4 for each adult.   ADMIT

1 Few of the applicants for the post of director had the necessary ....   QUALIFY

2 I'm not sure of the correct .... of these specialist art terms.   PRONOUNCE

3 Before the examination, the students on the arts foundation course devoted two weeks to ....   REVISE

4 Candidates are awarded a certificate on successful .... of the course.   COMPLETE

5 What's the .... to the problem of looking after these antiques?   SOLVE

6 The gallery needed the .... of the trustees before they could lend the painting to another museum.   PERMIT

7 The artist submitted paintings for .... in the summer exhibition.   INCLUDE

8 The student had learnt a lot and there was no .... of his earlier mistakes.   REPEAT

unit 17 A SENSE OF ACHIEVEMENT

Lead-in **1** Why should the people in the photographs feel a sense of achievement?
What have you done in your life that gives you a sense of satisfaction?
What kind of effort does it take to be successful?

2 Choose the correct word to fit the gap in each sentence.

> high-flier   precocious   handicap
> effort   under-achiever
> entrepreneur   potential   job
> concentration   setbacks

1 Michael was an .... at school, but as soon as he left his business career really took off.

2 She's twenty years old and has been running her own business for two years – no wonder people think she's a ....

3 Aileen's little boy is quite .... , he's only three and can already play tunes on the piano.

4 Joan trained hard in order to realise her ....

5 Tom has a speech impediment and battles hard to overcome his ....

6 It needed a tremendous .... but eventually the team beat their rivals.

7 What made Andrew stand out among his companions was his power of ....

8 There were a lot of .... but Stephanie never gave up.

9 At twenty-two, he's already a successful ....

10 The manager had had no formal training but had learnt everything on the ....

3 Choose the correct word to fit the gap in each sentence.

> boasts   risk   toll   weather
> pursue   rewards   commitment
> struggle   single-minded   victory

1 Alison is a .... young woman who is sure she will succeed.

2 Although Charles never .... about his achievements, he has every reason to feel proud of what he's done.

3 When she left school, Martha had already decided to .... an acting career.

4 Most actors have to .... when starting out on their chosen profession.

5 The skaters won a well-deserved ....

6 We gave the job to Paul because we were impressed by his ....

7 People who've worked hard expect to be able to enjoy the .... they've earned.

8 There'll be lot of difficulties but I'm sure we'll be able to .... them.

9 It's a calculated .... but one the boss is prepared to take.

10 It's fine to work hard, but remember that overwork takes its ....

Reading

A How would you feel if you were forced to stop studying before your studies were completed?

From scholar to entrepreneur

At the age of sixteen Simon Turner was a pupil at one of Britain's best, and most expensive, public schools. He was about to take his exams and expected to go to university to study Latin and Greek. 'That seems like a distant dream' he said. 'I don't expect I'll ever go to university now.' Simon's world was turned upside down when his parents took him away from the school because they could no longer afford to pay the fees. In fact, the fees had not been paid for two years. Simon's father's business, the source of the family's wealth, had been doing very badly. Simon knew nothing of this. 'My father borrowed heavily to keep the business going but neither I nor my mother realised that anything was wrong.' The family moved to a much smaller house and Simon attended a state school, but worse was to come. 'I think the stress was too much for my father and he died suddenly. The business had already gone bankrupt and I think he was overwhelmed by a sense of failure.'

When the company's assets had been sold to pay off the debts, there remained one small workshop and a few machines, which Simon inherited. 'In fact, it was the original workshop where my great-grandfather started the business in 1930. I was walking around it one day, when I made an important decision – I would, somehow, keep the family business going. I left school – I couldn't stand it any more. I tried to borrow money from the banks but they just laughed at me. I was still under eighteen and if they had lent me anything I would not have been legally obliged to repay. I didn't know what to do, but then I had an idea. Some of our former workers had got new jobs but because of the high unemployment rate, many were still unemployed. I went to see them and made them an offer. If they worked for me without pay for one year, I would pay them two years' salary when the company was a success. Most of them didn't take me seriously and didn't want to take the risk but I managed to persuade six of them to join me, so we started producing furniture again. I discovered some of my great-grandfather's original designs and copied them. This style of furniture turned out to be popular and soon we could hardly cope with the demand. For the first two years, I worked eighteen hours a day and slept on the premises. I was the manager, the designer, the accountant and the salesman and I had to make do without a secretary. I knew nothing about running a business. I just had to pick up the skills as I went along. It was trial and error. I made some mistakes but we pulled through.'

That was six years ago. Simon, still only twenty-four, has succeeded in doing what he set out to do. He employs one hundred workers – his original six are now directors of the company – and sells millions of pounds' worth of furniture every year. 'Looking back, I know I took a big risk. It could have been disastrous, but we managed to make a go of it. I feel a great sense of achievement but I am really proud that I've kept the family name alive.'

B What do these phrasal verbs mean?

Paragraph 1
1 took him away

Paragraph 2
2 pay off
3 make do without
4 pick up
5 pulled through

Paragraph 3
6 set out to do

C Are the statements *true* or *false*? Correct those that are wrong.

1 Simon was glad to leave public school.

2 The collapse of the business came as a surprise to him.

3 Simon's father had made no effort to save the business.

4 Simon's decision to keep the business going was made on impulse.

5 Simon had been happy at his new school.

6 The banks were immediately helpful.

7 The majority of his father's workforce found Simon's offer tempting.

8 There were few orders in the first two years.

9 Simon appreciated the efforts of the workers who joined him.

10 The business is now doing well.

Grammar: *gerund and infinitive*

1 **A** Complete these sentences with *one* word. You must use the *-ing* form of the verb. (Grammar Notes **17.1**).

EXAMPLE:
Although he was angry he remained silent. He didn't want to risk ....*upsetting*.... his boss.

1 He hated staff meetings and avoided .... to them whenever he could.

2 Because she felt nervous, Lucy practised .... her speech in front of the mirror.

3 Most of the students had finished .... the questions before the exam ended.

4 Kevin admitted .... a thief but denied .... the jewels.

5 My job involves .... with complaints from customers.

6 Sally dreaded .... to the dentist's.

7 I don't mind .... you to do this work.

8 Have you considered .... for a new job?

B A number of useful expressions and phrasal verbs are followed by the *gerund*. Complete these sentences with *one* word.

EXAMPLE: I am looking forward to *starting* my new job.

1 Patricia kept me .... for over an hour.

2 It's not worth .... that old radio. Buy a new one.

3 Mr Myers objects to .... in such a small office.

4 I can't help .... angry when you do such silly things.

5 John put off .... to see the doctor for as long as he could.

6 I can't stand .... obliged to be polite to those people.

7 It's no use .... him. He doesn't listen to my advice.

8 What about .... a picnic on Saturday?

2 A very large number of verbs are followed by the infinitive with *to*. Here are some of the most useful. Complete the sentences with the appropriate infinitive phrase.

to be tested	to have been working
to contact	to have witnessed
to have been killed	to have met

to be left	to be accused
not to accept	to have visited
to be living	

EXAMPLE: I would love *to have met* William Shakespeare.

1 Trevor advised us .... the police.

2 George was glad .... such an important event.

3 'I want .... alone,' said the film star to the persistent reporters.

4 The suspect is known .... the victim's house on the night of the murder.'

5 'He is thought .... in Malta at the present time,' said Inspector Collins.

6 I would not like .... of a crime I did not commit.

7 The victim is thought .... with poison.

8 These samples will have .... before a certificate is issued.

9 He is known .... for an Italian company in the mid-1980s.

10 After considering the matter carefully, Bernard decided .... the offer of promotion.

3 The verbs in this exercise are followed by the *infinitive* without *to*. Complete the following sentences.

EXAMPLE: The deadline is Friday. We must ....*finish*.... the work by then.

1 Sarah is only ten minutes late. Let's .... a little longer.

2 We could .... it by special messenger, if it's urgent.

3 You must .... your dog on the escalator.

4 I daren't .... into the water from this height.

5 You should .... the competition. You might ....

6 You needn't .... tomorrow. We'll post the photos to you.

7 The teacher made the children .... the work again.

8 I'd rather .... on holiday in September than in August.

9 You'd better not .... the meat any longer.

10 Julia didn't let me .... for the meal.

181

Listening 🔘

1 Listen to Kate talking about something that gives her a sense of satisfaction.

Answer the questions.

1 What does Kate say she wears when she goes swimming?

2 How does she get into the water?

3 What word does she use to describe her attitude to swimming?

4 How far does she swim?

5 What does she hate most?

6 How does she feel when she gets home?

2 Now listen to David. What aspects of having people round to eat does he say he enjoys?

Tick the points he mentions.

1 planning the menu

2 doing the shopping

3 preparing the vegetables

4 setting the table

5 choosing who to invite

6 getting things to run smoothly

7 choosing the drinks

8 being complimented on his cooking

English in Use

1 What is the difference between these two sentences? (Grammar Notes **17.2**)

James could read when he was three.
James was able to read the book despite the tiny print.

A Now look at the sentences and divide them into two groups, one referring to *general ability* and the other to *specific action*.

1 Martin was chosen as the translator for the group because he was the only one who could speak the language.

2 Henry could read and write before he started school.

3 The driver was able to steer the car out of the skid.

4 The fireman were able to put out the fire within half an hour.

5 Because Christopher could already play the piano, he found it relatively easy to master the organ.

B Now complete these sentences with the correct form of the verb in brackets.

1 Everyone said Rachel .... (do) much better if she tried.

2 .... you (find) the information we needed?

3 The policeman jumped into the river and .... (save) the drowning boy.

4 Anna .... (see) very well when she was wearing her new glasses.

2 Complete the sentences with *manage* or *succeed*.

EXAMPLES: The journalist <u>managed to finish</u> the report before the deadline.   MANAGE/FINISH

The mouse <u>succeeded in taking</u> the cheese from the trap without getting caught.   SUCCEED/TAKE

1 How did you .... an interview with the President?   MANAGE/GET

2 After a long hard struggle the climbers .... the summit. SUCCEED/REACH

3 After months of waiting the family finally .... an exit visa.   SUCCEED/GET

4 The prisoner .... by stealing the guard's keys.   MANAGE/ESCAPE

5 That case looks heavy. Can you .... it?   MANAGE/CARRY

6 The general .... his enemies.   SUCCEED/DEFEAT

7 Jane and Matthew .... all the preparations before their guests arrived.   MANAGE/FINISH

8 The conman .... everyone believe he was telling the truth. SUCCEED/MAKE

9 Following the accident, the police .... the road in time for the evening rush hour. MANAGE/CLEAR

10 Although he tried, James just couldn't .... himself understood. MANAGE/MAKE

Reading

A Before reading the text, discuss the following questions:
Who are the people you like going to see in films?
What makes someone a film star?
Do you have to be good-looking to be a successful film-star?

B Now read the article about Julia Roberts. Seven sentences have been removed from the article. Choose from the sentences A–H the one which fits each gap (1–7). There is one extra sentence that you do not need to use.

A STAR IS MADE

How to get a 14,000 per cent pay rise in three years

Mystic Pizza	$50,000
Steel Magnolias	$90,000
Pretty Woman	$300,000
Flatliners	$550,000
Sleeping with the Enemy	$1,000,000
Hook	$2,000,000
Dying Young	$3,000,000
Renegades	$7,000,000

Since she collected positive 'peanuts' for *Mystic Pizza*, Julia Roberts has become the highest paid actress in Hollywood. Then, Julia Roberts was just another unknown Southern girl trying to make it in the movies. (1) .... She is considered to be the hottest thing Hollywood has seen for many a year. She has already had two Oscar nominations and two Golden Globe nominations, for *Steel Magnolias* and *Pretty Woman*, and been named performer of the year by America's cinema owners.

The Julia Roberts story is a dramatic one, even by Hollywood standards. It begins in 1985, in a place called Smyrna, Georgia (population 30,981) where the school leaver suddenly decided to leave for New York, just three days after her graduation, determined to pursue an acting career. In classic show business tradition, she was 'discovered' walking along Columbus Avenue by a talent scout who helped fix a meeting with Bob McGowan, who offered to manage the then eighteen-year-old Ms Roberts. (2) .... 'Basically, I've learned on the job,' she says. 'It's an instinctive thing with me. I don't quite know what I'll be doing until it's done.'

Hollywood really began to take note after her memorable performance in *Mystic Pizza*. Elaine Goldsmith, her agent, says: (3) .... Roberts herself admits to such ambition. 'I wouldn't be in the business if I wasn't ambitious. But 'ambition' has bad connotations. It's not just money, greed, fame. My ambitions are to seek out new challenges, to discover new things about myself – maybe some thing I haven't wanted to deal with. I also want to be part of a group I respect, from whom I get ideas and creativity.'

'Men think Julia is extraordinarily beautiful,' says Sally Field, one of the producers of *Dying Young*. (4) .... And as always, luck enters into the phenomenon, with Roberts undoubtedly the right person in the right place at the right time. 'Julia's the new blood,' says one industry observer. 'No other actress in their 20s has her quotient of sex appeal.' (5) .... 'It's not necessary to know and I don't care.'

The last two years have been a period of non-stop work for Roberts. (6) .... Concerned friends say she is battling fatigue and is now capable of sleeping anywhere, in any position, at any time. In early July, she was rushed to the Cedars-Sinai Medical Centre and hospitalised with what she insists was a severe bout of flu. And then of course, there is the Great Wedding Cancellation. Due to be married to Kiefer Sutherland in a $500,000 ceremony on June 14, Roberts called off the whole thing with just three days to spare. The scandal heightened when she fled to Dublin with her former fiancé's best friend.

'They say I've had it easy,' says Roberts. 'But 'easy' on whose account? (7) .... I haven't struggled. But this is my journey, so who's to criticise or judge? Making movies, to me, is the best thing in the world. But at the risk of sounding ungrateful, it's very, very hard…'

A Roberts herself professes complete ignorance about the whole subject of just why she appeals to so many people.

B 'A lot of people went up for the roles in that movie, but when Julia wants something she goes after it with passion.'

C Just six movies later, she is the highest-paid actress in Hollywood and the only one who can instantly get a movie made just by signing on the dotted line.

D It has, however, taken its toll.

E 'And women think they went to school with her, that they can call her up and be her best friend… Something makes you care for her, watch her.'

F Sure, I haven't slept in the park.

G He suggested she abandon her southern accent and take some acting lessons, classes which she started but failed to complete.

H It's the commitment that has impressed those who have worked with her – this and her indifference to her looks.

Reading

A How do artists develop their talents?
Does their ability come from nature or training?

Alonzo Clemons: Sculptor

Alonzo Clemons was born in 1956. His mother recalls that he was a normal baby, although she considered him a precocious child because he seemed to learn so quickly. Even as a tiny toddler he showed remarkable interest in, and ability with, Play Doh (a type of plasticine), almost as if he were born to have something in his hands. A fall at age three caused brain injury that resulted in markedly slow development. At age twenty-five Alonzo could barely count to ten and could not handle money but was able to dress and feed himself, dust his room and catch the right bus to go to his job as a stable hand at a nearby ranch. There he would clean horse stalls and do housekeeping chores.

Sculpting, even in childhood days before the injury, seemed for him almost obsessional. At one point, when he was twelve and at a special school, it appeared that his obsession was getting in the way of his other learning – so much so that the clay was taken away to be used only as a reward for other behaviour designed more for his overall growth, particularly in speech and academic subjects. It was then that streaks of tar appeared in his bedding. Alonzo had sculpted from tar he had scraped from the school pavement with his fingernails. Today that obsessive attachment is to wax, which he transforms into remarkable sculptures by the perpetual motion of his skilled hands and fingers. In a single sitting of one hour he can produce, for example, a horse, a gorilla and a wildebeest. He kneads and presses the wax with his hands to form the sculpture, then uses his fingers to create the finer features and his fingernails for the minute markings that characterise his works. At the end of the day, his hands and fingers show the wear and tear of constant pressure. He remembers what he has seen only once and uses the picture in his mind as a model. He does not refer back to a photo and can sculpt in the dark.

In contrast to his skill is his handicap. His vocabulary is limited to several hundred words. His speech is impaired; for example, he often substitutes the word 'yet' for 'yes'. He usually responds to simple questions which one- and two-word replies. When asked how he does his sculpture, he replies, 'Hands' or 'God gives talent'. He loves to work quietly, without conversation. He seems most at peace when he works silently, usually with a slight, very contented smile. He seems capable of tremendous concentration and exclusion of the persons around him, no matter how large the crowd. He is exceedingly proud of his works and likes to accompany admirers silently from one piece to another, with a shy but almost boastful smile, content and pleased with what he sees and what he shows.

The demand for Alonzo's work has grown so that he has been able to quit his job at the stable. Buyers of his work are astounded to find that the artist happens to be mentally handicapped. He has earned enough for the purchase and renovation of a home next to his parents', which he uses as a full-time studio. Alonzo has never had a formal art lesson and probably never will. Yet, even in the absence of any such training, there has been a natural but dramatic progression from rather crude, static, highly accurate but relatively lifeless figures to pieces full of life, motion and movement. As his art has enlivened, so has Alonzo. His vocabulary, while still limited, has expanded. He is less shy, more spontaneous and better able to adapt to new situations. He is still unable to read and write but his verbal and nonverbal communication both show development. His obsessive sculpting has not hindered him but has actualised him; rather than being an impediment to his other communication skills, it has enhanced them.

B Answer these questions:

1 Alonzo has had artistic skills since
   A he was a baby.
   B his accident when he was three.
   C he went to a special school.
   D he got a daytime job.

2 His attitude to sculpture is that
   A it can be done without effort.
   B he can do it only in the right environment.
   C he will do it whatever situation he is in.
   D he must have the necessary materials.

3 When he is sculpting, Alonzo
   A has a model in front of him.
   B works from pictures.
   C uses mental images.
   D requires good light.

4 When people watch Alonzo at work, they are impressed by
   A how happy he looks.
   B his intense concentration.
   C his ability to talk to those around him.
   D his pride in his work.

5 How has Alonzo used the money he has made?
   A He is able to support his parents.
   B He has been able to afford a new house.
   C He had created a practical working environment.
   D He has invested in further training.

Talking Points

Section 1

What are the feelings of the winner?
What are the feelings of the person who came second?

Section 2

Read the following true stories.
Do you think that these people felt proud of what they had done?
Do you think they felt a sense of regret?

1   In 1912 Captain Robert Scott and four companions set out to be the first men to reach the South Pole. When they reached the South Pole they found that the Norwegian explorer Roald Amundsen had arrived four weeks earlier. Scott and his companions all died on the return journey. His diary was found in his tent and ends with the words 'We shall stick it out to the end, but we are getting weaker, of course, and the end cannot be far. It seems a pity but I do not think I can write more.'

2   In 1884 Hiram Maxim invented the first fully-automatic machine-gun.

3   On 20 July 1969 Neil Armstrong became the first man to set foot on the moon.

4   Marie Curie made important discoveries concerning radiation and won a Nobel prize, as did her husband, Pierre, and her daughter, Irene. Marie Curie and her daughter died as a result of exposure to radiation in their laboratories.

5   Percival Lowell predicted, by mathematical calculations, the existence of Pluto, which was discovered in 1930, fourteen years after his death.

6   In 1923 Gideon Sundback invented the zip.

7   Between 2 April and 31 May 1988, Remy Bricka walked 5,000 kilometres across the Atlantic Ocean, from Tenerife to Trinidad, on long water-skis.

Section 3

Which of the following would give you the greatest sense of personal achievement?

making an important archeological discovery
inventing a useful everyday device
making a medical discovery
being the first person to set foot on Mars
doing something that no-one else has ever done
writing a great novel, or creating a great work of art
winning an Olympic gold medal

Writing

Applying for a job

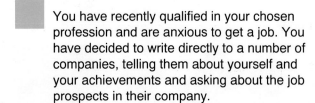 You have recently qualified in your chosen profession and are anxious to get a job. You have decided to write directly to a number of companies, telling them about yourself and your achievements and asking about the job prospects in their company.

Write this letter.

Look back to page 122 to check the layout and format of a letter to a company.

Prepare your letter by writing down the answers to these questions:

How old are you?

What are the important details about your education?

What qualifications have you got?

What languages do you speak?

Have you had any part-time jobs?

When can you attend for an interview?

When can you start work?

Can you drive?

Do you have computer skills?

Structure your letter into at least three paragraphs, including an introduction and conclusion.

Listening

Writing a song

Listen to James and answer the questions.

1 What three feelings does James get when he's written a good song?

2 Where does he do his composing?

3 What does he like about the instrument he uses?

4 What gives him the idea for a song?

5 What happens to him when he composes?

6 How does he feel when he finally goes to bed?

English in Use

1 Complete the sentences with the correct word from the list.

cheque	wages	pay	salary
fees	change	cash	notes
commission	interest	income	

1 .... in the fast food restaurant are paid at an hourly rate of £5.20.

2 The office manager earns an annual .... of £60,000.

3 What is the rate of .... for this job?

4 I have no small .... for the ticket machine.

5 You can pay in .... or by .... or credit card.

6 He's a good solicitor but his .... are high.

7 When completing this tax return you must declare your .... from all sources.

8 You earn .... on the money you keep in a building society.

9 This machine accepts coins but not ....

10 The salesman receives a .... on any sales he makes.

2 Complete each gap in the text with *one* suitable word.

A ten-year-old boy, Mark Edwards, has become the youngest member of SIGMA, an organisation which limits its membership to people with exceptionally high intelligence. Mark, who .... (1) the test at his home near London, has a level of intelligence .... (2) puts him in the top one .... (3) cent of the population.

Mark, a happy and unaffected boy, seems unconcerned .... (4) his success. His .... (5) interest is writing programs for his computer, though he is also very .... (6) on football. He hopes to be in the school .... (7) next year. So why was he interested .... (8) the test? He .... (9) it was his father's idea. 'That's right,' admits Tony Edwards, ... (10) is an accountant by profession. 'Mark does well enough at school, but we felt the teachers didn't recognise .... (11) intelligent he is. We want him to have special attention, and at the .... (12) he finishes his work before everyone else, and is a .... (13) bored.' Mark's mother, a university teacher of mathematics, has .... (14) giving her son extra lessons at home, but says he .... (15) benefit from more demanding teaching at .... (16).

Because of the publicity Mark has received, the school is now considering how they .... (17) help. There's no .... (18) of Mark having a teacher to himself but the headmaster, Derek Harrison, says all teachers will be considering how they can provide study programmes that stretch .... (19) the clever children .... (20) Mark.

3 A Phrasal Verbs

Complete the sentences with a phrasal verb based on *let*.

EXAMPLE: You needn't do the washing up tonight – I'll
.... you .... today.
            let   *off*

1 Most countries have a special day when it's traditional to .... fireworks,

2 So, Jamie, what time do your teachers .... you .... school every day?

3 Tim's quite unreliable – he's always .... his friends ....

4 The bad weather shows no sign of ....

5 When I knocked at the gates the porter .... me ....

B Complete the sentences with a phrasal verb based on *pass*.

EXAMPLE: The painting was a forgery but they tried to
.... it .... as the real thing.
            pass   *off*

1 Richard was hit on the head by an intruder and ....

2 My grandfather was ninety-two when he ....

3 There's nothing I like better than sitting on a bench in the park watching people ....

4 He was in a lot of pain following the accident but gradually it ....

5 As soon as I got the information, I .... it .... to the other people involved.

4 Word-formation

Complete the sentences with the correct form of the word in capitals.

EXAMPLE: It is .... to park on double yellow
            illegal
            lines.   LEGAL
            Tony always phones at the most
            inconvenient times when I'm involved in
            something important.   CONVENIENT
            No wonder Sally's getting fat – she finds
            cream cakes *irresistable* .   RESIST

1 The pharmacist couldn't read the prescription because the doctor's handwriting was ....   LEGIBLE

2 Buses on this route are quite .... so check the timetable.   FREQUENT

3 Sam writes well but his essays are full of .... information.   RELEVANT

4 Although we can provide some treatment, we are afraid this is an .... disease.   CURABLE

5 Tamsin acted in an .... way when she left the baby alone in the house.   RESPONSIBLE

6 People who can't read and write are ....   LITERATE

7 We didn't have much money for the trip so we stayed in .... accommodation.   EXPENSIVE

8 I couldn't follow Robert's argument because it was completely ....   LOGIC

9 Anne had a difficult childhood which has left her feeling ....   SECURE

10 Henry was under so much pressure that he reacted to the criticism in an .... way.   RATIONAL

TIME AFTER TIME

Lead-in **1** What is unusual about this painting?
What is the purpose of the building?
Could you manage without a watch?
Do you make an effort to be on time?
Do you get annoyed when people
are late?

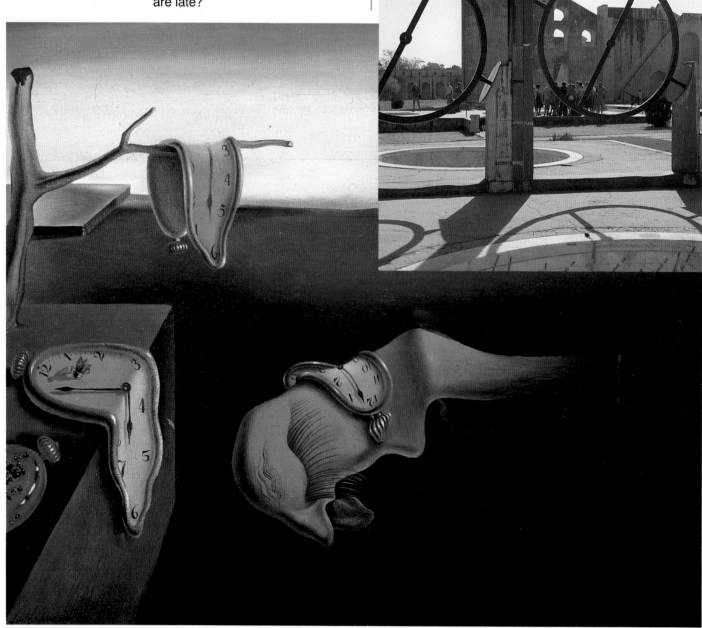

2 Choose the correct word or phrase to fit the gap in each sentence.

> calendar   bank holiday   leap
> agenda   clock   centenary
> working day   time zones
> millenium   diary

1 A year which has three hundred and sixty-six days is called a .... year.

2 John commutes to his job in London every ....

3 If you travel from London to Anchorage in Alaska you pass through nine ....

4 Because it was a .... we were unable to change money or do any shopping at all.

5 Next year the writer will have been dead for a hundred years and we will be celebrating his ....

6 A .... is the name we give to a period of a thousand years.

7 We've got lots of things to talk about as you'll see if you look at the .... for today's meeting.

8 I'm not sure I can come to dinner on Tuesday – let me just have a look at my ....

9 There's a .... in the kitchen if you want to see what day your birthday is.

10 Airlines state times of departure and arrival according to the twenty-four hour ....

3 Choose the correct word or phrase to fit the gap in each sentence.

> falls   black hole   speculate   digits
> pace   challenged   time span
> nostalgic   orbit   jet lag

1 My birthday .... on a Tuesday this year.

2 It takes a little over 365 days for the earth to .... the sun.

3 People travelling on long-distance flights have to suffer the effects of ....

4 The story deals with four generations of the same family and has a .... of over a hundred years.

5 Many scientists are concerned about the .... of change.

6 My father is very .... about the happy years of his childhood.

7 It's pointless to .... about what will happen in the future.

8 The teacher .... the student to provide evidence to support her theory.

9 Science fiction writers are fascinated by what happens when things disappear into a ....

10 How many .... are there in 10,000,000?

Reading

A Would you like to have a different number of days in the week, or weeks in the month?
Would there be any advantages in changing?
Can you think of any improvements that we could make to the calendar?

Give us back our eleven days!

The Earth takes 365.24219878 days to orbit the sun, which is extremely inconvenient for anyone who tries to devise a workable calendar. The problem is that the odd fractions of a day accumulate over time and eventually cause the calendar to be out of step with the seasons. Julius Caesar made an attempt to solve this problem in 46 B.C. Previous calendars were so badly wrong that Caesar started again with a new calendar that came to be known as the Julian calendar. He decided that the year 46 should have 445 days in order to start the new year at a time that was in step with the seasons. He also introduced the idea of a leap year to use up the fractions of a day but because he decided to have a leap year every three years instead of every four, his calendar was two hours and eleven minutes too long. In 8 B.C. a leap year every four years was introduced which meant that the calendar was then only eleven minutes too long but by the sixteenth century the error had accumulated to over ten days. Pope Gregory XIII then introduced a new calendar, the Gregorian calendar. This meant that in 1582 the day after October 4 was October 15. Britain refused to use this new calendar because it originated in Rome, and continued using the Julian calendar until 1752. By that time, having two different calendars was causing problems in international trade and the British government decided to change over to the Gregorian calendar. This meant that the date jumped eleven days. A number of not very well educated people in London could not understand what was happening and thought that they were losing eleven days of their lives! Mobs attacked government buildings yelling 'Give us back our eleven days!' The Julian calendar continued to be used in Russia until 1917.

In 1793 in France an entirely new calendar was devised. This had new names, appropriate to the seasons, for the months such as Thermidor (heat) which lasted from 19 July to 17 August and Brumaire (mist) which lasted from 22 October to 20 November. The weeks all had ten days and year one began in September 1792. There were still twelve months but all of them had thirty days. The odd days were official festivals. However, this revolutionary calendar was abandoned in 1806 and the Gregorian calendar was re-introduced. The Gregorian calendar, while not perfect, is quite efficient because it is in error by only 0.0003 days per year which means that it will be many centuries before any adjustment is necessary. There are other calendars still in use. There is a Muslim calendar, a Jewish calendar and a method of counting years in Japan from the date of accession of each emperor.

It would be possible to have a calendar in which the same date is on the same day every year. This would involve having a thirteen month year with twenty-eight days in each month. There have also been proposals to have a decimal day, that is, a day divided into ten hours.

B Find a word or phrase in the text which in context is similar in meaning to:

Paragraph 1
1 go round
2 small parts
3 tried
4 violent crowds
5 shouting

Paragraph 2
6 matching
7 change

Paragraph 3
8 mean
9 suggestions

C Work in pairs. Ask and answer the following questions.

1 What problem did Julius Caesar solve and how did he do it?

2 What is the purpose of a leap year?

3 What was wrong with the Julian calendar?

4 What happened in 8 B.C.?

5 What happened in 1582?

6 Why was the Gregorian calendar not universally adopted?

7 Why did some 18th century Londoners think that they were losing eleven days of their lives?

8 What do you think was the reason for the new calendar in 1793?

9 What were the advantages of the French calendar?

Grammar: *gerund and infinitive with or without to*

1 (Grammar Notes **18.1**). In the following sets of three sentences, use a *gerund* or an *infinitive* with *to* to complete each sentence. Use the word in capitals.

EXAMPLE:

MEET

Mr Franks is so old he can remember ___meeting___ Queen Victoria when he was a child.
In this sentence, the meeting with Queen Victoria happens first and Mr Franks remembers it afterwards.

John remembered ___to meet___ the client at the airport even though he hadn't written anything in his diary.
In this sentence, John remembers first and meets the client afterwards.

SIGN

1 I don't remember _____ this letter. I think someone forged my signature.

2 Make sure you remember _____ the cheque before posting it.

3 The artist didn't remember _____ this painting – or perhaps it isn't genuine and that's why there is no signature.

SEE

4 I'll never forget _____ his magnificent victory in the Olympic Games.

5 Don't forget _____ Mr Jenkins before you leave work.

6 'You didn't really forget _____ the dentist, you just didn't want to go, did you?' said Michael.

TURN

7 He tried _____ the handle but it was jammed and he couldn't move it.

8 He tried _____ the handle but the machine still wouldn't start.

9 'Try _____ your satellite dish a bit to the left. It might work better,' John advised me.

INFORM

10 When he was attacked by other prisoners, Mick regretted _____ the guards about the escape plot.

11 I regret _____ you that your application has been unsuccessful.

12 Martin regretted _____ the manager about his health problems – he failed to get promotion.

TALK

13 After describing his adventures in Patagonia, Captain Morgan went on _____ about his voyages in the Pacific.

14 Although his lecture was supposed to last one hour, Professor Dixon went on _____ until half the audience were asleep.

15 If you let him, Samuel will go on _____ for hours.

TAKE

16 After failing his driving test for the sixth time, Mr Brown decided to stop _____ it.

17 The views from the mountain road were magnificent, so we stopped _____ some photographs.

18 'Don't stop _____ the pills until you have completely recovered,' said the doctor.

2 Complete the following text with the correct form of the verb. You need the *gerund*, or the *infinitive* with *to*, or the *infinitive* without *to*. The first two have been done as examples.

Robert was tired of **taking** the train to work every day. He had **to catch** a very early train to be sure of (1 ARRIVE) at work in time. Often, delays due to bad weather and strikes prevented him from (2 GET) home in time to watch his favourite television programme. He objected to (3 PAY) such high fares for such a poor service. He decided (4 BUY) a bike. It might (5 BE) exhausting at first but he would soon get used to (6 CYCLE). He remembered (7 CYCLE) a lot as a child. In fact, he used (8 RIDE) his bike to school every day. He knew that bikes had improved a lot since those days and a friend advised him (9 BUY) a mountain bike and suggested (10 GET) some waterproof and windproof clothing as well. His first day of (11 CYCLE) to work went well. He chose his route so as to avoid (12 GO) up hills and he rode carefully because he didn't want to risk (13 HAVE) an accident. The weather was fine and there was little wind, so he enjoyed (14 RIDE). (15 BE) out in the open air made him (16 FEEL) invigorated. On the way home, however, he got a puncture. Fortunately, he had remembered (17 BRING) a puncture repair kit. When he had finished (18 MEND) the puncture, he looked around for the pump. He had forgotten (19 BRING) it!

Reading

A How good are you at mental arithmetic?
Can you remember telephone numbers easily?
How can people improve their ability to do calculations in their heads?

The calendar calculators

On what day of the week was your tenth birthday? In what year did your birthday fall on a Tuesday? In the year 2000, how many days are there between your birthday and Easter? What was the weather like the
5 day you turned 16? The year is 91360; on what day of the week will June 6th fall in that year? If you were still living in that year, how old would you be? Don't know? George does.

George and his identical twin brother, Charles, are
10 simply astounding. They are calendar calculators. Give them a date and they can give you the day of the week over a span of 80,000 years, 40,000 backward or 40,000 forward. Ask them to name in which years in the next 200 (or any 200) Easter will fall on March 23 and they
15 will name those years with lightning rapidity, faster than a computer and just as accurately. They can tell you what the weather was like on any day of their adult life, but they have forgotten your name by the end of a brief visit. They cannot count to 30 but they swap 20-
20 digit prime numbers for amusement. They cannot figure out the change from a ten-dollar bill for a six-dollar purchase, but they can factor with ease the number 111, or almost any number you name. They can remember 30 digits but cannot add. While there have been other
25 known calendar calculators, there have been none quite like George and Charles.

George and Charles were born three months prematurely. It was their mother's fourth pregnancy.

They were delivered by Caesarian section as two of a set
30 of triplets, two boys and a girl. The girl died within twelve hours. The boys were kept in incubators for two months. George held up his head at six months and sat at nine months, but did not walk or talk until he was 2½ years of age. Charles lagged behind George. Both displayed head
35 banging, hand biting and destructiveness. When they were 3, doctors recommended that they should live in a special hospital, but both remained at home. At age 6 George was already a calendar calculator. The twins were not especially close until age 9, when they were admitted
40 to a hospital where they stayed for 15 years. There they became inseparable and Charles became as interested in dates as his brother was. The fighting, biting and destructiveness continued there. In 1963 they were transferred to a different hospital, where their behaviour
45 improved. Both twins were severely short-sighted. Both boys had an exquisite sense of smell and frequently approached people and sniffed them. They could pick out their own slippers or clothes by smelling them. Both boys showed almost constant rocking and swaying movements.

50 George is boastful about his abilities. He also enjoys challenging visitors by asking them when their birthday is and then asking them in what years their birthday was on a Thursday. When the visitor cannot answer quickly, he recites the answer in a rather proud
55 and arrogant manner, and inquires why the visitor, whose birthday it is, cannot tell those dates when he, whose birthday it is not, is able to. When asked how he does it he says, 'It's fantastic that I can do that.'

B Find a word or phrase in the text which, in context, is similar in meaning to:

Paragraph 2
1 astonishing
2 period
3 extremely fast
4 exchange

Paragraph 3
5 too soon
6 developed more slowly
7 very delicate
8 smelled
9 moving from side to side

C Choose the correct answers, A, B, C or D

1 George and his brother can

   A count to 30
   B subtract $6 from $10
   C remember names
   D match days and dates

2 Charles became a calendar calculator when he was

   A between 3 and 6
   B between 6 and 9
   C between 9 and 15
   D between 9 and 24

3 Which of the following statements best describes George and Charles?

   A They are physically handicapped.
   B They are polite to visitors.
   C All their senses are very acute.
   D They are proud of their abilities.

English in Use

1 For, during, while

Complete the sentences with *for*, *during* or *while* (Grammar Notes **18.2**)

EXAMPLES:
They were married .... *for* .... ten years.
.... *During* .... his time in the navy, he visited more than fifty countries.
.... *While* .... Nigel was in hospital, he lost his job.

1 Both children were sick .... the flight.

2 Come and stay with us .... the weekend.

3 I visited Spain several times .... the 1980s.

4 He was sent to prison .... six years.

5 .... his time in prison he took several exams.

6 .... Mary was shopping she lost her purse.

7 We had to leave the building .... the police searched it.

8 .... the exam, Robert began to feel unwell.

9 My shoes were mended .... I waited.

10 The manager took several phone calls .... my interview.

2 Phrasal Verbs

In unit 10 we looked at phrasal verbs which have a noun form. Many phrasal verbs are used as adjectives. Complete the sentences with the correct word.

> stand-by   check-in   add-on   live-in
> pick-up   phone-in   walk-on
> follow-up   getaway   takeaway
> leftover   knockdown

1 The robbers rushed out of the bank and leapt into their .... car.

2 We gave the .... food to our dog.

3 Tom took his luggage to the .... desk at the airport.

4 Lord and Lady Chesterfield are looking for a .... housekeeper for their country mansion.

5 I bought a .... ticket because it was only half the price of a standard ticket and the flights were never full.

6 Sebastian was delighted to have purchased the antique chair at such a .... price.

7 A .... truck took the damaged vehicles away from the scene of the accident.

8 After the training course finished there were a number of .... sessions at which trainees could discuss any problems.

9 We bought a .... meal at our local Chinese restaurant.

10 Lucy was glad to have been given a .... part in such a famous musical.

11 This computer has many .... features that you can purchase at a later date.

12 .... programmes are very popular on commercial radio stations.

3 Word-formation

Complete the sentences with the correct form of the word in capitals. Note that in this and the next two units there will be a mixture of forms.

1 The postage charged on parcels depends on their ....   WEIGH

2 There are so few of these rhinos left they are regarded as an .... species.   DANGER

3 A roller was used to .... the grass before the match began.   FLAT

4 The glue is extremely .... so try not to get it on your fingers.   STICK

5 It was a hot day so John .... his tie.   LOOSE

6 There was no .... that Jack was the murderer.   PROVE

7 The water company sent out a .... so that no-one would forget to pay.   REMIND

8 The soldier was praised for his ....   BRAVE

9 The lecturer was a .... writer on political subjects.   PASSION

10 The marksman hit the target with his first ....   SHOOT

unit 19 EXPLORATION, ADVENTURE, INVENTION

Lead-in

1

A What is the difference between an explorer, a traveller and a tourist?
Was travelling more exciting in the past?

B What are these inventions?

A

B

Choose the correct word for the gap in each sentence.

> ventured   undaunted   arduous
> assault   transported
> hardship   supplies   exposure
> endurance   clung

1 The mountaineers took sufficient .... to last for three weeks.

2 Emily was prepared to put up with any .... that the expedition might involve.

3 The walkers were unprepared for a night in the open and were concerned about the dangers of ....

4 The explorer was determined to push himself to the limits of human ....

5 All the equipment had to be .... on horseback over the narrow mountain paths.

6 The climber .... to the cliff face to prevent himself from falling.

7 The team was to make their .... on the summit at dawn.

8 It was an .... journey lasting thirty-six hours.

9 A brave woman, she was .... by the discomforts she had to put up with.

10 With only a guide to help her, she .... into the remotest areas.

 Choose the correct word for the gap in each sentence.

> original   technical
> error   superseded   patent
> exploit   version   breakdown
> device   potential

1 The inventors decided which design worked best through a process of trial and ....

2 James is full of .... schemes, but he's not so good at putting them into practice.

3 To make sure no-one else copied her invention, Terry took out a ....

4 John doesn't have wonderful ideas himself, but he knows how to .... other people's.

5 This approach has considerable .... and is worth developing further.

6 The first .... of the machine was difficult to use but the second one is much easier to handle.

7 Sarah proudly explained that what she had in her hand was a .... for cutting hard-boiled eggs.

8 We had to solve a number of .... problems before we were able to market the machine.

9 The machine suffered a mechanical .... and could no longer be used.

10 This invention is so advanced that it will be many years before it is ....

Reading

Inventions

 A Which inventions have had the greatest effect on the way you live?

Work with a partner. See if you know what these inventions are. If you have difficulty deciding, look at the list given at the end.

1 In 1816 René Laënnec was walking near the Louvre in Paris when he noticed some children playing with long pieces of wood which they held to their ears. The next day he made the first version of something that no modern doctor could do without.

2 In 1902 Hubert Booth invented something which can now be found in almost every house. He got the idea by lying on the floor, placing a handkerchief over his mouth and sucking as hard as he could. His first machine was much larger than modern versions. A horse pulled it along the street from house to house.

3 In 1840 Rowland Hill invented something which doubled the number of letters posted in the following year. At first the things he invented were all small, black and cost one penny but now they come in all sizes, colours and prices.

4 In 1790 John Greenwood adapted his mother's spinning wheel to invent something which he could operate with his foot, leaving both hands free for the delicate work he performed on his patients. He was able to work more quickly, so his patients suffered less pain. Modern versions of this device are so fast that little, if any, pain is felt.

5 In 1813 George Manby watched firemen trying to put out a fire in a building in Edinburgh and noticed that they could not pump water as high as the fifth floor. He invented a device that could put out small fires immediately however high the building.

6 In 1903 Albert Parkhouse was working for a company which made lampshades. His boss was too mean to provide somewhere for the workers to hang their coats so Albert picked up a piece of wire from his workbench and twisted it into a shape we now find very familiar. His employer saw him do this, immediately realised the commercial potential of Albert's invention and patented it. Albert received nothing for his invention.

7 In 1797 Jacques Garnerin performed, over Paris, an extraordinary act of bravery, using a device of his own invention. He survived, as have thousands of people who have used modern versions of his invention in emergencies.

8 One morning in 1895 while looking in his mirror this man had the idea for something that would be used once and thrown away, and would therefore make him rich. It took him six more years to solve technical difficulties because he could not find a manufacturer who made steel that was thin enough but still strong. His product soon became immensely popular. Although it is used more than once, it soon wears out. It has made a daily chore quicker, easier and safer.

A parachute	E stethoscope
B razor blade	F dentist's drill
C postage stamp	G wire coat hanger
D vacuum cleaner	H fire extinguisher

B Explain the meaning of the following words and phrases:

Text 1
1 the first version

Text 4
2 adapted
3 device

Text 6
4 commercial potential
5 patented

Text 8
6 a daily chore

C Discuss in groups of three:

How important are these inventions in your life?
Have lives been saved by them?
Do they need improving?
Can you think of anything that has not yet been invented that would make life easier?

Grammar: *connectors*

 Compare these pairs of sentences. Their meaning is the same but a different connecting word has been used.(Grammar Notes **19.1**)

Jack continued working ....*although*.... he felt tired.
Jack continued working ....*despite*.... feeling tired.

Mary ran as fast as she could ....*but*.... she did not qualify for the team.
Mary ran as fast as she could. ....*However*...., she did not qualify for the team.

The villagers stored the potatoes ....*so that*.... they would have enough food for winter.
The villagers stored the potatoes ....*in order to*.... have enough food for winter.

Mike studied Latin ....*while*.... he was in prison.
Mike studied Latin ....*during*.... his time in prison.

You haven't completed the form correctly, ...*so*.... we can't accept your application.
You haven't completed the form correctly. ....*Therefore*...., we can't accept your application.

The fans cheered ....*as soon as*.... they saw their favourite footballer.
....*Immediately*.... they saw their favourite footballer, the fans cheered.

A Re-write these sentences using the word in brackets.

1 Ian didn't wear gloves although he was cold. (despite)

2 Jill had a bad cold. However, she decided to go ahead and make her speech. (but)

3 They started a fire in order to clear the land of trees. (so that)

4 During my holiday, I visited several museums and art galleries. (while)

5 There is no signature on this cheque. Therefore, the bank cannot give you money for it. (so)

6 Immediately the gates were opened, the crowd rushed in. (as soon as)

B Complete the sentences with the following words.

> as if
> not only ... but also
> whether ... or not
> in case
> even if

1 You have to hand in your paper now .... you have finished ....

2 Take a torch with you .... you have to come home in the dark.

3 Wear a lifejacket when you are in the canoe .... you are a good swimmer.

4 He is .... a champion athlete .... a first-class musician.

5 John looks .... he hasn't slept for several days.

C Complete the sentences.

1 The soldiers waited until
....

2 You can have £50 in cash or
....

3 They cannot be allowed into the stadium because
....

4 Jack put chains on his car wheels so that
....

5 He was allowed to begin his university course although
....

6 You can collect your car as soon as
....

7 Take gloves and a scarf with you in case
....

8 His novel did not win a prize even though
....

9 The police did not capture the escaped prisoner despite
....

10 He was not only the funniest comedian we had ever heard but also
....

Listening

My favourite invention

Listen to Claire talking about the invention in her home that she likes best.

Choose the best answer, A, B, C or D for each question.

1 Claire finds playing the piano

A requires intense concentration.
B is hard work.
C reduces stress.
D provides an emotional release.

2 Other members of her family

A encourage her to practise more.
B enjoy listening to her playing.
C want to play with her.
D leave the piano for her to use.

3 Claire appreciates

A the way the piano is constructed.
B the sound made by different keys.
C the effect she can produce on the piano.
D the way sounds combine.

4 One reason Claire gives for liking the piano is that

A she has always been able to improvise.
B she has worked hard to develop her technique.
C she has had a choice about what to play.
D she has progressed through a series of tests.

English in Use

For questions 1–15, read the text below and look carefully at each line. Some of the lines are correct, and some have a word which should not be there. Tick the correct lines and underline the wrong words in the incorrect lines.

EXAMPLES: 0 <u>from</u>
00 ✓

A terrible journey

0 When I left from your house last Sunday
00 I expected to get home in about four hours.
1 In fact, it took me much more longer than
2 that. It just became obvious that something
3 was wrong when the train had arrived an
4 hour in late. It then travelled at a very slow
5 speed up the line. The problem, so we were
6 told, it was flooding at a station ahead of us
7 which made it unsafe for the train to proceed.
8 Eventually, we had to get out of and wait for
9 a bus to take us to another station near. By
10 this time, it was the midnight and we were cold,
11 hungry and tired. Once we got us to the other
12 station, we were able to have travel on a
13 different line and the new train proceeded at a
14 normal speed up. We could also buy hot drinks.
15 But it took me ten hours to get home.

Reading

A What dangerous situations do you encounter in your normal life?
Have you ever done anything deliberately dangerous?
What activities are the most dangerous you can think of?

Clinging to life by the finger-tips

It is a picture of fear conquered. Stefan Glowacz clings to the overhang, his frail body suspended over a sickening void by his finger-tips. He has climbed a sheer cliff in his bare feet to get here.

5 As a child, Glowacz preferred to keep his feet firmly on the ground, playing sports like judo and football. But in his teens he overcame his fear of heights and began rock-climbing. The challenge of a dangerous sport, the individual pitted against uncompromising nature, drove him on, up tougher and tougher 10 ascents. Now at 26 he is one of the world's top exponents of the new, athletic solo-climbing in which the mountaineer is no longer a bearded man in a thick sweater, assaulting the rock-face with a barrage of special equipment and an army of porters, but a lone athlete, a slim figure in multi-coloured 15 Lycra who dances up the cliffs with just his or her bare hands and an agile brain as tools. The mountaineers' key-word is no longer assault, as in warfare, but 'problem' as in chess, a tactical, gymnastic search for a solution.

Like most beginners, Glowacz started by training on easy 20 slopes as part of a team, wearing a protective helmet and using ropes and bolts to help him up the rock-face. Gradually he became addicted to the 25 thrill and excitement, and wanted a greater challenge. He says: 'I wanted to push my body to its very limit, to be totally at one with the rocks and cliffs, so I took up solo-climbing.' It is a cruel variant of the gentle mountaineer's sport, involving 30 climbing without ropes or safety equipment.

For two years, Glowacz braved cliffs all over the world. He knew that one fall would be sufficient to kill him, but the pursuit of physical perfection drove him further and further, up 35 and up. Unfortunately for him, that fall came sooner than expected. A recent accident near his hometown of Munich left him with a broken wrist and heel – relatively minor injuries, but in centres of strength and agility crucial to his confidence. He suffered enough psychological damage to stop him climbing 40 for good. Glowacz will never go without his rope again but he remains one of the firmest supporters of the sport. He says: 'It is like a drug. The adrenaline, the buzz, that feeling when you get to the top cannot be compared to anything else.'

B Find the word or phrase in the text which is similar in meaning to:

Paragraph 1
1 delicate
2 emptiness

Paragraph 2
3 when he was an adolescent
4 more difficult
5 people with special skills
6 attacking
7 single
8 lively

Paragrapn 3
9 bit by bit
10 dependent on
11 as far as it could go

Paragraph 4
12 set himself against
13 need to achieve
14 essential

C Choose the best answer according to the text.

1 What makes Glowacz different from a traditional climber?

A He doesn't bother about what he wears.
B He likes danger.
C He doesn't rely on equipment.
D He has a large support team.

2 Glowacz's interest in climbing developed

A when he was a child.
B in his twenties.
C when he had to stop playing football.
D in his teens.

3 Which of these characteristics describes the solo-climber?

A a fashion follower
B a quick thinker
C a risk addict
D a fitness fanatic

4 According to Glowacz, what is the attraction of solo-climbing?

A being on your own
B not having to carry heavy equipment
C being close to nature
D not doing what everyone else has done

5 What is Glowacz's current situation?

A He plans to go solo-climbing again when he recovers from his injuries.
B He is afraid of the idea of another solo climb.
C He intends to climb again, but with a rope this time.
D He spends his time encouraging others to take up solo-climbing.

Reading

A What famous explorers have you heard of? What difficulties do explorers meet when they go into unfamiliar areas? What makes someone want to be an explorer or to travel to remote places? What makes travelling uncomfortable?

The Adventures of Isabella Bird

Isabella Lucy Bird, while not exactly an explorer, was one of the most intrepid lady travellers of the nineteenth century. She was born in 1831, the eldest daughter of a clergyman. During her childhood she suffered from ill health and took up swimming and riding to
5 build up her strength. In later life, she often justified her extraordinary journeys on the grounds that they were 'for the sake of her health'. In fact, many of her journeys were extremely arduous. At the age of sixty, for example, she travelled 4000 kilometres on horseback through Persia and Kurdistan. Her first journey, however,
10 was to America in 1854. She wrote a book, 'An Englishwoman in America', (1855), which was an immediate best-seller. She always made notes while travelling. In this way she was able to finance her travels. After her parents died, Isabella, feeling ill and depressed, began planning major expeditions. In 1872, she sailed to Australia,
15 New Zealand, the Pacific Islands, America and Canada. Her illness and depression disappeared as soon as she left Britain.

In her book, 'A Lady's Life in the Rockies' (1879) she describes her friendship with 'Rocky Mountain Jim', a cowboy with a wild reputation. She called him her 'dear desperado' and said that 'he was
20 a man any woman might love but no sane woman would marry'. In 1878 she visited Japan where she made a point of travelling to the most remote parts of the country, as far as the north of Hokkaido. She described her experiences in her book 'Unbeaten Tracks in Japan' (1880). She returned to England via Indonesia and the Middle East.

25 In 1881 she married Dr John Bishop and settled down to a peaceful domestic life in Edinburgh. Mrs Bishop began to suffer from ill health again, as did her husband, who died in 1886. Soon after her husband's death, Isabella set off for India, her health improving rapidly the further she was from Britain. She travelled widely in India and rode
30 on a yak through the highest Himalayan passes to Tibet. She met an army officer, Major Sawyer, and persuaded him to let her accompany him on a journey on horseback through Afghanistan, Persia and Kurdistan. These adventures led to another book, 'Journeys through Persia and Kurdistan' (1891). Outwardly, Isabella Bird was a
35 conventional, respectable, Victorian gentlewoman who seemed to be weak and frail, but she came alive when she found what she longed for, 'the savage freedom of the wilds'. She was undaunted by the hardships of long distance travel and did not hesitate to climb mountains, cross deserts, wade through rivers and swamps and hack
40 her way through jungles. Energetic, determined and resourceful, she let no-one stand in her way. She was not easily impressed. 'I care for no waterfall but Niagara', she once said. After her ride with Major Sawyer, she spent a few years in Edinburgh writing up her travels but her health began to fail and she felt restless, so she set off again.
45 Between 1894 and 1897, she visited Canada, Japan, Korea and China, always keeping away from cities and venturing into remote areas. Her final journey, at the age of seventy, was in Morocco, where she climbed in the Atlas mountains. She died in Edinburgh in 1904, her bags already packed for yet another journey.

B Choose the best meaning for the words and phrases from the text:

1 intrepid
  A fearful
  B brave
  C unusual

2 arduous
  A gentle
  B enjoyable
  C tough

3 major expeditions
  A short journey
  B long trips
  C relaxing holidays

4 sane
  A normal
  B sensible
  C well-educated

5 domestic life
  A living on a farm
  B having servants to help
  C home conditions

6 undaunted
  A not surprised
  B not confident
  C not frightened

7 resourceful
  A with plenty of money
  B full of ideas
  C showing aggression

C Work in pairs and answer the questions.

1 What was Isabella's family background?
2 How did she justify her travels?
3 How did she get the money from her journeys?
4 What effect did the death of her parents have on her life?
5 What usually happened to Isabella when she left England?
6 Who was Isabella's husband?
7 What was her married life like?
8 What contrast was there between Isabella's lifestyle and her outward appearance?
9 Where did she go on her last journey?

Talking Points

Section 1

What kind of environment is this to live in?
What things would you need in order to live here?
If you had to spend six months on this island alone,
what would you take with you?
If you were going as part of a group of four people,
would your choice of things to take be different?

Section 2

Discuss in groups of three:

Inventions in the home

Which inventions could you not live without?
Which inventions give you the most pleasure?
Which inventions cause the most irritation?
Which inventions would you get rid of if you could?

Listening

Sewing machines

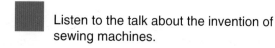 Listen to the talk about the invention of sewing machines.

Match the statements to the person each refers to.

> **People**
>
> A Barthélemy Thimonnier
> B Elias Howe
> C Walter Hunt
> D Isaac Singer

1 is the person usually associated with the invention of the sewing machine

2 produced the first sewing machine

3 had his business ruined by historical events

4 took action to stop people copying his invention

5 is known for the invention of another everyday object

6 was concerned about the social consequences of his invention

7 was cheated out of money due to him

8 returned sadly to his homeland

9 had to use the law in order to benefit from his invention

10 was forced to recognise the importance of another inventor

Writing

Telling a story

Professor Challenger, the famous archeologist, has been exploring the site of an ancient city in the Sahara desert. Four students are with him and one of them, John, has had a serious accident at the archeological site and both his legs are broken. Professor Challenger and his companions have decided to return to the nearest town to obtain medical treatment. Unfortunately, their vehicle has broken down in the desert and they cannot repair it. Professor Challenger and his students are considering what to do.

> We have only twenty litres of water – we need four litres a day each at least.

> John is getting worse – he won't last much longer in this heat – the temperature is over 40°C.

> There's plenty of water and food at the archeological site.

> Someone should walk to the road.

> A litre of water weighs a kilo.

> It's too hot to walk. We should wait until we are rescued.

> We should all stay together.

> The oasis is only 30 kilometres away. We could bring back water.

Using the information given, write a story which tells what happened to Professor Challenger and his students. The beginning of your story should include the information given here but you must decide what happens next and how the story ends. Write about 150 words.

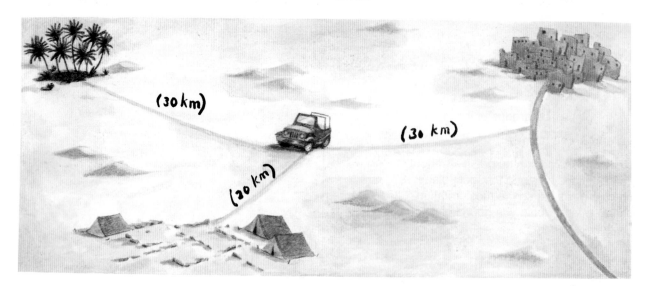

English in Use

1 Complete the text with one appropriate word.

Sally Brownlow, mother of three, is a mountain climber. If ....(1) talk to her about why she went climbing on the Eiger when she was pregnant with her first child, she'll tell you why she climbed this mountain and not ....(2). It doesn't seem to occur to her that ....(3) she did was at all unusual.

'The conditions were perfect, and ....(4) I was a bit worried about a fall, on this mountain it is not as likely ....(5) if you are climbing ....(6) it's very rocky', she says. But ....(7) did her doctor think? 'He supported me, and said I was better off ....(8) just sitting at home with my feet up.'

Five years ....(9) that climb, Sally has three young children to ....(10) after but she still climbs when she ....(11), though more often now it's in the hills of Wales nearer to the home she shares with ....(12) husband, Chris. The children are not yet old ....(13) to start climbing but they have all ....(14) encouraged to join their parents on long walks, being pushed or carried part of the way ....(15) they don't get too tired.

So what ambitions does Sally have ....(16) the future? ....(17) every climber I've ....(18) to, she regards Everest as the greatest ....(19), but it's an expensive operation and climbing there would mean leaving the children behind for a few months. Her real desire in the next few years is to ....(20) the children as climbers so that together they can climb some mountains nearer home in Europe.

2 Word-formation

Complete the sentences with the correct form of the word in capitals.

1 There is little .... when you have to share a tent with someone.   PRIVATE

2 When Tom cut his finger and it was difficult so stop the ....   BLEED

3 The rushing water in the river had made the banks ....   SLIP

4 The climbers huddled together for .... WARM

5 Tom Franklin, the famous explorer, has a .... to become anxious before setting off on an expedition.   TEND

6 The photographic film was kept in a special ....   CONTAIN

7 The .... of Mount Everest was the greatest achievement of his life.   CONQUER

8 The soldiers had nothing they could use to .... their tea.   SWEET

9 The expedition leader had underestimated the .... of the river.   WIDE

10 It was cold in the house because the central .... was not working.   HEAT

3 **A** Phrasal Verbs

Complete the sentences with a phrasal verb based on *do*.

EXAMPLE: I'm thirsty – I could __do with__ a cup of tea.

1 It's cold. .... your jacket before you go out.

2 The night before his operation William had to .... his dinner.

3 The car is really dirty – it could .... a good clean.

4 The council decided to .... conductors on its buses and just have drivers only.

B Complete the sentences with a phrasal verb based on *hold*.

EXAMPLE: The workers decided not to accept the offer, but to __hold out for__ a higher pay rise.

1 'Can I speak to Joan, please?' '........................ I'll just get her.'

2 Thieves .... a security van and stole two million pounds.

3 The city .... against its attackers for five weeks before it surrendered.

4 We'll get to the hotel before nightfall as long as we aren't .... in the traffic.

5 Passengers should .... tightly to the straps provided to ensure that they don't fall over.

6 The tent was .... by strong tent pegs.

unit 20 CONTRASTS

Lead-in **1** What can you see in the photo?
Who are the four tourists?
What is the reaction of the people
on the bench?

Choose the appropriate word for each sentence.

> natural fine plain simple
> second-hand mild scheduled soft
> experienced casual

1 Don't offer John any alcohol – he only likes .... drinks.

2 I don't like formal clothes, I prefer .... ones.

3 I can't eat curry that's too hot but I'm happy with one that's ....

4 Jane's not a sophisticated girl, she prefers .... pleasures.

5 There are no artificial flavourings in the yogurt, only .... ones.

6 The rainy spells this morning will give way to .... weather this afternoon.

7 Captain Robertson is no novice, in fact he's one of our most .... pilots.

8 All our children's clothes are .... because we can't afford new ones.

9 There were no seats left on the charter flight so we had to take a .... one.

10 I don't like milk chocolate, but I'm quite fond of ....

 Match each word in column *one* with the opposite in column *two*.

	1		2
1	victory	A	flop
2	success	B	danger
3	bravery	C	weakness
4	wealth	D	ignorance
5	hit	E	defeat
6	creation	F	cowardice
7	strength	G	poverty
8	knowledge	H	ugliness
9	safety	I	destruction
10	beauty	J	failure

Reading

A Before reading the article, discuss:
How do people's lifestyles change when they finish their studies and get a job?
Do the people themselves change?

B Now read the article where Helen describes her life. Seven sentences have been removed from the article. Choose from the sentences A–H the one which fits each gap (1–7). There is one extra sentence that you do not need to use.

Grow up and get a set of vegetable dishes

Helen describes her lifestyle

A year ago I had just graduated from university, just moved to London and just started my first job, as a secretary. (1) .... Twelve months later, I've discovered that no one ever seems to earn quite enough not to have to worry, and that having somewhere decent to live involves endless bills for taxes, services and repairs. As a student, I could invite friends to share scrambled eggs or a tin of baked beans. (2) .... Now that I have a house with a living-room, containing a table and four chairs, things have changed. Tables and chairs lead to tablecloths and place mats, and I invite friends for meals rather than just feeding them if they happen to be around at the right time. (3) .... I've started cutting recipes out of newspapers and spending whole days cooking, not to mention combing supermarkets for sun-dried tomatoes. I've actually begun to use my twenty-first birthday present, a set of matching vegetable dishes, for vegetables rather than for standing plants in.

(4) .... When I rented cheap, shared accommodation, the only thing I used to worry about was that nothing embarrassingly unhygienic would ooze out from under the fridge (or appear inside it). (5) .... Spills on carpets were rubbed in or ignored. Now that I am a householder, I whizz around spraying polish from a can, and I hoover under the furniture as well as round it. I hover around people with drinks in their hands, waiting to shove mats under glasses that might leave rings on polished surfaces. I am barely able to be polite if someone tips up a glass on the light grey carpet.

My sister is still a student. (6) .... She complains about the fact that I can't stay up all night when I've got work the next day, but she regularly comes to raid my fridge and use the washing machine. (7) .... I'm not sure whether that's because I want to welcome her to the real world, or to stop being reminded of the other one.

A I've got more fussy about surroundings as well as food.

B She sighs ostentatiously now when I send her to fetch a cloth after a minor accident such as knocking over a glass.

C I was looking forward to earning some real money after four years of watching every penny as a student, and to living in my own place rather than a grotty student room.

D She graduates this summer, and I can't wait.

E The friends are the same friends I had before, but now they seem to expect three courses.

F Cleaning the fridge was nobody's responsibility.

G None of them would raise an eyebrow at being expected to sit on the edge of a bed and balance a plate on their knees.

H Having a flat of my own hasn't turned out at all the way I expected.

Grammar: *adverbs*

 A (Grammar Notes **20.1**) Look at these words and phrases. Which tell you *how*? *where*? *when*? *how long*?

> quickly   badly   well   fast   easily
> at home   in the park   on Saturday
> yesterday   at five o'clock   for
> two days   for six years

Place the words in brackets in the correct position in the sentence.

EXAMPLE:
I saw them walking. (yesterday evening, through the park, quickly)
I saw them walking quickly through the park yesterday evening.

What is the order of adverbs in this example?

1 I met them.   (on Saturday, at the football match)

2 I saw Mary with her fiancé. (in a restaurant, yesterday)

3 The champion ran.
          (slowly, after his victory, round the stadium)

4 The burglar has to stay.   (for three years, in prison)

5 She was arrested for driving.
          (on the motorway, too fast, yesterday)

B What question do these words answer?

> often   sometimes   never   rarely
> always   hardly ever   usually   seldom

Place the words in brackets in the correct position in the sentence.

EXAMPLES:
He is always late.   (always)
He never arrives on time.   (never)
He should never have been chosen for the team. (never)

1 Our team wins a match.   (rarely)

2 We will get there on time.   (never)

3 I have seen such interesting fossils.   (rarely)

4 He arrives at 9am.   (hardly ever)

5 The brushes should be cleaned before being used
  again.   (always)

6 I can understand what she says.   (usually)

C And what question do these words answer?

> definitely   possibly   absolutely
> undoubtedly   obviously   just

Place the word in brackets in the correct position in the sentence.

EXAMPLES:
He is   definitely   the best sculptor alive today.
                    (definitely)
She   absolutely   detests beetroot.   (absolutely)
He would   possibly   have won if he had trained
harder.   (possibly)
According to witnesses, he   just   walked into the
sea.   (just)

1 Samuel Castro was an imposter.   (obviously)

2 David will win the race.   (definitely)

3 He has spent a lot of time in the sun.   (obviously)

4 They have committed these crimes together.
                    (undoubtedly)

5 He might have given the map to his brother. (possibly)

6 She removed the ring and walked away.   (just)

D Although there is some flexibility about the position of adverbs in English, the following sentences definitely have the adverb in the wrong position. The order is clearly wrong and the writer has obviously made a mistake. Can you re-write them correctly?

1 Jenny wasn't worried about the faulty lock – just she thought it was a nuisance.

2 Professor Jones wants to stop immediately this project.

3 I have received this morning a letter from you.

4 The pilot safely landed.

5 Helen needed desperately new clothes.

6 He forgot easily people's names.

7 Just I wanted to let you know about it.

8 I always am the last person to know.

English in Use: *common errors*

 These sentences contains errors which are common in the First Certificate examination. Write out the sentences correctly.

1 He gave me some advices about buying furnitures.

2 Be careful not to loose your money.

3 Before to go on holiday, we had the car serviced.

4 I suggest you to ask for a refund.

5 Last year we couldn't visited New York.

6 He succeeded to win the race.

7 They prevented the man to leave.

8 He works like an accounts clerk.

9 His parents made him to take the exam.

10 It's no point waiting any longer.

11 It's a two-hours flight.

12 The society should not tolerate this kind of behaviour.

13 I like to remind the good times.

14 I sat in a red and comfortable chair.

15 People are very lucky for having a new hospital in their town.

16 It was such a nice weather we had a picnic.

17 John watches television the most of the time.

18 He is 25 years.

19 At my college, you have the possibility to play tennis.

20 Mr Brown is on holidays.

 Else

To express the ideas of something extra and additional we can use the word *else* in combination with many other words.

what	where	how	or (*twice*)
much	everybody	anywhere	nobody
someone	anyone	something	
anything	nothing	somewhere	

EXAMPLE:

I have <u>nothing else</u> to tell you.

<u>What else</u> did you do on holiday apart from swimming and sunbathing?

Complete the sentences using a word from the list.

1 It's not my book. It must be .... else's.

2 The tickets must be in the house. They can't be .... else.

3 'Have you .... else to declare?' said the customs officer.

4 'There is .... else I want to discuss with you,' said Jane. 'Can we talk about it now?'

5 We must win the match – .... else matters but winning.

6 Is .... else coming to the meeting, or just David?

7 The house is empty – Mark must be living .... else.

8 .... else are you going to buy with the prize money?

9 .... else have you been in France apart from Paris?

10 Of course he stole the money. .... else could he afford such an expensive car?

11 .... else enjoyed the film but Paul hated it.

12 'You must pay the fine by Friday .... else you will be re-arrested,' said my solicitor.

13 The doctor has sedated the patient. There isn't .... else he can do at the moment.

14 John apologised to me but .... else did.

15 'Hand over the money immediately .... else!' shouted the robber.

Reading and Listening

A Have you ever heard two completely different accounts of the same incident? How reliable are witnesses? Do people's memories let them down?

Now look at the first text.

B Now listen to Mrs Roberts's version of this incident. Make a list of the differences between the two stories. Which version do you believe? What questions would you ask? What other steps would you take to establish the truth?

C Now read this text. Then listen to a different version of the same event.

The store detective's story

I observed a middle-aged lady, whose name I later discovered to be Roberts, enter the store at about 2.30 pm. She was carrying a large shopping bag which appeared to be empty. She walked directly to
5 the children's clothes department and spent about five minutes looking around. She then approached a counter on which children's pullovers were displayed. I saw her place four pullovers in her bag and immediately leave the counter. She did not
10 attempt to attract the attention of the shop assistant who had just finished talking to another customer. Mrs Roberts walked directly out of the store and did not stop at any of the cash desks, all of which were in operation. I followed her out of the
15 store and observed her get into her car, remove one of the pullovers from her bag and put it on a small child. There was one other child and a man in the car. I opened the car door, identified myself as a store detective, placed my hand on Mrs Robert's
20 shoulder and informed her that I was arresting her. I was immediately subjected to a torrent of abuse both from Mrs Roberts and her husband. I asked Mrs Roberts to get out of the car and accompany me to the store manager's office. Her response was
25 to push the car door open in such a way that it struck me on the knee, tore open the leg of my trousers and caused a deep cut that required first-aid treatment. At the same time, Mr Roberts got out of the car on the other side and advanced
30 towards me, making threats of further violence. At this point, three of my colleagues appeared on the scene. We were able to assist Mrs Roberts out of the car and escort her to the manager's office where she remained until a police car arrived to take her to
35 the police station where she was charged with theft. I recovered the three pullovers, all the same colour, green, and the same size.

The doorman's story

On the night in question, I was standing at the door of the club with one colleague. We were performing our duties as security doormen. That means that we have to decide whether people who
5 wish to enter the club comply with the club's dress code and standard of behaviour. We wear evening dress but members are merely required to be smartly dressed. At about 11.30 four youths approached us and attempted to walk straight
10 into the club without saying anything. We stood in the doorway to prevent this. All four were obviously drunk – two were still holding beer glasses. They were dressed in a very scruffy way. We do not allow people wearing trainers into the
15 club. Three youths drifted away but one came back and subjected us to a stream of bad language. He then attempted to push past us into the club. In order to prevent him from doing this, I was obliged to apply an armlock and to escort
20 him down the street for about fifty metres. He protested loudly but when I left him, he seemed perfectly all right.

Reading

Mission Accomplished

Commander Cassius, pilot and navigator of the starship *Belisarius*, examined the astral map on the screen in front of him. This was the last map that the ship's computer could provide him with. He would soon be moving into a totally unmapped area of the
5 universe. That, after all, was his mission – to complete *The Great Map Of All The Galaxies*. No ship had ever travelled into these regions except possibly, over two hundred years ago, the starship *Bellerephon*, whose mutinous crew had fled in this direction after a battle with a starfleet patrol, but after the damage it had suffered
10 the *Bellerophon* must have broken up within days. As he calculated the ship's course, he was aware of a low hum, gradually coming closer. It was the domestic robot bringing his dinner. The robot slid into view, quietly placed a tray on a small table about two metres away and departed. Cassius was distracted for a few
15 minutes by a difficult navigational problem. When he looked up, his dinner was crawling towards the edge of the table. This had happened once before and he had spent hours looking for it. He flicked his tongue. There was a sudden *thwack*, a little squeal, a loud gulp and dinner was over. He completed his calculations and
20 opened the ship's log. There was little to write. There had been little to write for the last fifty years. He had, according to instructions, improved the maps of earlier navigators, correcting an error here and there. But the most inspiring part of his mission, the search for intelligent life, had come to nothing. He had
25 discovered no intelligent life. Perhaps his friend Julius had been right – the chances of a major discovery were so small that it was not worth the sacrifice he had chosen to make. Julius, along with the rest of the crew had left the ship fifty years ago and returned to their home planet. He, Cassius, had continued alone, knowing that
30 he could never return. When he had completed his map, all the information stored on the computer would be transmitted the vast distance back to base, but the procedure for doing this would result in his own death and the destruction of the ship. Only one life would be lost – apart from him the crew were robots. Simply
35 completing *The Great Map Of All The Galaxies* would ensure that his name lived for ever, but he had hoped for something more.

Cassius had one last planetary system to survey and his map would be complete. He approached the third planet revolving around a bright yellow sun. It was an attractive blue and green colour, quite
40 similar to his own planet. Suddenly, he saw on his screen a distress signal – there was no doubt about it. He was picking up a starship distress signal from the surface of the planet! He switched off the automatic pilot and guided the ship towards the surface.

The exit hatch jammed as it had fifty years ago. He did the
45 same thing he had done then. He coiled his powerful tail around the handle and wrenched it aside. As the air rushed in, he was struck by its freshness. He felt invigorated. He slid down into the water and swam towards the shore. As he got nearer he was astonished to see twenty or thirty creatures running towards
50 him. They were clearly alien – they had only two arms and legs – but not unattractive. Their rapid movements and animated expressions suggested that, at last, he had found intelligent life. Although he was outnumbered he felt no fear – the tallest of these creatures was no more than 2 metres in height. From the
55 difference in clothes and certain superficial physical differences it appeared that, as on his own planet, they were divided into two sexes. He was totally amazed when one of the creatures stepped forward, cupped both hands round its mouth and addressed him, not only in his own language but also in the honorific terms of
60 address appropriate for a starship commander. Looking above the trees, he saw the explanation, a face like, or almost like, his own. He recognised the face of Lieutenant Portia, one of the officers who had joined the *Bellerophon's* mutineers.

'.......... and the only one to survive our crash on this planet.'

65 'But your appearance hasn't changed. You look the same as in the starfleet *Wanted* posters!'

'I know. There is something about this planet – it slows down the aging process. It would do the same for you.'

'You realise that it is my duty to escort you to the nearest starfleet
70 base to face trial, or failing that, to execute you on the spot.'

'You cannot do the former and why should you do the latter? If you carry out your orders, we will both die. Forget about the great map. Live on this planet – with me.'

Work with a partner. Ask and answer these questions.

1 What does Cassius look like? Refer to his age, size, eating habits and body-shape.

2 What happens when Cassius has his dinner?

3 Why did Julius leave the ship?

4 What will happen when Cassius transmits his information back to base?

5 How long has Cassius been on board the ship?

6 Why did he decide to land the ship on a planet?

7 Where did he land?

8 What surprised him first?

9 How did the aliens address him?

10 If you were Cassius, what would you do?

Talking Points

Section 1

Describe what you can see in the photos.
How typical are these scenes?

Section 2

Which of these words would you use to describe
boys?

brave	imaginative
gentle	helpful
rough	practical
sweet	noisy
caring	

Would you use the same words to describe girls?
Are there any other words you would use to
describe boys?
What about girls?

Section 3

Discuss these questions in groups:

What sort of things are little boys aged under
five interested in?
Are little girls interested in the same things?
Do people use a different tone of voice when
speaking to boys and girls?
What kind of toys are traditionally associated
with boys and girls in your country?
Are there any toys that parents discourage boys
or girls from playing with?
Why are certain colours thought appropriate for
girls and others for boys?
Are the differences in behaviour of boys and
girls due to the way they are brought up or
due to the differences in their nature?

Listening

Town and country

A Listen to four people discussing living in the country and living in the town. Complete the summary of their discussion. Use phrases of between *two* and *five* words.

Mandy says that she appreciates the good points of both country living and town living but lives in a town now because it is very .... (1) in the country. However, she admits that the country is ideal for .... (2). Kate believes that the country is full of .... (3) but David disagrees and says he would love .... (4). In fact, he has compromised by living in Richmond which is near London but has a lot of .... (5). James loves living in .... (6) but thinks it would be best to have .... (7). Kate points out that you need to .... (8) to do that. David used to have .... (9) as James but now thinks that cities are no longer .... (10) to live. James thinks he would .... (11) if he had to live in the country. David says that your opinion about the .... (12) depends on what your values are. Kate points out that there is much more to do in a town but David wonders if people who live in towns take advantage of what is available. Mandy points out that if you .... (13) it is difficult to get out and enjoy what a city has to offer but adds that children from the country really love the .... (14) in cities and seem to prefer them to .... (15).

Writing

Arguing a point of view

A When arguing for a point of view, you will find the following phrases useful. Look at the example, which is about living in a historical city centre, and put the words and phrases below in the appropriate place. Use each word or phrase once only.

on the other hand	besides
furthermore	in addition
first and foremost	both positive and negative aspects
while	

The centres of many historical towns have been turned into conservation areas. How does this affect the people who live there, and what are the advantages of living in such a place? .... (1), if you live in the centre of town, you are close to all the amenities and right in the heart of things. .... (2) to this, in a historical city centre you will be surrounded by old buildings of historic and architectural importance. .... (3), a flat or house in this area is likely to be full of character. .... (4), there are some disadvantages. Old towns had smaller streets than we expect today, and they weren't designed for cars. This means that .... (5) the streets may look appealing, it's quite difficult for cars to manoeuvre, and parking can be an absolute nightmare. .... (6) this practical difficulty, historical towns often attract tourists, so that at certain times of the year, the town doesn't seem to belong to the people who live there.

So there are .... (7) to living in historical centres, and if you're thinking of living there you need to weigh up the pros and cons.

B An English-language newspaper is going to publish a series of articles about young people and money. It has asked young people to write and tell them their views. Write to the paper, indicating how you feel about this question: is it a good idea for students at school or college to have part-time jobs to earn their own spending money? Write between 120 and 180 words.

English in Use

 A Phrasal Verbs

What is the difference in meaning between these sentences?

The explorers ....*got over*.... the river by building a raft.
Jack ....*got over*.... the shock of losing his job by starting his own small business.

In the first sentence *got over* has the meaning of 'crossed the river'. In the second sentence *got over* has the meaning of 'recovered from'. Look at these sentences and match the phrasal verb with the meaning given below.

1 The children have run out of the house.
2 We have run out of sugar.
3 John turned up the heating.
4 Nobody turned up for the meeting.
5 Jane came round to my house last Saturday.
6 After the accident, Mike came round in hospital.
7 They came across the lake in a rowing boat.
8 I came across some old documents in the attic.
9 Bernard asked the vet to put his dog down because it was old and sick.
10 Sarah put her baby down in the cot.

a placed in a horizontal position
b increased
c found by chance
d haven't got any left
e visited
f cause to die
g gone out quickly
h regained consciousness
i arrived
j crossed

B Now do this exercise in the same way.

1 The farmers rounded up the cows by helicopter.
2 I rounded up the number from 99.25 to 100.
3 The burglar ran off when he heard the alarm.
4 I ran off ten copies of my report.
5 Mrs Thompson decided to take in lodgers to increase her income.
6 The students couldn't take in all the facts and figures that they heard.
7 Richard set off on his journey at 6am.
8 He set off the rockets in the firework display.
9 The dog suddenly went for me.
10 The directors of the company went for Plan B.

a increased to the next whole number
b launched
c gathered
d accept
e fled
f chose
g printed
h attacked
i started
j comprehend and remember

2 Word-formation

Complete the sentences with the correct form of the word in capitals.

EXAMPLE: It was an act of ....*heroism*.... to jump into the river and save the boy.   HERO

1 The .... took place in full daylight.   ROB

2 Tim's a man with great .... of character.   STRONG

3 My new shoes were extremely .... and pinched my toes.   COMFORT

4 Diana heaved a sigh of .... when she heard she has passed the exam.   RELIEVE

5 I don't leave the children alone because they are very ....   QUARREL

6 Caroline is .... to remarks about her appearance and easily gets upset.   SENSE

7 She's a .... child who's too used to having her own way.   SPOIL

8 We were kept so busy on the course that we could never complain of ....   BORE

9 Rachel possesses remarkable powers of .... – nothing will distract her when she's working.   CONCENTRATE

10 The hospital is sure the operation will be ....   SUCCESS

Exam Practice 4

1 (Exam Hints: Paper 3, Part 5)

For questions 1–10, read the text below. Use the word given in capitals at the end of each line to form a word that fits in the space in the same line. There is an example at the beginning (0).

Computer crime

Most people find that computers (0) ___enable___ them to do their work	ABLE
with greater (1) .... For a few, the attraction of computers lies	EFFICIENT
in the many (2) .... they offer for committing crimes. Criminals	POSSIBLE
may use computers to transfer large sums of money (3)	LEGAL
Amateur computer experts may get a feeling of (4) .... by	EXCITE
obtaining secret information. These (5) .... may not always	ACTIVE
receive a lot of (6) .... because companies, especially financial	PUBLIC
institutions, do not want to reveal the (7) .... of their computer	WEAK
systems. Total computer (8) .... is possible but such a system	SECURE
would be expensive to build and (9) .... to use. In reality,	CONVENIENT
companies must balance the (10) .... of their computer system	PROTECT
with the ease with which employees can make use of it.	

2 (Exam Hints: Paper 1)

You are going to read a magazine article about trips to the seaside. For questions 1–14, choose from the places (A–D). Some of the places may be chosen more than once. There is an example at the beginning (0). For question 15, choose the answer (A, B, C or D) which you think fits best according to the text.

Places
A Eastbourne
B Weston-Super-Mare
C Northumbria
D Aldeburgh

Which of the places the writer visited:

0 was the one the family considered the best?
...........D...........

1 has an exceptionally wide, sandy beach?

2/3 provided an opportunity for the study of marine creatures (2 answers)? ....

4 had a hotel well-situated for touring? ....

5 had a hotel with facilities for sport? ....

6 was visited by few people? ....

7 had the hotel with the best food? ....

8 gave people the chance to listen to music? ....

9 allowed her to stay within sight of the sea?
....

10 caused one child to get very excited about an animal? ....

11 had an atmosphere different from the modern world?
....

12/13 provided the group with sunny weather (2 answers)? ....

14 allowed her and the children to enjoy a train ride?
....

15 Who is the magazine article written for?

A children thinking about possible holidays
B elderly people wishing to visit places reminding them of their childhood
C students exploring the coast
D parents with young children

Listening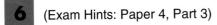

5 (Exam Hints: Paper 4, Part 2)

You will hear Angela describing how she looks after her horse. For questions 1–10, complete the sentences which summarise what the speaker says. You will need to write a word or short phrase in each space.

Angela's horse is kept in a (1) ....

Every day Angela checks Toffee's (2) ....

Infection here makes it impossible to (3) ....

Toffee often gets covered in (4) ....

To overcome this problem, Angela uses a special (5) ....

It is important not to remove the oils in a horse's (6) ....

It is essential that what they (7) .... is clean.

Their teeth should be filed (8) ....

They need (9) .... against tetanus and equine flu.

To keep them warm and dry in winter, they wear a (10) ....

6 (Exam Hints: Paper 4, Part 3)

You will hear five different men talking about complaints about things bought in shops or from companies. For questions 1–5, choose from the list A–F the sentence that best describes what happened in each case. Use the letters only once. There is one extra letter which you do not need to use.

A He was surprised by what happened.

B He had to take matters further.

C He failed to get the service he was promised.

D He refused to pay more money.

E He got what he wanted but was not pleased.

F He was pleased at first but then disappointed.

Speaker 1 ....

Speaker 2 ....

Speaker 3 ....

Speaker 4 ....

Speaker 5 ....

7 (Exam Hints: Paper 4, Part 4)

You will hear two Australian students answering questions about a trip to Europe. Answer questions 1–7 by referring to the list of cities (A–E). Write the letter for each city in the space provided after the statement to which it refers.

A Amsterdam
B Athens
C Dublin
D London
E Paris

1 This was considered the best place for shopping.
....

2 This provided the chance to see paintings.
....

3 This city provided cheap entertainment.
....

4 Most of this city can be seen without using public transport. ....

5 This place was considered by the students to have the best buildings. ....

6 There were problems with the weather in this place.
....

7 This is the place they are leaving from.
....

GRAMMAR NOTES

Unit 1

In Unit 1 there are exercises on the *present simple*, *present continuous*, *too* and *superlative adjectives*.

Present Simple 1.1

Affirmative:	I (you, we) like oranges
	He (she, it) likes oranges
Negative:	I don't like oranges
	He doesn't like oranges
Questions:	Do you like oranges?
	Does he like oranges?
	Don't you like oranges?
	Doesn't he like oranges?
Short answers:	Yes, I do
	No, I don't
	Yes, he does
	No, he doesn't
Tag questions:	You live in Manchester, don't you?
	She drives a BMW, doesn't she?

There are full and contracted forms 'do not/don't,' 'does not/doesn't'

You use the *present simple* for:

1	*Habitual states and activities*	He catches the train every day. She lives in a flat.
2	*Things which are facts*	Lions eat meat.
3	*Future facts*	The train leaves at 10 a.m. tomorrow.
4	*Jokes and dramatic stories*	This man comes in and says ...
5	*Commentaries (e.g. football matches)*	Jones passes the ball to Smith...
6	*Thoughts and feelings*	I understand it now. I feel so happy.
7	*Declarations*	I name this ship 'Adventure'.
8	*Giving instructions and directions*	You add the eggs and then ... You go down this street and turn left.
9	*Newspaper headlines*	Brown wins the championship (*this means that he has already won*)

Present Continuous 1.2

The *present continuous* is formed with the present form of *to be* and the *-ing* form of the verb.

Affirmative:	I'm cooking dinner now. Can you phone back later?
	You're checking the numbers, aren't you?
	She's parking her car.
	We're looking for stolen goods.
	They're waiting for an answer.

There are full forms and contracted forms:

I am/*I'm*, you are/*you're*, he is/*he's*, she is/*she's*, it is/*it's*, we are/*we're*, they are/*they're*

Negative:	I'm not doing anything now.
	You aren't/You're not cleaning it properly
	He isn't/He's not writing it down.
	We aren't/We're not enjoying this film.
	They aren't/They're not writing it down.
Questions:	*These are formed by inversion.*
	Are you enjoying the meal?
	Is the doctor examining the patient?
Short answers:	Yes, I am. No, I'm not.
	Yes, you are. No, you're not/No, you aren't.
	Yes, he is. No, he's not. No, he isn't.
	Yes, we are. No, we're not. No, we aren't.
	Yes, they are. No, they're not. No, they aren't.
Tags:	Am I? Aren't I?
	Are you? Aren't you?
	Is she? Isn't she?
	Are we? Aren't we?
	Are they? Aren't they?

Spelling rules

One-syllable infinitives with a short vowel followed by a consonant double the final consonant: *swim – swimming*.

One-syllable infinitives with a long vowel and ending with a consonant do not double the final consonant. *meet – meeting.*

Infinitives ending in *-e* lose the *-e* and add *-ing*: *take – taking*

Infinitives ending in *-y* add *-ing*: *study – studying*

Infinitives ending in *-ie* change to *-y* and add *-ing*: *die – dying*

If the infinitive has two syllables and the stress is on the second, the final consonant doubles: *begin – beginning*

If the infinitive has two syllables and the stress is on the first, the final consonant does not double: *profit – profiting*

(*travel – travelling* is an exception in British English.)

You use the *present continuous*:

1 *For what is happening at the moment of speaking.*
   The toast is burning!

2 *For what is going on now; before now and after now.*
   I'm studying French this year.

Note sentences of this type refer to past, present and future activity.

3 *For planned events in the future.*
   I'm meeting Tom at 4 p.m. tomorrow.

4 *For expressing annoyance at people's habitual behaviour in combination with such words as 'always', 'constantly', 'forever'*
   Our neighbour is always having noisy parties.

Note: verbs of perception and feeling do not occur in the *present continuous* unless there is a change in the meaning of the word.

For example: 'see' when it means 'see with the eyes' is unlikely to occur in the *present continuous* but when it means 'meet' it occurs in such sentences as 'I'm seeing (meeting) John on Friday'.

Similarly, 'think' when it means 'give an opinion' occurs in the *present simple* form 'I think it is a good idea' but when it means 'the process of thinking' it is *present continuous*, 'I am still thinking about your suggestion'.

Too   1.3

The coffee is too hot to drink.
This means that it is impossible to drink the coffee. Do not confuse 'too' with 'very'.

This coffee is very hot – just how I like it.
This means that it is possible to drink the coffee.

Comparative and superlative adjectives   1.4

hot – hotter – hottest
successful – more successful – most successful

One syllable words add *-er* and *-est*. Words with three or more syllables are preceded by *more* and *most*. If a word has two syllables it may have *-er* and *-est*: *heavy-heavier-heaviest* or it may have *more* and *most*: *pleasant-more pleasant-most pleasant*

Unit 2

This unit covers the *past simple*, and *countable* and *uncountable* nouns.

Past Simple   2.1

Affirmative
Regular verbs form the past by adding *-ed* to the infinitive, or just *-d* if the infinitive ends with *-e*. One-syllable infinitives with a short vowel will double the final consonant.

Infinitive	Simple Past
like	I liked the film very much.
crash	He crashed his car into a tree.
chop	She chopped up the wood.

Irregular verbs do not add *-ed*. They change the vowel.

| *give* | He gave me some money. |
| *run* | He ran to the police station. |

Some irregular verbs do not change from the infinitive form.

| *cut* | He cut the string round the parcel. |
| *let* | He let the birds go free. |

Negative
Both regular and irregular verbs form the negative in the same way, by using *did not* or *didn't* in front of the infinitive.

For example:
He didn't like the film very much.
He didn't crash his car into a field.
She didn't chop up the wood.

Questions
Both regular and irregular form questions using *did* and the *infinitive* form of the verb.

For example:
Did you see him?
Did you like the film?

Short answers: Yes, I did. No, I didn't.

Tags: did you? didn't you?

The *past simple* is used for:

1 *Describing states and actions in the past which the speaker regards as complete.*

223

When did you meet him?
We met him in 1970.

Note: the *past simple* is often used with phrases that refer to past time such as 'five years ago', 'in 1970', 'yesterday', 'last week'.

2   *For describing hypothetical situations which have not yet happened.*

It's time we left.
I'd rather you came tomorrow.
If I knew the answer, I would tell you.
I wish I knew the answer.

Countable and Uncountable Nouns   2.2

English nouns are divided into *two* groups: *countable* (or *count* nouns) and *uncountable* (or *mass* nouns). The distinction is very important. The words that we can or cannot put in front of a noun depend on whether it is countable or uncountable.

Characteristics of **countable** nouns

There is a singular form and a plural form e.g. cup, cups. We can say:

I need a cup.
Where is the cup?
This cup is broken.
That cup is too small.
Cups cost 50p each.
The cups are broken.
These cups are expensive.
Those cups are cheaper.
There aren't many cups on the shelf.
There are a lot of cups on the shelf.
Here are some cups.
There aren't any cups.
We have a few cups.
We have few cups – we'd better buy some more.

Remember that *many*, and *(a) few* are used with plural countable nouns.

Characteristics of **uncountable** nouns

The noun is followed by a singular verb. There is no plural form. We can say:

I need advice on this matter.
This advice is useless.
The advice he gave me was useful.
You shouldn't listen to that advice.
He gave me a great deal of advice but I didn't take it.
He gave me some advice.
He didn't give me any advice.
He didn't give me much advice.
He gave me a lot of advice.

He gave me a little advice.
He gave me little advice – it wasn't worth asking him.

Remember that *much*, *a great deal of*, and *(a) little* are used with uncountable nouns. *A lot of* is used with both *countables* and *uncountables* and in positive statements, negative statements and questions. It is, therefore, a very useful expression which you are unlikely to make mistakes with.

Some words can be both *countable* and *uncountable* and if you look at these you will see why the distinction is a meaningful distinction. The meaning of a word changes according to whether it is used as a *countable* or an *uncountable* noun.

We need to put some glass in the window. (Uncountable)
This means the material 'glass'.
I need a glass. (Countable)
This means something you drink out of.
Give me a cloth to wipe the table. (Countable)
This means something for cleaning.
He chose some cloth to make a suit. (Uncountable)
This means material for making clothes.

What is the difference between these sentences? Which one of the four seems very unlikely?

1   He put chicken in the sandwiches.
2   He put a chicken in the sandwiches.
3   Coffee costs £4 a pound.
4   Would you like a coffee?

Note that the following words are *uncountable*: 'advice', 'furniture', 'information', 'spaghetti', 'money', 'news'.

Uncountable nouns are often used with words such as 'a bit of', 'a piece of' or more precise words such as 'a bottle of'.

He gave me a bit of advice.
I bought a bottle of milk.

The reason for this is that we regard *countable* nouns as limited, separate units and *uncountable* nouns as a mass without clear limits. By using 'a bit of' and so on we can regard *uncountable* nouns as units.

Some nouns, especially to do with food and drink, such as wine and cheese, normally occur as *uncountable* nouns. But sometimes you will see them with a singular and plural form.

This is a very nice cheese. (countable singular)
This means that the type of cheese (e.g. Cheddar) that you are eating is very nice.
If you mean that the cheese that you are actually eating is very nice you say:
This is very nice cheese. (uncountable)
This shop sells many cheeses. (countable plural)
This means that the shop sells many varieties of cheese. It doesn't tell you about the total amount.

This shop sells a lot of cheese. (uncountable)
This means that the amount of cheese sold in the shop is very large. It doesn't tell you how many varieties are sold.
This shop doesn't sell much cheese. (uncountable)
This means that the amount of cheese is very small.
This shop sells many cheeses (countable plural) but not much cheese (uncountable).
This means that the shop sells many different cheeses but not much cheese in total.

Unit 3

In Unit 3 you look at the *past continuous* and the *past simple*, *hope* and *expect*, *gain*, *win* and *earn*, and *to be/become/get used to + -ing*.

Past Continuous   3.1

Affirmative: You form the *past continuous* with the past tense of *to be* and the *-ing* form of the verb.

I (he, she,) *was eating* breakfast when the postman arrived.
We (you, they) *were waiting* for the bus when the accident happened.

Negative: John *wasn't* (*was not*) *listening* to what his father said.
The students *weren't* (*were not*) *paying* attention to the lecture.

Questions: *Was* he *doing* his homework when you visited him?
Were you *living* in London at that time?

Short answers: Yes, I was. No, I wasn't.
Yes, they were. No, they weren't.

Tag questions: You were waiting for him, *weren't you*?
He wasn't telling the truth, *was he*?

You use the *past continuous* for:

1   *Describing ongoing actions and events, when we are not concerned about when they started or when they finished. Often it describes the background to another event.*

I was reading when I heard loud noises from next door.

2   *For arrangements in the past.*

We were leaving at dawn.
(*This is the past form of the present continuous used for arrangements.*)

When you use the *past continuous* to describe the background against which a past simple action takes place, it doesn't matter what the order of tenses in the sentence is.

He found some gold coins when he was walking in the forest.

When he was walking in the forest, he found some gold coins.

Hope and Expect   3.2

When you use the word *expect* you are almost certain or have a very good reason to believe that something will, in fact, happen. You have prior knowledge that makes you think that the event is almost certain.

She is expecting a baby.   (*because she is pregnant*)
We expect John to pass the exam.   (*because he is a bright student*).
We expected him to arrive at 9 a.m.   (*this was the arrangement*)

When you use the word *hope* you say what you want to happen, but you are not certain.

I hope I get the job   (*but I might not*)
She is hoping to have a baby.   (*but she is not pregnant yet*).
I hope to arrive by 6 p.m.   (*but I'm not sure*)

Gain, Win, Earn   3.3

You use *gain* to express the idea of *increase*.

He gained a lot of experience.
The car gained speed.
She gained a reputation for efficiency.

You use *win* to express the idea of victory.

He won the race.

You use *earn* with reference to money.

She earns £50,000 a year.

To be used to, to get used to, to become used to   3.4

If you are not used to doing something, then you feel uncomfortable when you do it because you have not done it very often. If you are used to doing something then you feel very comfortable doing it and probably find it easy because you have done it many times before. It is possible, however, that you will never get used to doing some things even if you do them many times, because you dislike those things so much.

For three years I got up at 5 a.m., but I never got used to it.

This means that getting up early was always difficult and strange even after three years.

Remember that these expressions refer to how you feel, not to the number of times you have done something. *Get* and *become* refer to the process of change and often occur in continuous and perfect tenses.

John isn't used to driving this car.

This means that John has not driven the car (much) before and is not enjoying it because he finds the controls very different from his normal car. If he drives the car for long enough, however, he will be able to say:

I have got used to driving it now.

This means that he has now reached the state of feeling comfortable and at ease when driving the car.

John may say:
I am getting used to it.

This means that he is feeling less uncomfortable than before but isn't completely comfortable yet. When you have difficulties operating a new machine, or doing things in a different way from before, people often try to reassure you by saying:

Don't worry. You'll soon get used to it.

Unit 4

This unit looks at ways of talking about *the future, other, the other, another, others, journey, trip,* etc. and *so* and *neither*.

The future   4.1

There are a number of ways of talking about the future in English.

For things that you have already formed the intention of doing before you speak about them, use *going to*.

I'm going to apply for that job.

When *going to* is used for objects it means that there is clear evidence now for what is going to happen.

That wall is going to fall down.

This means that we have seen some indication, movement, for example, that this is likely to happen.

For arrangements that you have already made, and which might be in your diary, use the *present continuous*.

I'm meeting Mr Thomas at 3.30 tomorrow afternoon.

For things which happen at fixed times in the future, and may appear on timetables and itineraries, use the *present simple*.

Your flight leaves at 10 a.m. tomorrow.

'll

For things that you spontaneously decide to do and say as soon as you think of them, use *'ll*.

That case looks very heavy. I'll help you carry it.

Be careful not to say 'I help …' in these situations. The *present simple* is not correct for spontaneous offers and responses.

For things that the speaker regards as simple, straightforward facts about the future.

I'll see you on Tuesday.
You'll receive the goods early next week.

Note that the full form *will* is not very common in spoken English. We can use it for *requests*:

Will you come this way, please? (*Would* or *could* are also possible) and *will* can be used in short answers.

Yes, I will (*expressing agreement to do something*).

The contracted form *'ll* is much more common than *will*. You should always use the contracted form in speech.

When you are imagining now future activities that will last for some time, use the *future continuous*.

This time next year we'll be working in a different office.

Won't

This is used to express refusal. It is used for both people and things.

I won't do as you say.
The machine won't give me my money back.

Again, it is much more common than the full form *will not*, which in most circumstances sounds so strong that it is almost aggressive. You are likely to hear *will* and *will not* when people are arguing.

The other, another, the others, others   4.2

You say *the other* when there are only two items or two groups.

Here is one glove – where is the other one?
Some children have arrived but where are the other children?

(Be careful not to make *other* plural when it is followed by a plural noun.)
You say 'the other girl' (one of two girls) and 'the other girls' (one group of girls of two groups)
We use *another* when we choose the second or third item from a group.

He ate one cake and then another and another and another.
We managed to get another person into the car.

The others refers to a known group of people.
Six of us are here but where are the others?

Others refers to an unknown group of people.
Many others had failed to reach the South Pole, but Amundsen succeeded.

Words to do with travel   4.3

You use *voyage* for a journey by sea.
A *journey* is on land, by train or car for example.
A *cruise* is a holiday on a ship.
A *trip* means going somewhere, staying and coming back.
A *trip* is two *journeys* (going and coming back).
A *trip* is often short but not necessarily so.
A *flight* is by air.
A *pilgrimage* is a religious journey.
Travel is either a verb *to travel* or an adjective as in *a travel agent* or an uncountable noun as in '*Travel in the 21st century*' but not a singular noun. It is wrong to say 'The travel lasted two days'. You should say 'The journey (or voyage or whatever) lasted two days).
Travels is a plural noun meaning the same as *journeys* but used only for explorers and other people who travel a lot.

So, neither (or nor)   4.4

You use both these words to agree with what someone has said. *So* agrees with positive statements.

I like cats. *So do I.*
If you want to disagree you say *I don't.*

Neither agrees with negative statements.

I didn't go to the concert. *Neither did I.*
If you wish to disagree, you say *I did.*

You use the auxiliary verb followed by the pronoun or noun. In the case of modal verbs, you use the same modal verb.

I must go now. *So must I.*
She can't swim. *Neither can her brother.*

Unit 5

This unit look at sentences beginning with *if*.

If sentences   5.1

A The first kind of sentence practised in this unit has the pattern:

If + present simple + will + infinitive

If you wait a moment, I'll get the parcel.

It refers to things that the speaker thinks are likely or almost certain to happen if a condition is met.

If Chelsea play as they usually *do*, they will win the match.
The speaker clearly expects Chelsea to win.

When the *if* clause begins a sentence, you put a comma at the end of the clause. When the *if* clause ends a sentence you do not put a comma.

If you ask him, he'll tell you the answer.
He'll tell you the answer if you ask him.

You can use other present tenses and modal verbs in this type of sentence.

If you are thinking of buying a new television, you will get a bargain at 'TV Superstore'.
If you can speak French, they will pay you extra.
If you buy ten, you can get a discount.

B The second kind of sentence has the pattern:

If + past simple + would + infinitive

If I had enough money, I would lend it to you.
You can use this pattern for things which are unlikely.

If I went on a diet, I would lose weight.
This is possible, but the speaker has no intention of doing so – it is very unlikely.

If we had our own spaceship, we could travel to Mars.
This is clearly not going to happen – it is impossible.

You can use modal verbs in both clauses.

If humans could extract oxygen from water, they could live under the sea.

You must be careful not to put *would* after *if*. It is incorrect to say:

*If I would work harder, I would pass my exam.

Would does come after *if* in some polite expressions such as:

If you would wait a few moments, I will fetch the manager.

Unit 6

This unit looks at the *passives*, *anybody*, *nobody*, etc., *must be/could be* and *too/enough*.

Passives   6.1

Sentences can be transformed into the passive by following four very simple rules.

Example:

Active The police took the documents away.
Passive The documents were taken away by the police.

Step 1: Identify the *object* (the documents) and write it down:
The documents …

Step 2: Look at the active sentence and notice the tense of the verb. It is past simple so write down the past simple form of *to be*. Remember that 'documents' is plural so you need to write down *were*.
The documents were …

Step 3: Write down the *past participle* of the verb. The past particle of *took* is *taken*.
The documents were taken away …

Step 4: Consider whether you need to say *by* followed by the subject of the original sentence (the police). It isn't always necessary but in this case it is.
The documents were taken away by the police.

Transforming sentences from active to passive and vice versa is a popular examination task. Remember, however, that the reason for using the passive is that we want to start the sentence with the most important thing. We say: *Professor Brown was killed by lightning* because *Professor Brown* is more important than the *lightning*. This sentence would sound strange if you transformed it into the active. Another reason for using the passive is when you do not know who did something. We say: *My car was stolen* because we do not know who stole it and even if we did, we might not want to mention that person first and our car second.

Anyone, anybody   6.2

You can use these words in negative sentences.
There isn't anyone there = *There is no-one there.*

You can use them in questions.
Does anyone know the answer? No, no-one. or Yes, I think someone does.

You can use them in statements.
Anyone can do it. This means that it is very easy to do.
Anyone can go to the party – you don't need an invitation. This means that there are no restrictions.

It is the same with *anywhere* and *any*.
Put the books anywhere you like. This means that it doesn't matter where you put them.
She will be satisfied with any record by 'Queen'. This means that

she likes all the records so you don't need to be selective.

Must be, could be   6.3

That must be Professor Moriarty. This means that you are almost sure.
That could be Professor Moriarty. This means that you are not sure but it is possible that you are right.
If we put these words on a scale, it looks like this.

He may be the man the police are looking for.	*possible*
He might be …	*possible*
He could be …	*very possible*
He must be …	*almost certain*
He is …	*certain*

Too   6.4

Do not confuse *too* with *very*.

It is very cold but we are going to play football.
This means that despite the cold we will play football.

It is too cold to play football.
This means that we will not play football because of the cold. Too conveys the idea that something is impossible.

Enough

You use *enough* before nouns and after adjectives.

John isn't old enough to drive a car.
We haven't got enough money to buy this car.

Unit 7

This unit looks at the *present perfect simple*.

The present perfect   7.1

Whichever way you use the *present perfect*, it is always relevant to *now*. The point of view from which events and action are seen is *now*. This is why it is called the *present* perfect. The present perfect refers to past events but they are past events which are relevant to *now* and seen from *now*. We can, however, sub-divide the various uses of the present perfect.

A *For saying what happened in the past but not saying when.*

Jane has studied the history of art.

This sentence does not tell us when Jane studied this. It suggests, for example, that since she has studied it she may now be able to answer our questions about painting.

B *For referring to recent past events.*

John has just phoned.

This happened a short time ago. When the present perfect refers to recent past events, you can use *just*. Remember that the present perfect is not only for the recent past:

This castle has stood here for a thousand years.

Note that it doesn't matter whether the event or action is complete or not. Often the present perfect does refer to completed events and actions.

Vincent has sold all his paintings.

This means that he has none left so the selling is complete.

But it also refers to events and actions which are not complete.
I have worked here for fifteen years. (*and I continue to work here*)
We have interviewed ten candidates so far. (*and we will interview more*)

You can use *just*, *so far*, *yet*, *already*, *ever* and *never* with the present perfect.

You cannot use *ago*, *last week*, *in 1970*. These tell you exactly when things happened and are used with past tenses.
When you want to say that you moved to London six months ago and that you are living there now, you say:

I have lived in London for six months/since January.

Be careful not to say:
*I am in London since six months.

However you may say:
I am in London for six months.
This means that the total length of your stay is six months. If you say this, people will think that you have just arrived. You might say this to the immigration officer on arrival.

Unit 8

This unit looks at the *present perfect continuous*.

Present perfect continuous   8.1

You form the *present perfect continuous* by adding the *-ing* form of the verb to the *present perfect simple* of *to be*.

Form

Affirmative: I (you, we, they) have been working since 9 a.m.

He (she, it) has been working for six hours.
The contracted forms are I've, you've, we've, they've, he's, she's, it's.

Negative: I have not (haven't) been studying hard.
She has not (hasn't) been feeling well lately.

Questions: Have you been reading this book?
Has he been taking the medicine?

Short answers: Yes, I have. No, I haven't.
Yes, he has. No, he hasn't.

Tag questions: You've been working hard, haven't you?
He's been waiting for a long time, hasn't he?

Use

You use the *present perfect continuous* to refer to actions and events which began in the past and continue at the moment of speaking, or have stopped but are relevant to the present or will continue into the future.

For example:
I've been driving for four hours.
This means that you have just stopped or are continuing to drive – the context will make this clear.

I've been working in the garden all morning.
If, when you say this you are washing your hands, then your work in the garden has finished but you can say this as you continue to work.

It's been raining for six hours.
This means it started raining six hours ago, is raining now and will continue into the future.

You can also use the *present perfect continuous* to refer to repeated activity over time.

For example:
I've been trying to phone him all morning.
This means that I have dialled his number many times but without getting an answer.

You can use the *present perfect continuous* to explain something that can be seen.

For example:
Why is your house in such a mess?
I've been re-decorating.

The   8.2

You use *the*:

for countries that have 'United' or 'Union' in the name;

for geographical features: 'the North Pole', 'the Tropic of Capricorn', 'the Himalayas' 'the Middle East', 'the Sahara';

in expressions which clearly refer to one thing: 'the best', 'the worst', the first, the same;

for double comparative constructions: 'the bigger, the better', 'the more, the merrier';

for families: 'The Robinsons', 'the Joneses' – *this means all the members of a nuclear family*;

when using a singular countable noun to refer to a type of animal or machine:
The cow has been domesticated for thousands of years.
The car has transformed our lives;

for groups of people where the adjective is used as a collective noun: 'the poor', 'the rich', 'the old', 'the blind'.

You do not use *the*:

for countries that do not have 'Union, United or Republic' in their name: France (but *the* Republic of France), Holland, Japan, Germany, Greece. There are a few exceptions: the Netherlands, the Lebanon;

for abstract words such as 'nature', 'society', 'crime'.
Note the difference between:
The President was determined to reduce crime. (*crime in general*)
The crime he committed was very serious. (*one particular crime*)

You do not use *the* for uncountable nouns used in a general way:

Spinach is good for you.
John is good at swimming.

or in expressions such as 'at school', 'in church', 'in court', 'in hospital' when the sentence refers to the basic function of the place mentioned.
For example: He went to school. *This means he went to be educated.* He went to the school. *This means for a purpose which is not education.*

Unit 9

This unit looks at *relatives* (*who*, *which*, *that* and *whose*). They join clauses together in one sentence. Without them, you would have to write in very short sentences.

Relatives 9.1

a Defining clauses (subject) – who, that, which

The girl was happy. She had won first prize.
The girl who had won first prize was happy.

The word *who* replaces *she* in the second sentence. We use *who* for people and *which* for things.

The car was stolen. It has been recovered.

The car which was stolen has been recovered.

We can use *that* for both people and things.
The girl that had won first prize was happy.
The car that was stolen has now been recovered.

The only information that we have about 'the girl' and 'the car' is given by the words *who/that had won first prize* and *which/that was stolen*. This information helps us to identify the girl and the car.
We call these clauses *defining relative clauses*.

b Defining clauses (object) – contact clauses

In the examples above, *who*, *which* or *that* replace 'she' and 'it' – the subjects of the sentences. In the examples below we are going to replace the 'object' of the sentences.

He's the man. The policeman arrested him.
He's the man the policeman arrested.

Notice that there is no relative here. It is known as a *contact clause*. We can also say:

He's the man that the policeman arrested. But 'that' is not *necessary.*
He's the man whom the policeman arrested.
'Whom' is now extremely formal, almost unknown in spoken English and rare except in the most formal writing.
He's the man who the policeman arrested.
Some people regard this as incorrect (preferring 'whom') but it is commonly used.

It is best to use *contact clauses*. Be careful *not* to write:

He is the man who he gave me the money.
Here is the television I bought it this morning.

These are incorrect. The relative or contact clause replaces the pronoun.

c Non-defining clauses – who, whom

None of the sentences that we have looked at so far contained commas. But sometimes you will read sentences like this:

Mr Brown, who called yesterday, is coming to dinner.

The words *who called yesterday* do not define or identify Mr Brown, whose name we already know. They merely give us extra information about him. These clauses are called *non-defining relative clauses*. In these clauses we do not use *that*. We use *who* or *whom* for people.

Janet has just won some money. She is going on holiday.
Janet, who has just won some money, is going on holiday.
Who replaces 'she' – the subject of the second sentence.

Jack Scott is back in prison. The police recaptured him this morning.
Jack Scott, whom/who the police recaptured this morning, is back in prison.

It is traditionally correct to use *whom* but *who* is often seen nowadays. *Whom/who* replace 'him' – the object of the second sentence.

d Non-defining clauses – which

When we are referring to things, we use *which* for both subject and object.

'The Titanic' has been photographed lying on the seabed. It struck an iceberg in 1912.
'The Titanic', which struck an iceberg in 1912, has been photographed lying on the seabed.

The painting by Goya has been found. Thieves stole it last week.
The painting by Goya, which thieves stole last week, has been found.

e Whose

We can use *whose* to replace possessive words such as 'his', 'her', 'their' in both defining and non-defining relative clauses.

The boy was pleased. His painting impressed the judges.
The boy whose painting impressed the judges was pleased.

Michael Smith has won the prize again. His photographs won first prize last year.
Michael Smith, whose photographs won first prize last year, has won the prize again.

Unit 10

Modal verbs   10.1

The information on modal verbs is sufficient to help you do the exercises on modal verbs. It is not a fully comprehensive study of these verbs.

Should can be used in two ways:

1   To express a present obligation.
    You should pay him the money you owe him (*it is your duty to do so – not as strong as 'must'*)

2   To say that something is probable, either now or soon.
    You should see the train any minute now. (*you expect to see it soon*)

Might is used to say that something is possible but not very likely.
We might arrive in time (*but I doubt it*)

Could is used for a stronger sense of possibility.
Our team could win the match. (*it is possible*)

Must can be used in two ways:

1   To express strong obligation.
    You must arrive before 9 a.m.

    The opposite of this meaning is *must not*.
    You must not be late.

2   To make deductions based on evidence.
    That must be the man we are looking for. He fits the description we have.

    The opposite of this meaning is *can't be*.
    That can't be the man we are looking for. He looks nothing like this photograph.

Should have + past participle can be used in two ways:

1   To make a reasonable assumption about what has happened.
    Jack should have reached the airport by now. (*but we are not sure*)

2   To refer to a past obligation.
    He should have given us the information. (*but he didn't*)

Could have + past participle can be used in three ways:

1   For things that you were able to do but did not do.
    We could have finished the job in three days. (*but we didn't*)

2   For things that were possible but did not happen
    You could have lost all your money. (*but you didn't*)

3   For making guesses about what has happened.
    John could have missed the train or he could have got lost. (*we don't know*)

Must have + past participle is used for deductions that we are fairly certain about and probably have evidence for.
He must have walked this way. Look at the footprints in the snow.

The opposite of this meaning is *couldn't have* or *can't have*.
He can't have come this way. There are no footprints in the snow.

Might have + past participle can be used in two ways.

1   For things that were possible but did not happen.
    You might have warned me. (*but you didn't – this is a complaint*)

2   For making guesses about what has happened.
    Jack might have forgotten his appointment.

If we arrange sentences according to how certain the speaker is, the order is as follows:

They might have reached the airport by now. (*not really sure*)
They could have reached the airport by now. (*possible*)
They should have reached the airport by now. (*very likely*)
They must have reached the airport by now. (*almost certain*)

any-, some-, no-, every-   10.2

Make sure you understand the difference between *anything/anyone* and *no-one/nothing*.

Anyone can solve that problem, means that the problem is very easy, so everybody (or anyone you ask) knows the answer.

No-one can solve that problem, means that the problem is impossibly difficult.

You can eat anything you like, means that you have a completely free choice about what you eat.

There was nothing to eat, means a complete absence of food. In order to express the same meaning using *anything* you must say: There wasn't anything to eat. Note that He didn't say anything, and He said nothing, mean the same but the second sentence is more emphatic.

Used to   10.3

Form

Affirmative:	I *used to* live in Bristol.
Negative:	He *didn't use to* drive to work but he does now.
Question:	*Did* your parents *use to* live in that house.
	Didn't you *use to* work for the Bank of England.
Short forms:	Yes, I did. No, I didn't.
Tags:	You *used to* live there, *didn't* you?
	He *didn't use to* like gardening, *did* he?

Used to refers to regular, habitual activity in the past. It is only used for the past. It has no present form. If you want to talk about habitual activity in the present, you need the *present simple* or the *present simple* and *usually*.

We get up early *or*
We usually get up early.
These are the present equivalents of:
We used to get up early.

Used to is similar in meaning to the *simple past* but emphasises that an action or event continued for a long time or was often repeated.
These sentences are very similar in meaning:

When I was at university, I cycled a lot.
When I was at university, I used to cycle a lot.

Make sure that you can distinguish between *used to + infinitive* and *to be used to + -ing* and the regular verb *to use + noun*.

Compare these three sentences:
John *used to work* in a restaurant.
Sheila *isn't used to working* such long hours.
We used a knife to open the tin.

Like, as, as if, alike   10.4

When you want to say that two things or people are separate but similar you use *like*.

Your house looks *like* mine.
This means that the two houses are similar in appearance.
We can also say:
These two houses look *alike*.

When you use *as* you are referring to one thing or person, not two.

John works *as* a doctor.
This means that John and the doctor are the same person. John is a doctor. You are referring to one person, not comparing two.

He eats *like* a horse.
This means that he eats a lot – like a horse. It does not mean that he is a horse.
If you use 'as' in this sentence it can only mean that he goes into a field and eats grass.

He looks *as if* he knows what he is doing.
This means that he appears to be very confident. This impression may or may not be true.

You can also say, 'He looks *like* he knows what he is doing', *but this is rather colloquial.*

About to   10.5

He is *about* to speak.
This means that he will speak in the next few seconds but hasn't started yet.

She was *about* to leave work when the telephone rang.
This means that the telephone rang just before she left – so she didn't leave until later.

Bound to   10.6

Bound is from the verb *bind – bound – bound*. Literally, it means to 'tie up'.

His hands were bound behind his back.

But *to be bound* also means that something is certain to happen.

She is *bound to pass* the exam.
This means that she is certain to pass – there is no doubt about it.

The train *is bound for* Glasgow.
This means that the train is on its way to Glasgow.

A few, few   10.7

You use these words in front of plural nouns.
We have *a few* tomatoes so we can make some soup.
This means that we have a small number of tomatoes but we have enough. It has a positive meaning.

Few people are interested in this subject. We will have to cancel the course next year.
This means that the number is so small that the course is not worth running. It has a negative meaning.

A little, little

You use these words in front of uncountable nouns.

There is *a little* flour, so I can make a small cake.
This means that there is a small amount of flour, but just enough for a cake.

They have *little* food left – they cannot survive for much longer.
This means that the amount of food is so small that they may soon starve to death. It is very negative.

We can also use these words as nouns.
The patient has eaten *a little* today.
This is good news – he is getting better.
The patient has eaten *little* today.
This is bad news – he is not getting better.

Unit 11

The past perfect   11.1

Form

You form the *past perfect* with the past of *have* (*had*) and the past participle of the verb.

Affirmative:	I (you, he, she, we, they) had finished work before the inspectors arrived. *Contracted forms*: I'd, you'd, etc.
Negative:	We hadn't (had not) seen so much money before.
Questions:	Had they studied the map before they set off?
Tag questions:	He hadn't used that type of machine before, had he? She had gone before you arrived, hadn't she?

Use

You use the *past perfect* when you look back on the past from a point in the past. Therefore, it is necessary to know what the point in the past is. You can indicate this by using the *past simple* in the same sentence.
For example:
In the garden of my new house there was
    (*point in the past – past simple*)
a lot of rubbish which the builders had left behind.
    (*before the point in the past – past perfect*)

You can indicate the point in the past by mentioning a specific time.

By 10 a.m. (*point in the past*) we had taken (*before the point in the past*) orders from fifty customers.
You can indicate the point in the past in another sentence.
John left the army in 1990 (*point in the past*). He had served twenty years (*before the point in the past*).

You do not use the past perfect for a series of consecutive events in the past. You use the past simple.
For example:
The soldier picked up his gun, took aim and fired.

You use the past perfect in third conditional sentences.
For example:

If I had known the painting was by Goya (*but I didn't know*), I would have bought it (*but I didn't buy it*).

You can use the past perfect after *if only* and *I wish*.
For example:

I wish I had studied harder (*but I didn't*)
If only I hadn't sold that painting (*but I did*).

You use the past perfect in reported speech. It can replace both the present perfect and the past simple.
For example:

Direct Speech:	'Our school has won the competition,' Peter told John.
Reported Speech:	Peter told John that their school had won the competition.
Direct Speech:	'I sold my car yesterday,' Mary told Elizabeth.
Reported Speech:	Mary told Elizabeth that she had sold her car the day before.

When you use the words *after*, *before* with the part of the sentence that refers to the point before the past, you can use the *past simple* instead of the *past perfect*.
For example:

After I finished my homework, I watched television.
After I had finished my homework, I watched television.

The reason you can use the *past simple* instead of the *past perfect* is that the meaning of the word *after* is enough to express the meaning that one thing happened after another. If you use the word *when* you do need to use the *past perfect* to convey your meaning. *For example*:

When the police entered the house, the robbers had left.
This means that the robbers left before the police arrived. The two events did not happen at the same time.

When the police entered the house, the robbers left.
This means that the two events happened at the same time.

In spoken English it can be difficult to hear the *past perfect* tense, especially if the main verb begins with /d/ or /t/. *For example*:

He'd taken the car away before I arrived.
In this sentence, although you may not be able to hear 'He'd' the word 'taken' should tell you that the *past perfect* is being used, because the past would be 'I took'.

However, in this sentence:

I'd decided to reject the offer before I got the letter

you may hear 'I'd decided' as 'I decided'. However, this is unlikely to lead to any serious misunderstanding. Native-speakers of English can't hear the difference either.

When you use the *past perfect continuous*, as with other continuous sentences, it is because you want to say that something happened over a period of time.

We had been working for six hours before we were able to have a break.

Wound, injury, damage   11.2

Wound is both a noun (*a wound*) and a regular verb (*to wound*). You use *wound* when the skin is clearly cut or penetrated, by a knife or bullet for example. You can use *wound*, therefore, when people have been fighting in battles.
Injury is both a noun (*an injury, injuries*) and a regular verb (*to injure*). You use it in connection with accidents. However, if you are referring very precisely to a cut on the skin, you can say *wound* even if it has been caused by an accident.
For example:

The nurse removed bits of glass from the wound.

Damage is an uncountable noun (*damage*) and a regular verb (*to damage*). It is used for objects, not people. However, you can use *damage* for internal organs – brain *damage*, for example. Note that *damage*, because it is uncountable, has no plural and is preceded by 'a lot of', 'much', etc. The word *damages* means a sum of money which is paid by someone who has committed libel or slander.

For example:

The judge ordered him to pay £20,000 damages.

Cure, treat, heal   11.3

If the doctor can *cure* you, you make a complete recovery. The doctor will *treat* you, by giving you medicines for example, but there is no guarantee that the treatment will cause the illness to go away. It may, or it may not. That is why we can say: *We can treat this disease but there is no cure for it.* This means that doctors will be able to make you feel better, but they cannot make you healthy again. When we use the word *heal* we are referring to the way in which skin which has been cut, gradually returns to normal. *Minor wounds will heal by themselves, without treatment.* We can also use this word metaphorically.
For example:

Only time can heal a broken heart.
Time heals all wounds.

Unit 12

If sentences   12.1

Sentences with this pattern (usually called the *third conditional*)

If we had repaired (past perfect) the wall, it would have cost (would have + past participle) £500.

mean that something did not happen.
We did not repair the wall and therefore we did not spend £500.
The idea that 'it did not happen' is true only if both parts of the sentence are positive. If they are negative, then something did happen.

If you hadn't reminded me about the tickets, I would not have remembered to bring them.
This means that you did remind me and I did remember.

Sometimes, one half of the sentence is negative and the other half positive.
For example:

If the spy hadn't warned the soldiers, they would have walked into an ambush.
This means that the spy did warn the soldiers and they didn't walk into an ambush.
Note that the contracted forms are 'I wouldn't've remembered' and 'they would've walked'.

It is possible to have a variety of patterns after *if*. The pattern you have studied in this unit refers to the past, but it is correct to say:

If we had won the first prize (*but we did not*), we would be on holiday in Tahiti now (*but we are not*).

Bath, bathe, sunbathe   12.2

To bath means to have a bath, usually in a bath in a bathroom.
To bathe means to swim, usually in the sea. It also means to clean with water, for example: The nurse bathed the cut with water
To sunbathe means to lie in the sun until your skin becomes darker – it has nothing to do with water. Don't write *I had a sunbath on the beach.
You should write, 'I sunbathed on the beach.' The noun is *sunbathing*.

Short answers   12.3

To form a short answer to a question, you use the auxiliary verb or the main verb in the case of modal verbs, *be* and *have*.
Remember that short answers are not contracted – you use the full form.

For example:

You're a doctor, aren't you. Yes, I am (*not I'm*).

But *negative* short answers can be contracted.
He's late, isn't he? No, he isn't.

What, which   12.4

What can be followed by an infinitive with to or a clause. The clause beginning with *what* is the subject or object of the sentence.
For example:

What he said was beyond belief.
He didn't know what to do.

In these sentences *what* does not refer to a noun in another part of the sentence – it is the subject or object of the rest of the sentence.
In contrast, *which* does refer to a word which precedes it in the sentence:

He gave me a painting which his grandfather had left him.

In this sentence, *which* refers to *painting*.

Unit 13

13.1   For revision of past tenses, see units 2, 4, 8 and 11.

Adjectives in -*ed* and -*ing*.   13.2

There are many pairs of adjectives such as *interesting* and *interested*.

If you read an *interesting* book, you are *interested* in that book.
If you go on a *tiring* journey, you will feel *tired*.
The words ending with -*ed* describe how people feel. The words ending with -*ing* describe what people or things are.
For example:

He is a very interesting writer. I am interested in what he writes.

Remind, remember, memorise, reminder, memory, souvenir   13.3

If you *remind* someone to do something, you say or do something that makes another person remember something that they might have forgotten.
For example:

I reminded Peter to buy the tickets.
If I hadn't, he probably would have forgotten.

Things that you see can remind you of other things.
For example:

These mountains remind me of the Swiss Alps.

A *reminder* is something that reminds people. If someone has not paid a bill, they might be sent a reminder.

Memory is your capacity to remember. You can lose your memory, improve your memory, have a good or bad memory. *Memories* are the specific things that you remember. *To memorise* is to learn things by heart.
For example:

The politician memorised his speech so that he wouldn't need to use notes.

A *souvenir* is an object that reminds you of a holiday or a similar experience.

Unit 14

14.1   For revision of *if*-sentences, see units 5 and 12.

Unless   14.2

If you don't pay in full, you can't have a discount.

You can re-write this as:

Unless you pay in full, you can't have a discount.

Rob, steal   14.3

If you steal something, you take away with you the thing that you steal.

He stole the painting.
This means that he took the painting away.
If you rob something, the thing that you rob stays where it is.
He robbed the art gallery.
This means that the art gallery stays where it is.
The sentence does not tell us what was stolen.
We *cannot* say:
He stole the art gallery.

Fault, blame   14.4

To *blame* a person means to believe that he or she is responsible for an accident or mistake.

I blame John for not finishing the work in time.
John is to blame for not finishing the work in time.

If you blame someone for something, you think that the accident or mistake is his or her *fault*.

It is John's fault that the work was not finished in time.

Blame describes the way people feel about the person they think is responsible.

The   14.5

The difference between:

He went to prison

and

He went to the prison

is that the first sentence means that he was a prisoner and the second sentence means that he was not a prisoner but went to the prison for some other reason – to work, for example. Writing or not writing *the* makes a big difference to the meaning.
If we say:

Bill is in hospital. *This means that he is ill.*
The most common mistake is to write *the* when it is not necessary. Other words for which the same difference in meaning occurs are: *court, university, college, church* and *school.*

He is at university. *This means he is a student.*

He works for the university. *This means he is not a student or a teacher. He does some sort of job for the university.*

Unit 15

Indirect Speech   15.1

Indirect Speech is often tested in the First Certificate and other examinations. It is, however, a rather artificial exercise. In real life, people either simply repeat the words they heard. *For example*:

Martin picks up the phone and hears Bill say 'I'll be late'. He then puts the phone down and says to his friends, *'Bill says he'll be late.'*
or they paraphrase, using different words to express the same meaning. However, sometimes we do follow the rules for changing direct speech to indirect speech, especially if the time and place are different from the original time and place. The changes are as follows:

Tense changes

present simple	**past simple**
'Where does Tom work?' John asked me.	John asked me where Tom worked.
present continuous	**past continuous**
'What is Jane doing?' Mary asked me.	Mary asked what Jane was doing.
present perfect	**past perfect**
'Why has Bob left?' Tony asked me.	Tony asked me why Bob had left.
past simple	**past perfect (or past simple)**
'What did Lynne say?' Sally asked me.	Sally asked me what Lynne had said *or* Sally asked me what Lynne said.
past continuous	**past perfect continuous**
'What was Jane doing?' Mary asked me.	Mary asked me what Jane had been doing. *or* Mary asked me what Jane was doing.
will	**would**
'Will you be coming to the party, Peter?' asked Martina.	Martina asked Peter if he would be coming to the party.

Past perfect verbs do not change. Modal verbs do not normally change although *must* may change to *had to* and *can* may change to *could*. Much depends on the exact meaning that you want to express.

Time words will change if the time has changed.
'Will you see John today, Bill?' asked Peter.
Peter asked Bill if he would see John on that day.

'Are you leaving tomorrow?' Martin asked me.
Martin asked me if I was leaving the next day.

'Did you go to Paris last year?' Lynne asked me.
Lynne asked me if I had gone to Paris the year before/the previous year.

'Are you going to live in Athens next year?' Diana asked me.
Diana asked me if I was going to live in Athens *the next year/the following year*.

Note that if you are reporting this question in the same year that it was asked, it is not necessary to change 'next year'.

Place words will change if the place has changed.

'How long are you going to live here?' she asked me.
She asked me how long I was going to live *there*.
'Do you like this hotel?' he asked me.
He asked me if I liked *that/the hotel*.

Note that if you are in the same place when you report the question, the place words will not change.

Changes in word order

Note that in direct questions the verb comes in the middle of the sentence:
'Where is the receipt, Nigel?' Lynne asked.

But in indirect questions the verb is *at the end*:

Lynne asked Nigel where the receipt *was*.

Unit 16

Indirect Speech (2)   16.1

When changing *indirect speech* into *direct speech* you have to apply in reverse the changes you make when you change direct speech into indirect speech. In addition, you have to pay attention to the punctuation. You need speech marks at the beginning and end of the spoken words and the full stop comes right at the end, not after the spoken words.

Jenny told me that she was leaving the next day.
'I'm leaving tomorrow,' Jenny told me.

You may need to add a question mark.
Tom asked me if I knew what the answer was.
'Do you know what the answer is?' Tom asked me.

Paraphrasing direct speech

Sometimes instead of keeping the exact words that the speaker used and making various tense changes, we can express the same meaning with other words. We use different words in order to express more clearly the meaning of what the speaker said.
For example, if Tom says:
'Why don't we have a picnic?' he is not really asking a question. He is making a suggestion.
If we say: *Tom asked why we didn't have a picnic*, it sounds as if he is asking a question or even making a complaint.

It is better to say: *Tom suggested having a picnic* because this is a truer reflection of his meaning.
Words frequently used in this way are

accuse someone of + *-ing*
apologise to someone for + *-ing*
admit + *-ing*
deny + *-ing*
suggest + *-ing* **or** that + pronoun + should
tell (not) + (to) infinitive
promise + (to) infinitive
refuse + (to) infinitive

So, such (a)   16.2

So is followed by *adjectives*
The soup was so hot I couldn't eat it.

Such (a)
This is followed by a noun or an adjective plus noun. If it is a singular noun, you need *such a*.

It was such a slow train that I arrived late for the meeting.

If it is an uncountable noun or a plural countable noun, you need *such*.

They were such large tablets that I couldn't swallow them.
It was such poor quality oil that it damaged my car engine.

I wish, if only   16.3

If you have regrets about something you don't have or can't do, use *wish/if only + past*.
I wish I had a ticket for that concert. (*but I don't*)
I wish I knew the answer. (*but I don't*)

If you have regrets about something you didn't do, use *wish/if only + past perfect*.
I wish I had arrived at the station in time to catch the fast train. (*but I didn't*)

You may have regrets about situations which actually exist.
I wish I didn't have to work such long hours. (*but I do*)

You may have regrets about things you did.
I wish I hadn't bought this car. (*but I did*)

For wishes about the future, use *wish/if only + would*.
I wish it would stop raining.
I wish they would stop making so much noise.

Note that it is incorrect to say *I wish I would… Do not say *I wish I would be rich (*this is a mistake*). You should say: I wish I were rich.

When *would* is used after *wish*, the sentence expresses the idea of willingness (or lack of it) or habit. Do not say: I wish it would be sunny tomorrow. To express this meaning you say: I hope it will be sunny tomorrow. If you say: I wish you would come to my party, it means that the person has already refused to come. If this has not happened, you say: I hope you will *come to my party*. The sentence: I hope John will *arrive on time*, expresses a hope about the future but the sentence: I wish John would *arrive on time*, is a complaint about his habitual lateness.

Unit 17

Gerund (1) and infinitive   17.1

Some of the most common words and phrases followed by the gerund form are:

enjoy	consider
mind	involve
avoid	risk
practise	admit
deny	dread
prevent … from	apologise … for
accuse … of	succeed in
to be used to	not worth
object to	can't stand
can't help	keep
it's no use	look forward to.

Phrasal verbs are followed by the *gerund*, as are prepositions.
Some verbs are followed by the infinitive with *to*. Some of the most common are *want, advise, decide, ought*
Many verbs are followed by infinitives without *to*. Most modal verbs are in this category – *must, can, could, may, might, shall, should*

Note that the infinitive can take a number of different forms. *For example*:

We must leave. (*infinitive* without *to*)
I want to leave. (*infinitive* with *to*)
This work will have to be left until tomorrow. (*passive infinitive*)
The building seems to have been destroyed. (*perfect passive infinitive*)
Our guests seem to be leaving now. (*continuous infinitive*)
They seem to have left. (*perfect infinitive*)
They seem to have been waiting for a long time. (*perfect continuous infinitive*)

To make them negative, you put *not* in front of the infinitive.

He seems not to have been informed.

Could, was able to, manage to, succeed in   17.2

Could does not mean successful completion of a specific task. It refers to general ability only.

I could swim when I was six.
This sentence means that you had learned to swim by the age of six, but tells us nothing about your particular achievements.

I could swim the Channel when I was twelve.
This sentence means that you had the ability to swim the Channel. It is not clear whether you actually did so. If you mean that a particular event really took place, do not use could. Use managed to, succeeded in *or* was able to.

I could swim the Channel if I wanted to.
This sentence means that if, in the future, you attempted to swim the Channel, you think you would succeed.

I succeeded in swimming the Channel when I was twelve.
This sentence means that you actually did so.

Therefore, if you want to say that you successfully performed a specific act on a specific occasion, use *succeed in + -ing*. You can also use *was able to* and *managed to* (if you want to emphasise the difficulty).

The climbers could see the top of Mount Everest. (*This is correct – seeing is a general ability*).
After three more hours, they managed to reach the top ('could' *would not be correct here*).
They had succeeded where many others had failed ('could' would not be correct here).

If the sentence is negative, you can use *couldn't, wasn't able to, didn't manage to, didn't succeed in*.
The following sentences all mean the same, except that *didn't manage to* emphasises difficulty and *didn't succeed in* emphasises lack of success.

He couldn't lift/wasn't able to lift/didn't manage to lift, didn't succeed in lifting 200 kilograms.

A Note on Suggest   17.3

You can use *suggest* with a gerund.

I suggest going for a picnic.
This will be understood to be a suggestion that includes everyone present including the speaker.

You can also say:

I suggest that you should take it back to the shop and complain.
This is a suggestion that applies to the person ('you') who is addressed and doesn't include the speaker.

When you use the pattern
suggest + that + pronoun + should + verb
I suggest that you should apply for the job

you can direct the suggestion at a person or persons by using the appropriate pronoun. Be careful *not* to use the infinitive after *suggest*.

Unit 18

Gerund and infinitive with and without to   **18.1**

Some verbs have a different meaning according to whether they are followed by a *gerund* or an *infinitive*. This difference depends on a general principle that you can apply to most of these verbs. Look at these sentences:

1   John remembered to buy the tickets.
2   John remembered serving that customer.

Why is there an infinitive *to buy* in the first sentence and a gerund, *serving* in the second sentence? To understand the reason for this you must consider the *mental activity* (*remembered*) and the *action* (*to buy, serving*).

Which happened first, the mental activity or the action? In the first sentence the mental activity came first and the action (*to buy*) came second, as a consequence of *John remembered*.

In the second sentence the action (*serving*) came first and the mental activity (*John remembered*) came second. When the mental activity comes first, you need an *infinitive* and when it comes second, you need a *gerund*. It has nothing to do with the tense of the verb.

The same principle applies to *forget*, *stop*, *go on* and *regret*.

He stopped to have lunch.
This means that he stopped whatever he was doing, the sentence doesn't tell us what that was, and then had lunch. Stopped comes first, to have lunch second.

He stopped speaking.
This means that he was speaking and then he stopped and was silent.
Speaking came first, stopped came second.

There is a slightly different explanation for *try*. Compare these sentences:

1   Jack tried to lift the suitcase but it was too heavy.
2   The doctor tried speaking to the patient in three different languages, but there was no response.

In the first sentence, *to lift* the suitcase is in fact impossible for Jack. Jack made an attempt but failed. In the second sentence, the doctor had no difficulty in speaking the three languages – this was easy. The problem was that the patient did not understand them. There is no sense of difficulty here – but no certainty of success. *Try speaking* in this sentence means to experiment and see what is effective. You can use *try + -ing* form when you are making suggestions or giving advice.

During, for, while   **18.2**

Compare these sentences.

1   He was in hospital for three weeks.
2   During his three weeks in hospital, he had two operations.

The first sentence means that he was in hospital continuously for three weeks. *For* covers the whole period.

The second sentence means that on two occasions in a three-week period, he had operations – but not for the entire three weeks.
During means at certain times within a specified period. Compare these sentences.

We flew for ten hours non-stop.
During the flight, we had two meals.

During cannot be followed by specific time references such as 'five days', 'ten years'. It is incorrect to say:
*We watched the film during two hours.

You *should* say:
We watched the film for two hours.

or *possibly*:
The film lasted two hours.

Both *for* and *during* are prepositions and are followed by nouns. *While* is a conjunction and is followed by a verb.
While he was in hospital, he had two operations.

Unit 19

Connectors   **19.1**

Expressing contrast

You can contrast two ideas by using the words *despite*, *although*.

Despite is a preposition and must be followed by a noun, pronoun or gerund.

Despite his illness, he went to work.
Despite feeling ill, he went to work.
Despite the fact that he was ill, he went to work.
He was ill. Despite that, he went to work.

You can change the order of the clauses.
He went to work despite his illness.

Note that *in spite of* means the same as *despite*.

Although is a conjunction and is followed by a verb.

Although he was ill, he went to work.
He went to work although he was ill.

Even though is a stronger form of *although*.
Even though he was in great pain, he didn't make a sound.

You can use *though* instead of *although* but note that in spoken English *though* is used in this way.
It's a nice restaurant. It's a bit expensive, though.

You cannot use *although* in this final position.
You can use *but* and *however* to express contrast but *however* must begin a sentence.

He entered the competition five years running but he never won a prize.
He entered the competition five years running. However, he never won a prize.

Expressing purpose

You can express purpose by using the words *so that, in order to*. These words are followed by different verb patterns.

He bought some wood in order to build some kitchen units.
He bought some wood so that he could build some kitchen units.
They froze the food so that they would be able to eat in the winter.
They froze the food in order to be able to eat in the winter.

Expressing consequence

You can use *so, therefore* to express consequence but *therefore* must be the first word in a sentence.

The pilot failed his medical test, so he had to stop flying.
The pilot failed his medical. Therefore, he had to stop flying.

Expressing time differences

You can use *before, after, as soon as, until, when, while* to express time relationships. Note that these words are not followed by *will* or *would*.

I will telephone John when I finish work. (*not 'I will finish').*
When we have dug the garden, we will plant some rose-bushes. (*not 'we will have dug')*

Note that *while* can show that two things happened at the same time.
He mended my shoes while I waited.

When can show that one thing happened after another.
When I threw a stone at the pigeons, they flew away.

Since can indicate *time*

I have lived here since I was ten/since 1980/since January.

Since can also indicate *reason*

Since you got the highest mark, you will get the prize.
This means the same as:
Because you got the highest mark, you will get the prize.

As can also indicate *time* and *reason*
As we climbed higher, the air became thinner. (*time*)
As Mike is ill, you must take his place. (*reason*)

You can use *in case* to refer to possible future events which require you to take precautions. We don't use *will* or *would* after *in case.*

We took sandwiches in case we couldn't get any food on the train.
Peter always carried a spare inner tube in case he got a puncture.
Take your umbrella in case it rains.

Unit 20

Adverbs and adverbial phrases   20.1

You can divide adverbs and adverbial phrases into five groups, according to the information that they give you.

1   Some adverbs tell you *how*. These are called adverbs of manner.
    He wrote the letter quickly.

2   Some adverbs tell you *where*. These are called adverbs of place.
    She put the book on the table.

3   Some adverbs tell you *when*. These are called adverbs of time.
    We met them at five o'clock.

Note that these kinds of adverbs come towards the end of the sentence, after the object or after the verb if there is no object. For additional emphasis, you can start a sentence with an adverb.

Quickly, he seized the revolver and loaded it.

You should *not* place an adverb between the verb and the object.

*He drew quickly his gun. (This is *wrong*.)
If these three types of adverb occur in one sentence, the normal order is *manner, place, time*.
Peter played badly (*manner*) *at Wembley* (*place*) *on Saturday* (*time*).

4   Some adverbs tell you *how often*. These are called adverbs of frequency.
    always, sometimes, often, never, usually, seldom, hardly ever, rarely.
    When you use a simple tense of the verb *to be* (I am, etc. I was, etc.) these adverbs come after the verb.

    She is never on time.
    They were always short of money.

    When you use simple tenses of other verbs, these adverbs come before the verb.

    Andrew always walks to work.
    We usually worked on Saturday mornings.

    If the verb includes an auxiliary, which is the case with continuous, perfect and passive tenses, these adverbs usually come after the first auxiliary.

I have always enjoyed his novels.
He would never have got the job without his uncle's help.
The offices are usually cleaned at night.

5 Some adverbs tell you *how much*. These are called adverbs of degree:
definitely, absolutely, obviously, possibly, just, certainly
These adverbs follow the pattern of adverbs of frequency.

He is definitely the right man for the job.
He was obviously telling lies.
He would certainly have been chosen for the team if he hadn't been injured.

A note on hardly   20.2

Some adverbs have the same form as the adjective. This is the case with *hard*.

He is a hard worker. (*adjective*)
He works hard. (*adverb*)
Hardly is a different word with a negative meaning.
He does hardly any work. *This means that he does very little work.*
They hardly ever arrive on time. *This means that they are usually late.*

Adjectives ending in -ly

Although many adjectives form adverbs by adding *-ly* (quick, quickly), there are some adjectives which end in *-ly*. The most common are:

friendly, lively, lovely, ugly, silly, cowardly, motherly

To use these words adverbally, you have to say 'in a friendly way', etc.

He was very friendly. (*adjective*)
He spoke to me in a friendly way. (*adverb*)

EXAM HINTS

These exam hints give advice on how to approach the questions in the *Exam Practice* sections.

Paper 1 – Reading

In the exam, there will be four reading texts. Give yourself time to do all four reading texts. Don't spend too long on one that you find difficult, reducing time for the others. Allow time at the end for checking your answers.

Remember that there are different ways of reading

- fast to get a general idea of what the piece is about (*skimming*)
- looking through the text to locate the answers to specific questions (*scanning*)
- reading slowly and carefully to understand detail.

Don't worry if there are words in a text you do not already know. Just concentrate on answering the questions. Use the context to help you guess what any unknown words might mean.

In *multiple-matching tasks*, take one of the people (or places, etc.) from the list of choices and match against the questions. Do this for all the choices in turn.

When *choosing headings*, remember that important information is often contained in the first and last sentences of each paragraph, so pay special attention to these. For *summary sentences*, check that the sentence you choose covers all the information in the paragraph.

In the *gapped text exercise*, look carefully at the sentence that comes before and the one that comes after the gap, and make sure that the extract you choose fits both. When you have completed all the spaces, always read through the whole text to check that it all reads well.

In *multiple-choice questions*, look carefully at the possible choices and first decide those that are clearly wrong. Then choose the correct answer from the ones that are left. Keep looking back at the relevant parts of the text to check you are right. If you really don't know, then guess. Do **not** leave a blank answer.

Take care in transferring answers to the answer sheet. When you have finished, **check** what you have written down.

Paper 3 – Use of English

Part 1

Always read the whole text before choosing the right word.

When choosing a word consider the **meaning** and the **grammatical pattern** in which the word will fit. One of the words may have the right meaning but it may need to be followed by an infinitive and not by the gerund that is in the passage.

Learn the differences in meaning between similar words, e.g. *demand* and *ask* or *think* and *consider*.

Learn the grammatical patterns that follow such words as *suggest* or *warn*. Learn such words in phrases, not in isolation.

Associate words with prepositions. Note how words with similar meanings are followed by different prepositions, e.g. *keen on*, *enthusiastic about*, *interested in*.

Pay attention to the differences between phrasal verbs. You may have to choose between phrasal verbs with different particles, e.g. *take up*, *take over*.

Study how linking words such as *despite* and *although* fit into sentences.

If necessary, guess. Do **not** leave blank spaces.

Part 2

Always read the whole text before you decide what the missing words are.

Most of the words you need are short, structural words such as *if*, *was*, *has* and *whose*.

Look closely at verb patterns which may require an auxiliary or modal verb, especially passive structures and perfect and continuous tenses.

Consider if a connecting word such as *which*, *although* or *but* is needed.

Study the different uses of prepositions such as *for*, *during* and *by*.

Try closing your eyes and re-telling the text in your head. This may produce the missing word that you need.

Part 3

You must use the key word given. Do **not** change this word. The key word may be in any position in the phrase.

You must use a minimum of two and a maximum of five words.

Pay special attention to learning complete phrases, such as *to look forward to -ing, to accuse someone of -ing, to mistake X for Y, to warn someone not to do something.*

Do not worry about contractions. You can write *hasn't* or *has not.* Using a contraction will not reduce the words from six to five. There must be a maximum of five words whether the full or short form is used.

On the exam answer sheet, you only have to write the missing words. Take care that you do not include words that are already on the paper before or after the missing words.

Part 4

Read the whole text first. Begin to make your decisions on the second reading.

Remember that 3–5 lines are correct.

Some lines have extra words that are wrong. You have to identify these and write them on the answer sheet. You do not have to correct the sentences.

There are **no** missing words.

You may make two kinds of mistakes. You may think that correct lines contain wrong words or that wrong lines are correct.

Read the whole sentence. Wrong words may seem to be correct if you look at a phrase of three or four words. If you study the complete sentence you will see that they are wrong.

Pay special attention to articles, auxiliary and modal verbs, prepositions, phrasal verbs, comparatives and relatives.

Part 5

Study the title and read the whole text before you begin to write down the answers.

You may have to add suffixes, e.g. *perform →
performance* or prefixes, e.g. *wrap → unwrap.*

You may have to change the middle part of a word, e.g. *long → length.*

You may have to make two changes, e.g. *know →
unknown.*

You may have to form compound words, e.g. *snow →
snowflake.*

Sometimes the new word must be a plural. Check the grammar of the sentence carefully.

It is best to study word formation methodically. When you learn a new word, make sure that you know all the forms in which it can appear, as a noun, adjective, adverb or verb, e.g. *rely, reliable, unreliable, reliability, reliably, reliance.*

Paper 4 – Listening

Answer each question in the way required; if a letter (A, B, C, etc.) is needed, use this; if a few words are asked for, don't write a long answer.

In **Part 1**, don't choose your answer simply because you have heard a word that appears in one of the choices. Listen to the context in which the information appears. This may show that the word you have heard is not the answer. Listen to all the information provided.

In **Part 2**, where you have to write the answers, make sure you keep your answers short and relevant.

In **Part 3**, again, listen for the meaning. Don't just spot the words. Listen to the context in which they occur. Remember that the choice of answer will require you to analyse the information you are given.

Part 4 has a variety of different formats (matching, multiple-choice, True/False). Again, listen carefully to the context in which the words occur and think about the meaning of what you have heard before choosing your answer.

Take care in transferring answers to the answer sheet.